Mechanical Analysis of China's Macro Economic Structure

Xiaojiang Zhang

Mechanical Analysis of China's Macro Economic Structure

Fundamentals Behind Its Macro Investment Strategy Formulation

Springer

Xiaojiang Zhang
Hangzhou, Zhejiang, China

ISBN 978-981-15-3839-1 ISBN 978-981-15-3840-7 (eBook)
https://doi.org/10.1007/978-981-15-3840-7

This Springer imprint is published by the registered company Springer Nature Singapore Pte Ltd.
The registered company address is: 152 Beach Road, #21-01/04 Gateway East, Singapore 189721, Singapore

Introduction

This is the first book ever published in the world to decipher and piece together the major interactive and sequential operating and investment flow dynamics within the complex Chinese macro-economic structure, in an effort to guide global investors to formulate their own macro-assessment and investment strategy in or related to China. Different from USA that had a relatively short and ascending economic past, China endured a much longer history with quite a few volatile economic cycles. With that lesson of history in the background as country's guiding economic management principle, within the current geographical, industrial and financial landscape, China's economic policy and management superstructure, combined with regional government, financial community, industrial community, consumers and other entity types, together form a huge and complex operating flow dynamics, within which macro-condition can be assessed and understood, industrial investment opportunities be identified and strategies be formulated by interested global and domestic investors.

Given the complex and fluid nature of the current global economic order and the sizable influence of Chinese economy to the global economic growth and balance, the importance for reaching that clarity on China macro-mechanics cannot be overstated.

I thank you for your interest. All constructive feedback is welcomed at my email address, xiaojiang_john_zhang@yahoo.com.

Contents

Chapter 1
The History of China's Economic Structure Management

The Opium War in 1840 and many interactions with the western world since then, shook China to its core, and with them, fundamentally different economic management thoughts and practices arrived on shore. But well before those more recent interactions, China had a recorded history in economics and economic management, which could be summarized into some very long up and down economic cycles, a few of which were quite volatile. That economic history has continued to shape China's management rationale over its vast and complex economy up to this day. Thus, to fully grasp the central theme of China's current economic management philosophy, it is important to first understand that history background.

1.1 Land Distribution, Meritocracy and the Rise of Qin Empire

The delineation of Chinese economic history could be grouped into the following periods: Pre-Qin 2070 BC–221 BC; Qin 221 BC–207 BC; Han 207 BC–Pre-Tang AD 618; Tang AD 618–Pre Song AD 960; Song AD 960–Pre Ming AD 1368; and Ming AD 1368–End of Qing AD 1911. Economic history before Qin lacked detailed documentation.

1.1.1 Economic Structure Before Qin–221 BC

The Pre-Qin era included Xia dynasty, 2070 BC–1600 BC; Shang dynasty, 1600 BC–1046 BC; West Zhou, 1046 BC–770 BC; and East Zhou, 770 BC–221 BC. East Zhou period could be further divided into Spring Autumn Period, 770 BC–476 BC and Warring States Period, 476 BC–221 BC. For the Pre-Qin period, according to the *Book of Han, Monograph on Food and Currency*, the prevalent Grid Field Farming

X. Zhang, *Mechanical Analysis of China's Macro Economic Structure*,
https://doi.org/10.1007/978-981-15-3840-7_1

System, which sometimes was also referred to as Well Field System, was described as such: a square-shaped parcel of land was divided into 9 equivalent square pieces, with the surrounding 8 pieces designated for private farming, the 20% of the center piece for dwelling and water well, the rest 80% of the center piece for public farming. Each male peasant or slave farming labor was given a parcel of land (100 Mu), about the size of the one of the nine squares, roughly equivalent to $140 \times 140\ m^2$. For non-farming populations, e.g., those in bureaucracy, industries and commerce, a family of 5 would be counted as one farming labor, and farmland would be allocated to accordingly. Tax collection rate was 10%.

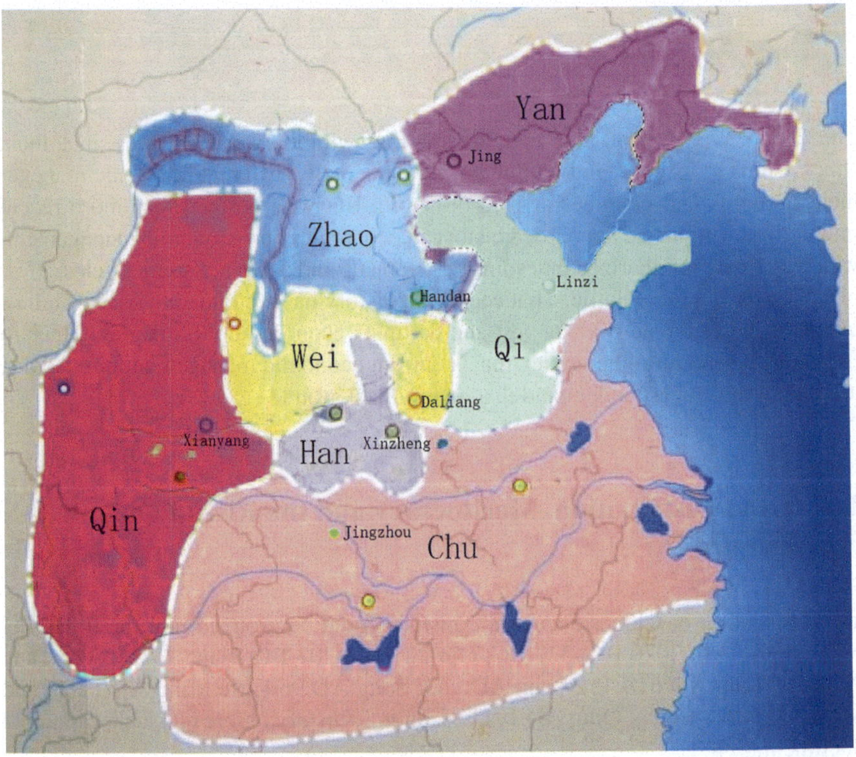

7 kingdoms during Warring States Period (476 BC–221 BC)

During the East Zhou period, especially during the Warring States period spanning from 476 to 221 BC, the Grid Field System was collapsing, as the 7 major antagonist kingdoms battled each other for supremacy and the need to secure food supplies for their respectively ever increasing sizes of armies was urgent. It was also just prior and during this period, China produced some of its brightest philosophers and politicians ever in history. One of them was a legalist named Li Kui (455 BC–395 BC) from kingdom Wei. In the *Book of Han, Monograph on Food and Currency*, he reckoned that crop price at too high level could harm consumers, and crop price at too low level could harm farmers. To reduce price volatility he classified each year's crop harvest into 6 levels. Three levels for good harvesting, better, best, and three levels for poor harvesting, poorer, poorest. Tax collection was set to 6 different levels accordingly. The highest amount of the harvest tax collected during best harvest year was redistributed out during poorest harvest year, better for poorer, good for poor, respectively. In this harvest tax collection and redistribution process, the objective of muted price volatility was achieved.

Price volatility marked the coming of agricultural market economy. To protect market ownership rights in that economy, Li Kui's tried to introduce meritocracy in then mostly aristocratic society and to protect the land ownership of those who were not from aristocrat bloodline. He also was responsible for one of the first legalist masterpiece, the Legal Essence, which provided legislation on personal safety and properties. In the years followed, while legalist and Confucianism thoughts both gained their prominence and became the main schools of thoughts used for governing China up to the its opening in the nineteenth century, on the economic front, the legalist thoughts had exerted much larger influence than the Confucianism thoughts.

1.1.2 Shang Yang and Land Reform

Shang Yang (395 BC–338 BC), a staunch legalist, left a lasting mark in China's political and economic history and remained a controversial figure up to this day. His was originally from Wei where he witnessed and learnt from the many reform initiatives started and implemented by Li Kui, and went on to serve in Qin's royal court. Legalists preferred rule of law as the governing tool by the king, with all the executive power taken from feudal lords to be fully concentrated into the hands of the high kings. This was very appealing for a king since it offered policy implementation efficiency during a truly chaotic time. After winning royal support, Shang Yang abolished the Grid-Field farming system in Qin that mostly befit the rigid aristocratic hierarchy, in favor of feudal land ownership that was often associated with military meritocracy at that time. The land reform greatly benefited the growth of Qin's agricultural economy. Commerce was suppressed in order to focus the economy on agricultural production.

1.1.3 The County Administrative System and Military Meritocracy

Shang Yang also took steps to reform Qin's administrative system. County administrative system was introduced using career bureaucrats as managers reporting to kings. This greatly strengthened the hands of Qin's kings. To mobilize the populace on war front, high social status would only be given to those with military success and be taken away from aristocrats without military success. The result was a super efficient and highly motivated army.

1.1.4 The Demise of an Unsustainable Revenue System

While Shang Yang's reform expanded the agricultural output and streamlined the kingdom's regional management, quoted tax rate was very high, possibly at 50% to support the brutal war efforts and large construction projects that had been the trademark of the Qin dynasty, which included expansive palaces, terracotta army-guarded mausoleum and the Great Wall. Even with expanded farmland ownership and output, the fiscal burden was too high to be sustainable without paid tributes from conquered land.

In summary, via land reform, bureaucratic reform, and military meritocracy reform, the legalist policy implementation by Shang Yang generated wealth, created the most militant and efficient kingdom in Warring States Period eventually unifying China by 221 BC.

1.2 Han's Imperial Success and Subsequent Class Divide

Overburdening its commoners with tax and labor work, Qin dynasty quickly collapsed in 207 BC. It was replaced by Han dynasty. How to fund military operations against different northern tribes, became a perennial fiscal issue throughout Chinese economic history.

1.2.1 Brutal War Against the Northern Tribes

It was during this time that a northern tribe, the Hun nomads that some considered the descendants of Xia, became a formidable force. Before Qin, the Great Wall was a fragmented line of defense. Northern tribes lacked the technology of iron making, neither did they have stable food supply of an agricultural economy. Food and textile demand were acute, especially when several cold winters or severe droughts were encountered consecutively. Once county administrative system replaced smaller kingdoms and local feudal lords within the empire, pieces of wall were connected and manned by large amount of well-armored soldiers, trades were often blocked, and small scaled skirmishing and looting then became large battles, involving hundreds of thousands of soldiers from both sides. In one battle, Han's first emperor Liu Bang, a strong military leader at the time, was encircled with his 320,000-strong army by 400,000 riders from the North, according to *The Record by Sima Qian*. Acknowledging its relative weakness against the Huns, for quite some years, Han had been enduring humiliating postures from northern tribes. The aging empress Lv who was the caretaker of the empire after Liu Bang once received a taunting marriage proposal from the north and had to diplomatically turning it down after an internal debate against military escalation.

1.2.2 Agriculture Versus Commerce Debate

The need for economic recovery was real after the ravage incurred during the collapse of Qin dynasty. In 178 BC, Jia Yi presented his emperor his policy proposal, emphasizing the need for agricultural production. He argued that the quick demise of Qin dynasty was due to its ill treatment of the commoners and advocated the production and storage of agricultural goods as the most important mandates for people's livelihood and a dynasty's survival, therefore denounced the stringent country-first approach by Qin's legalist. But he shared one core belief with Shang in terms of slighting businessmen and commerce, considering commerce not the most important service to be provided for the general society, and its quick-profit thinking and accompanying wealth flaunting actions demoralizing for agricultural society. His thought system regarding agricultural production and its importance to a dynasty's stability was noted by many later rulers and was highly regarded by Mao Zedong.

1.2.3 Confucius, Legalist, Salt and Iron Nationalization

Bringing up the agricultural production alone was not enough for securing empire's border region. As the northern tribes' demands for textile, iron and food supplies from south of the Great Wall were real and large-scale military invasions routine occurrence, war became inevitable. Composed of many battles stretched over a long period of time across the entire northern frontier, the military campaign was a huge military success for China that stabilized the vast frontier border region for the first time since the collapse of Qin. According to *The Record by Sima Qian*, the largest battle occurred in 119 BC. Han army with about 500,000 infantry, 100,000 cavaliers, 140,000 horses were sent forming a multi-prompt offence across the Mongolian desert. The brutal campaign extracted heavy tolls from both sides in terms of human lives and resources. On China's side, the loss ratio for soldiers was put down at 30%, and only 30,000 out of 140,000 horses returned. The battle was a turning point on China's long conflict versus the Hun tribe, eventually producing geo-consequence for the entire Eurasia continent as the Hun tribe gradually migrated westward.

Lacking military mobility, agricultural society was ill equipped to fend off large scale horse-riding cavalry invasion, unless substantial economic resources were diverted to raising military horses, building wheeled equipment and training capable mobile regiments. After the first 70 or so years of peace, Han empire was prosperous and ready to bring balance to the northern front, but much more was needed to fund the war effort. Emperor Liu Che (156 BC–87 BC) eventually implemented nationalization of the iron and salt industries for funding his military campaign. Iron was chosen for material's essential usage in agricultural plow and military equipment and therefore industry's capability to generate high revenue. There was also room for technological and efficiency improvement with the scale of production after nationalization. Just as important, for its weight and production facility requirement, iron production site could be easily monitored and controlled to prevent private production and smuggling. Salt was chosen since boiling seawater was costly without industrial coal capability, and access to limited number of salt mines on land in terms of 7 salt wells or salt lakes could be easily controlled. Salt was also an essential food ingredient, without which, an army could quickly lose its fighting capacity. Their easiness for control and absolute necessity made iron and salt industries suitable for nationalization to generate revenue to cover large budgetary shortfall in military campaign and other government initiatives.

The disagreement over salt and iron nationalization led to a rare open and heated economic policy debate in China. Famously called Salt and Iron Debate, it was recorded by Huan Kuan. The con side argued for laissez faire economic policy, mainly from Confucianism belief that whatever government took was taken from the people hence unnecessarily impoverishing the people and bad for the ruling of the empire. The nationalization also translated into monopoly of ironwork with poor product quality. The pro side, led by Sang Hongyang, argued that budgetary shortfall could only be covered and government function be maintained with nationalization of those high profit industries. While con side won morale high ground, the pro side's policy implementations mostly remained in place after the debate, without which, government would find it hard to fund its military and other budgetary initiatives.

The recorded debate was studied up to this day by subsequent generations of China's management elite. Two key conclusions could be drawn: 1st, practicality should always be a prerequisite for any economic policy proposal; 2nd, nationalization of certain industries could play an important role in fulfilling essential governing role, including revenue generation and wealth gap management.

1.2.4 Social Inequality and the Age of Noblemen

The nationalization of iron and salt industries was not enough for combined expenditure for war and other projects. High tax and fines for prevalent taxing dodging practice drove many farmers and wealthy individuals into bankruptcy. Regional strong lords emerged with land ownership consolidation. Much of resources evaporated from regional management via budgetary constraint that local bureaucrats also fell to the influence of those strong lords. The consequence was the enlarged class-divide and weakened central government. Economic and social polarization continued and Han dynasty eventually fell into internal chaos and collapsed in AD 220. The Three-Kingdom period lasted from AD 220 to AD 280. Jin was a short-lived dynasty from AD 265 to AD 420, overlapping with Jin was the 16-Kingdom Period from AD 304 to

AD 439. Wealth flaunting was appalling during this time. A famous incident involved a wealthy official (Shi Chong, AD 249–AD 300) using patterned silk fabric to create his personal passage more than 17 km long. Balance of economic wealth distribution was only partially restored and prosperity came after Tang dynasty claimed throne.

In summary, Han's iron and salt nationalization was partially successfully for balancing central government's budget. More resources were needed and taken to fund government, exacerbating a class divide and the empire consumed by internal military conflict.

1.3 Tang's Social, Economic and Territorial Success

Sui Dynasty (AD 581–AD 618) and Tang Dynasty (AD 618–AD 907) implemented many successful policy initiatives lasted well after their ruling failed. The most famous of those initiatives, included the Imperial Examination and Grand Canal system.

1.3.1 The Imperial Examination and Social Mobility

The demand from competing kingdoms for best policy ideas to survive created a level playing field for many during Warring States Period and Qin, but mobility and class divide became more serious social issues since Han. During the time of Emperor Liu Che, in AD 107, the size of impoverished migrant refugee was more than 2 million (*The Record by Sima Qian*), relative to the total population estimated at between 30 and 40 million (36 million estimated in AD 134). The migrant refugee issue persisted throughout the Han dynasty and their rebellion was directly responsible for its downfall. While the size of deprived population often decreased during subsequent dynasty change, the root cause of class divide never went away and solution at system level was required. The bloody military aristocracy in Qin while effective in motivating the mass, it was aimed at creating an effective war machine during a chaotic period and brought deep reflection after astonishingly quick collapsing of Qin, which was supposed to last for thousands of years to come by its architect. Since Han, royal relatives, large landlords, warlords and high level bureaucrats together formed an entrenched upper class within the society that created such a rigid social divide, and the poor were in such a dire state, reflected by the number of migrant refugee, the social fabric became unstable and a solution was required.

To bring class mobility into the society, Imperial Examination system was experimented in Sui and was formally introduced in Tang. There were three key points for taking the exams: 1st, there was no need for reference by officials; 2nd, admission was solely based upon written exams; 3rd, the exams were held regularly. Good exam results would bring people into management class and hence possibly elite social circles. The exam system evolved over the 1400 years or so period during its existence in terms of content coverage and other mechanical details. Exams would be organized at multiple levels. 1st level of passage makes a person eligible for being a student for later formal exams. Formal exams are organized at provincial and national level. Top examinees at national level could go directly to the top echelon of the national governance.

The social impact of this systematic policy initiative could not be overestimated when a famous high king, Li Shimin, was quoted saying: "Now all the brightest are in my pocket". As the examination system helped to provide social mobility to the general population previously under-privileged, it also reduced the likelihood of unsatisfied intellectuals rising up to lead challenges against the ruling of a dynasty. The system produced a new bureaucratic establishment, pulling people from urban, rural and far-flung regions, displayed a rudimentary form of representation that was a great social advance at the time. Its main economic effect was wealth redistribution to more general population.

1.3.2 The Grand Canal and the Revenue Flow from the South

Sui was the first dynasty to link many of the regional waterways together to create the Grand Canal. This canal was continuously dredged and upgraded in Tang. Linking the most the Northeast corner south of the Great Wall (Beijing), Southeast Yangzi Delta, where Shanghai and Hangzhou are located, to Luo Yang in the mid-western section, which was the political center at the time. This was strategic for both economic and military importance for the whole empire. Finally, the political center in the mid-western section during that time, the terracotta land that included Chang An and Luo Yang, and the relatively barren Northeast military outpost Beijing, could be economically supported by the fertile south. To certain extent, this economic pattern persisted up to this day, even though the economic model and means of transportation are fundamentally different.

The connection to the fertile south also had a class impact. The fertile south made self-sufficient small family farming a viable choice, and their support and the Imperial Exam System together had reduced empire's reliance on large landlords from the north.

1.3.3 Decentralized Command Centers and the Age of Warlords

To reduce central government expenditure and its economic dependency on regional aristocrats, Tang set up regional military command centers that also had controls on local economic resources. This was budget-savvy in the early stage of a dynasty, during which its governance was effective and military strength solid. Later the combined military and economic management structure generated environment for regional military leaders unrestrained by central government economic support and internal warfare broke out. The dynasty never regained effective central control until Song dynasty separated the economic and military management lines.

In summary, Sui and Tang tried to close the social and economic class divide by instituting Imperial Exam, and reducing budgetary shortfall by completing the Grand Canal therefore they could reach the fertile south and lessen dependency on northern regional lords. But to reduce military and government expenditure, its distributed military command system produced a breeding ground for internal separatist warfare. Every ruler since then remained constantly vigilant regarding close formation of regional military and economic relationship.

1.4 Song's Comprehensive Reform and the Conquest by the Mongols

1.4.1 Centralized Military and Its Budgetary Consequence

Taking lessons from Tang, Song (AD 960–AD 1279) discarded decentralized military management and adhered strictly to centralized military commanding structure with civilian bureaucrats in charge. The most capable military regiments, the imperial guard regiments, were stationed in large numbers close the capital city, Kai Feng, to protect the empire. The capital city was selected for its central position and control over the Grand Canal and therefore the central government could maintain forward military posture over the empire, but it had no natural geographic advantage in terms of defense parameter setup. To compensate for the lack of natural defense parameter, the size of imperial guard regiments had always been large.

1.4.2 Green Sprout Reform and Corruption

Based upon land productivity, Song government classified farmland into 3 categories, good, average and poor. Each counted labor would be given a parcel of land 100 Mu in good quality, or 150 Mu in average quality, or 200 Mu in poor quality. The tax bases for all the above three scenarios would be set at 100 Mu. Tax rate was set at 30% (*Book of Song, Monograph on Food and Currency*). This was a stable economic situation for a period.

But with hostilities on both northern and western border, the size of the central imperial guards grew larger over time, close to one million strong at some time point. The cost to maintain an army with such a large size was difficult even for Song with relatively developed economy in their time. Also fresh on the memory was the fall of both Han and Tang that could be directly attributed to large mass of impoverished peasants deprived of land ownership. Comprehensive reform was sought and rolled out by Wang Anshi, between AD 1068 and AD 1085, with support from ambitious emperor, for bettering farmer's capability to weather a bad harvest, to improve budgetary condition and to strengthen the military.

Similar to those policies proposed by Li Kui during Warring States Period, one of the key ideas was to make loans to farmers by the government when needed. The interest rate of the issued loans was limited at no more than 20% (*Book of Song, Monograph on Food and Currency*), a rate much lower than the interest rate charged by the loan shops in general at the time. Since the loan were issued by the government, in theory they would increase government revenue stream, reduce the likelihood of farmer bankruptcy if farmers could now get loan to plant seeds during spring. Other important proposals included buying low at one place and selling high at another place, privatizing raising horses for the military.

Those reforms policies were controversial since it redistributed wealth within economy without corresponding bureaucratic reform. The reform was short-lived and empire was not significantly strengthened, followed by the dramatic takeover of the capital by Jin from the North. One of the most horrible scene for any royal court in Chinese history occurred in AD 1126–AD 1127. Most of the royal families were captured, including the current emperor, the retired emperor, the empress, princes, princesses, extended relatives, close to 10,000 royal families, many of them tortured on their route to north, and women became sex slaves. This event was named the Shame of Jing Kang. The Dynasty fled south and was eventually conquered by Mongols. In the last battle on Hainan, more than 100,000 committed suicide by jumping into the sea. The carnage was called the battle of Ya Shan. Many historians attributed to The Shame of Jing Kang and Battle of Ya Shan, at least partially, to the failed reform started by Wang Anshi. Wang was one of the best literature writers in his time and in centuries, a tested bureaucrat known for impeccable moral background and keen insight into economic affairs, plus solid support by his high king. His failure to successfully carry out a systematic reform and bring substantial benefit for a ruling dynasty had a lasting impression for all subsequent reform-minded royal rulers and bureaucrats on what a daunting task a systematic reform could be.

Yuan dynasty's rule lasted from AD 1271 to AD 1368. During this period, the Grand Canal no longer took the detour by first running southwest from Beijing to Luo Yang, then southeastward to Yangtze Delta. This was because the central western region, which was the power base for Tang's ruling class, was unimportant to the new dynasty that ruled from Beijing. Therefore the man-made waterway took a more straight line from Beijing in the North to Yantze Delta in the South. This routing change had the economic impact of further lessening the importance of central western region, but created new commercial activities and prosperities in cities along the banks of current waterway.

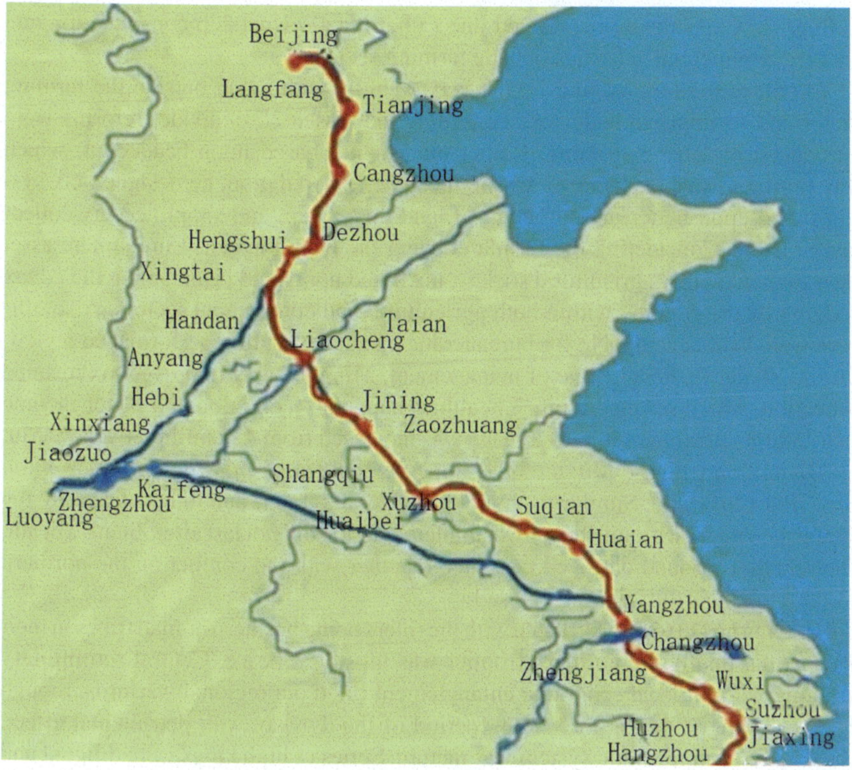

Map of the Grand Canal in Tang–Song (Blue) and Yuan (Red)

In summary, during Song dynasty, the Imperial Exam system and Grand Canal system were well functioning. To reverse the trend of regional military separatists movement since Tang dynasty, civilian rule of centralized military management structure was strictly enforced. Cost to maintain the strength of military with such management structure was high, especially with the presence of military conflict on both northern and western frontier. Reform to improve budgetary condition and reduce farming sector cost, via nationalization of small loan financing and buying low selling high from region to region failed due to bureaucratic resistance.

1.5 Ming–Qing

During Ming dynasty (AD 1368–AD 1644), the Imperial Exam System was mature and capable of elevating some of the brightest from the general population into the ruling class. Civilian rule of the military was secure. War with the northern tribes was continuous and costly. Commercial activities outside farming sector started to flourish. Class divide reemerged due to both land ownership consolidation and untaxed commercial activities outside farming sector.

To reduce the tax dodging by the very wealthy within and outside the farming sector and to improve budgetary condition and lessen class divide, reforms were introduced by Zhang Juzheng. Rather than taxing based upon headcount, which was similar to sales tax spread among the general population, he designed tax system based upon better measurement of land ownership, and simplified tax collection practice. Considering the farmland being the most important investment asset class in then mainly agricultural society, tax based upon land ownership reduced tax dodging by the wealthy within both agricultural and commercial sectors. Also officials were held accountable for bureaucratic agenda execution performance review. During Zhang Juzheng's time of management, Ming dynasty improved tax revenue collection, which resulted a much healthier budgetary condition and better income distribution. Taxable farmland acreage was increased from 422 million Chinese Mu, to 701 million Chinese Mu, a 65.8% improvement (*Book of Ming, Monograph on Food and Currency*). Similar to the fate of Han and Tang, due to resistance by the established interest group, the reform implementation did not last after Zhang's death. The rebellion of land-deprived peasants, together with the conflict on the northern border took their toll. Ming collapsed.

For Qing (AD 1636–AD 1911), with the rulers being northern nomad tribes in their origination, finally the northern frontier was mostly at peace. Centralized military structure without local economic entanglement ruled out regional warlords, though this was changed during the ending period of the dynasty with detrimental effect. The empire's bureaucratic system was mature. Series of high kings were diligent and they continuously focused on fine-tuning the empire system to prevent any unwanted introduction of drastic idea or changes similar to those brought by the likes of Wang Anshi.

1.5.1 Political Business Interest Group—Jin and Hui

Business people as a social class started to emerge in Ming and Qing, with Jin group and Hui group the two best-known groups. During Ming dynasty, to support soldiers manning the northern front, government rewarded business people willing to haul supplies to northern military fortresses with vouchers for monopolized salt sales, which was very profitable at that time. Those with geographical proximity to the northern fortresses prospered on this business model, especially in Shanxi province, Jin for short, within which an important northern fortress city, Datong, was situated, hence the formation of the Jin business group. This supplies for salt business model evolved over time, gradually relying less on military demand after the peace arrived on the northern border during Qin, more on commerce along the straightened Grand Canal. Hence the formation of the business group in Anhui, Hui for short. It is worth noting that both Jin and Hui groups relied heavily on good will from the government for granting monopoly business privileges to prosper in their respective fields. Hence their behaviors somewhat had more in common with the current western military industrial complex, and less so with the corporations in civilian sectors.

1.5.2 Epic of an Agricultural Economic Structure

With more stability on the periphery of the empire, functioning Grand Canal, properly centralized military commanding structure, thorough taxation based upon land ownership to minimize class divide, Imperial Exam System facilitating social mobility, the high kings of Qing were finally satisfied and turned attention to mopping out any sign of systematic idiosyncrasy. The development of agricultural society development was at its peak. The population in China soared, from less than 100 million in the beginning of the Qing dynasty, to more than 400 million, right before the 1840 Opium War (*Book of Qing, Monograph on Food and Currency*).

1.5.3 Collapse of Domestic System Under Foreign Pressure

Perceived eternal stability at hand in the earlier nineteenth century proved to be rather short-lived. The renowned Imperial Exam System had run its course. While it had broadened imperial representation, major side effects also became evident. 1st issue originated from its deep embedding into the class hierarchy making societal intellectual pursuit very focused upon climbing the bureaucracy ladder. 2nd issue originated from content coverage of the exam. To broaden the exam system's social reach, the testing coverage was restricted to the content of a relatively small set of books to reduce preparation cost, punishing broad knowledge-based thinking. These two effects became impediments for modern societal and economic development, within which broad knowledge base and innovative thinking are essential. The system was abolished in 1906 shortly before Qing's end.

Long and successful pursuit of social stability came with a huge cost. Compared with Warring States period, Han and Tang dynasty, lacking in free thinking led to the lack of innovation. The empire was eerily quiet. Jin and Hui business groups could not represent independent interest groups, and were content with collecting their dough via government handout. Scaled indigenous industrialization did not come and productivity growth stalled relative to western peers. The gap in terms of technology and economic efficiency was so large, Qing collapsed amid both internal and external difficulties and China took on a long arduous journey of reform with continuous self-reflection.

1.6 Earlier Twentieth Century Chaos

Qing collapsed in 1911 and at last China became a republic, though the scaled industrialization did not set foot until much later. So called "May 4th Event" occurred in 1919, as people yearned for a more complete break from the old tradition and hoped that a complete new system could rejuvenate the nation. Many crucial thought leaders emerged during and after this important event, a rarity when looking back, since deviation from old school thinking in China was much harder than being acknowledged. It was said during this period, Mao Zedong and Deng Xiaoping formed their beliefs and became communists.

The collapse of Qing was followed by bloody internal conflicts. Warlords fought each other, often with the backings from various foreign countries. The end of Sino-Japan war in 1945, followed by a 4-year civil war, saw a unified country. There was a brief war on Korea peninsular from 1950 to 1953. In 1953, the first 5-year plan was put in action, hence the start of modern economic history in China.

1.7 Summaries and Conclusions

1.7.1 Economic Geography History

Geography always played an important part in Chinese economic history. Well-developed agricultural economy first appeared in China in the mid to downstream Yellow River, with center of gravity being Luo Yang in Henan province. After Qin's rise from a fertile basin area surrounded by high mountains on the upstream of the Yellow River, with Xi An/ Xian Yang as its center, that basin area remained both the economic and political center for China throughout the Qin, Han and Tang dynasties for its natural resources and advantageous defensive position. Difficult to be attacked by potential hostile from the east plain, it was also difficult to be supplied by the rest of the country. Over the course of history, as country's expansive south and east became more developed, economic sustainability and connectivity consideration gained more weight and empire's economic center gradually shifted eastward, first to Kaifeng in Song dynasty, finally settled on Beijing–Shanghai–Hangzhou corridor directly connected by the Grand Canal through the Ming and Qing dynasty. While the most active economic regions at this time are Beijing, Yangtze River Delta and Pearl River Delta, the light of history could well one day shone favorably again upon Xi An, Luo Yang and other place with historical significance.

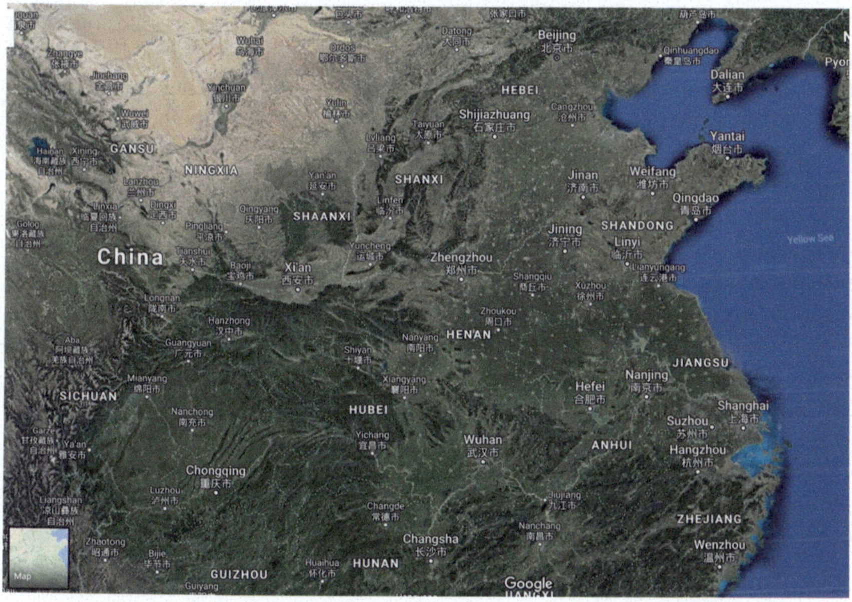

China geography. Courtesy from Google Map. *Source* https://www.google.com/maps

1.7.2 Risks for Economic Reforms

It is worth noting that major reform events in Chinese economic history that touched upon important interests of the establishment often brought severe retribution, which had been the cases for Li Kui (455 BC–395 BC), Wu Qi (440 BC–381 BC), Shang Yang (395 BC–338 BC), Sang Hongyang (?–80 BC), Wang Anshi (AD 1021–AD 1086) and Zhang Juzheng (AD 1525–AD 1582). Li Kui, Shang Yang, Wu Qi and Sang Hongyang were killed, and Wang Anshi was banished. After Zhang Juzheng died on his duty, his surviving family members were ostracized, with one of his two sons starved to death. Real risks should always be part of calculation for any real reform process.

1.7.3 Competing Objectives for Economic Structure Design

Looking back at the course of long Chinese history, the economic management teams eventually learnt to try to manage the balance of the following competing objectives: 1st, achieving economic development versus managing accompanying social class divide; 2nd, nationalizing certain industries for government revenue and lessening class divide versus growing the market enterprises; 3rd, central economic control for stability versus regional management efficiency; 4th, social representation via Imperial Exam for mobility versus modern society need for free thinking and innovation (this remains to be the most difficult to solve). At different time points, some objectives are more important than the others. Failure to recognize or solve critical problems or manage the balance of different objectives within a certain timeframe could bring enduring severe consequences. This sense of history lesson and ambivalence toward short-term gain are quite ubiquitous among the management elite in comparison to US, which has a relatively short history and country's economic trajectory was mostly upward-sloped.

In modern era, debates have raged on how to prioritize those objectives and what is the best way to achieve them amid economic slowdown and external trade conflict. The most controversial ones include the appropriate amount of influence central government should wield in economy, the appropriate amount of weight SOEs should possess in various sectors, how to rekindle government/SOE interest in economic growth without bringing in uncontrollable corruption and how to embrace open economic system without sacrifice economic sovereignty.

Chapter 2
The Birth of Chinese Modern Economic Structure

Recognizing the need to play catch-up, Qing's bureaucrats started indigenous industrial modernization effort after the Opium War. Western-educated professionals streaming in since then, plus large number of skilled workers in northeastern and coastal China being trained during semi-colonization period, provided human resource foundation for later development. Though this process of modernization never stopped, it failed to gain enough momentum until more recent period, when a series of 5-year planning, open market reform, FDI and Internet together led to the creation of current industrial, financial, and regional economic structure.

2.1 The First 5-Year Plan and the Soviet Support

There were cases of large economic modernization attempts at national level in world economic history, but few countries had carried out a relatively fast and successful implementation in a sized economy. The first such example occurred in Soviet Union when it was measured by heavy industrial output increase in a short 20-year period. An important contributing factor for its success was that before the Soviet revolution, Czar's Russia had already mastered certain level of industrial sophistication and could manufacture indigenously complicated engineering work such as dreadnaught battleship. Comparatively, China did not have a Peter I equivalent at the top during its dynasty times and had much humbler starting point for its economic transformation. The first scaled industrialization push in China came after the end of the Korean War. Dubbed China's first 5-year plan (1953–1957) and centered around so-called "156 projects", it was carried out with extensive Soviet technology transferring. With 19.6 billion CNY invested in total, those projects covered 91 modern industries and were crucial for China's modern economic structure. Never a country of China's size received a technological transferring to such an extent in modern economic history.

X. Zhang, *Mechanical Analysis of China's Macro Economic Structure*,
https://doi.org/10.1007/978-981-15-3840-7_2

At the end of the first 5-year plan in 1957, in the steel sector, capacity at the pre-existing large steel mill at An Shan in Liao Ning province was expanded. Two new large steel mills were constructed, one at Wu Han and the other one at Bao Tou. Steel production was 4.12 million tons versus 1.35 million tons in 1952. Truck production was 4000 compared with 0 in 1952. Coal production rose to 113 million tons from 63.53 million tons. It was extraordinary in retrospective considering that China could not produce indigenously small caliber cannons in Sino-Japan war period.

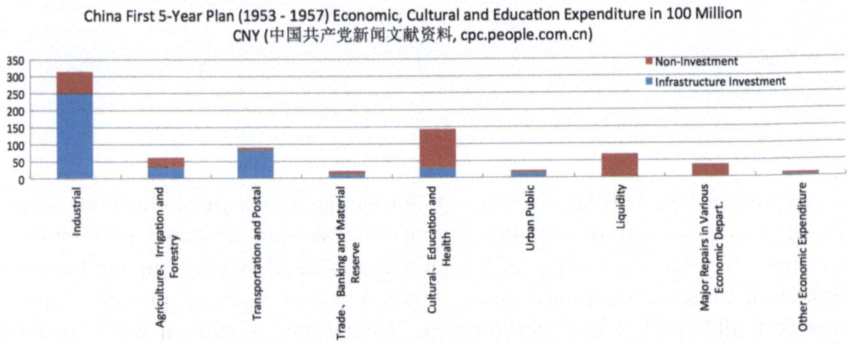

At macro structure level, at the end of the 1st 5-year period, though China's industrial output as percentage of GDP was increased from 26.7 to 36% and its industrial capacity and capabilities were greatly expanded, the depth of its industrial development in terms of indigenous R&D was lacking compared with that of the Soviet Union. This was demonstrated by the very slow technological progress on auto, shipping and other manufacturing industries after relationship with Soviet soured and technology transferring being cut off. The number of enrolled college students was at a low 671,000 figure within a total population of close to 600 million. But the problem only became clear later on and the initial fast speed of industrial growth at the time created an overly optimistic environment, which partially led to many political and economic events occurring with large social and economic consequences.

Some of the issues are more structural. 1st was the level of nationalization. Public enterprises accounted for 61.3% of GDP, Co-op 4.4%, public and private collaborative 22.1%. These three categories combined accounted for 87.7% of China's GDP, based upon People's Congress report in 1955. That level of nationalization was unprecedented in China's economic history. There are three distinctive schools of thoughts regarding privatization versus nationalization. The 1st school was led by Chairman Mao. Well versed in Chinese political and economical history, he remained guarded towards any sign of emerging aristocracy and tumultuous period that could subsequently occur. The 2nd school was represented by Chen Yun. A socialist economist in nature, he tried to adhere to economic rules regarding balancing budgetary revenue and expenditure, credit loan and deposit, material supply and demand, foreign exchange inflow and outflow. These were advanced concepts to many other officials during the time from agricultural background without prior exposure to modern governance. Also aware of the mainly agricultural nature of then

Chinese economy, he was against industrialization at all cost, arguing that the industrialization should be based upon agricultural growth so citizen's basic well-being would not be compromised during industrial investment expansion. Chen favored an economy mainly composed of nationalized segments supplemented with market enterprises. The 3rd school was represented by Deng Xiaoping. Bounded by neither shadow of history nor Soviet economic methodology, Deng's strongest forte was his pragmatism and biggest concerns need to be addressed would decide his stand on large economic issues. Growing up in a time filled with civil war chaos and facing the dire need to improve living standard, he chose to let loose of economic force, while introducing many of the free thinking concepts in the bureaucracy mostly without letting loose the party architecture.

2.2 Deng's Economic Reform

There are usually 6 stages involved in a country's industrial transformation. The 1st stage is the opening up of the general population and economic structure to free up labor and resources; the 2nd stage is the industrialization by family-owned enterprises; the 3rd stage is the scaled industrialization; the 4th stage involves scaled infrastructure investment to accommodate scaled industrialization; the 5th stage involves advanced stage of industrialization; the 6th stage is the formation of the welfare state.

On the eve of Deng's economic reform, China already had a unified single market, a relatively well-educated industrial workforce, a Soviet-originated industrial backbone and a slew of experiences of industrialization trials and errors and serious after-thoughts. During Deng's 20-plus years of economic management in what he codified as a muddling-through process, "feel the stone and cross the river", he managed to accomplish China's first 3 stages of industrial transformation. For the 1st stage communal production in agricultural sector was discarded, inefficient state-owned enterprises cutback to free up underutilized labor force and resources; For the 2nd stage the emergence of family enterprises in countryside, many of which involved in the export sector, and privatization of previously public-owned enterprises, combined to form the industrialization of the family-owned business; the 3rd stage involved scaled industrialization, as the market grew and enterprises grew their capacities in response.

This roadmap of industrialization looked clear only in retrospect, as each large country's industrialization path proved to be unique, and the process full of unexpected difficulties. Deng's successful economic turnaround were centered upon a couple of key policy principles: 1st was to let farmers and small enterprises manage their own practice, hence release individual aspiration for wealth creation; 2nd was the let go of the many inefficient public enterprises, which freed up resources but had a large social backlash; 3rd was the special economic zone with preferential tax policy and improved infrastructure. The political and business atmosphere was relatively open after many of the tumultuous events. The family-owned business, communal or not, and standing public enterprises often produced for the export market that could afford improved quality. As it went on, those improved products also found their way back to the domestic market, further boosting this group of more capable producers.

The 4th stage came after China's entry into WTO. There was also a large CNY devaluation to reflect then China's tacit acknowledge of its industrial inefficiency, against much internal opposition. With the accumulative effect of past Soviet technology infusion, primitive industrialization, formation of a unified single market, 20-plus years of reforms, difficult privatization, labor force education, WTO entry and currency devaluation, export-driven growth gathered momentum, and trade surplus and wealth accumulation led to the real estate purchase boom, which in turn led to government's improved budgetary condition for national and municipal infrastructure fixed investment. That investment further fed into the real estate investment growth. Export, real estate and fixed investment formed the main drivers of China's stage 4 industrialization.

Unlike the first three stages, much more planning and coordination were involved in the 4th stage, at which point China analyzed industrialization trials by other countries and could also draw from its own past success and failure experience for industrial management. Based upon past industrial experience, domestic industry protection policies were calibrated. The dominating positions by the multinational companies during that period, and their from time to time predatory M&A practice in China generated significant controversies. In the process of opening up, for example, China lost many of its cosmetic, personal care name brands to P&G and others, film industry to Kodak and Fuji and large segment of the auto industry to international automakers. The intended "market share for technology swap" strategy to grow domestic employment with improved living standard did not materialize in many segments. International companies would often take over domestic flagship name brands, and after gaining local market knowledge and distribution channel, retire domestic brand name and its management team. Boeing's canceling of MD80 collaboration with China also led to the realization of aviation industry's importance. The concern over MNCs led to the blockage of bid on Xuzhou Construction Machinery Group (XCMG) by Carlyle Group. On the financial side, international financial industry's capability to change macro liquidity condition, exert heavy influence and the overall messy handling of the aftermath of Asian Financial crisis created atmosphere for protecting domestic financial institutions and markets as well. But the protection policy of the considered key domestic industries, especially the financial and auto industries, proved to be controversial, as both state-owned auto industries and financial industries failed to become truly globally competitive in their respective segments.

Also noted for this stage 4 was the learning from other countries experience for industrial planning. Japan's past practice to promote rising sectors such as automobiles and plan ahead an orderly decline of sunset sectors were difficult to emulate, especially due to the lack of capacity concentration for certain domestic segments such as auto and steel industries and internal economic competition among regions in

China. On the other hand, export supply chain's crucial role in bringing up domestic industrial capability to international standard for Japan and 4 Asian tigers was evident, and railroad's role in generating industrial efficiency in German and US industrialization was clear. Large planning effort and investment implementation were carried out to improve port, aviation and railroad infrastructure. The continuous infrastructure investment enhanced the export efficiency, generated income, increased real estate value and improved budgetary condition. Those interactive forces, the past successful industrialization and present difficulty in upgrading into more advanced knowledge-based economy, and changing dynamics of domestic and international economic condition, form the basic picture of current stage of economy, which is in a transition from stage 4 to stage 5.

2.3 Current Industrial Landscape

Using NBSC definition, at the broadest level, economic activities are to be grouped into three categories: primary, secondary, and tertiary industry. Primary industry includes various sectors within agricultural industry such as farming, forestry, fishing, animal husbandry, and associated small scale manufacturing activities; secondary industry includes industrial sectors such as manufacturing, mining, and construction. Industries that do not belong to the first two categories are included in the tertiary industry, many of which are service components, such as transportation, IT, lodging, and real estate services. In terms of contribution to GDP, based upon NBSC data since 1998, the primary industry's share stayed at low level, the secondary industry's share had been volatile and overall on a decreasing trajectory, and the tertiary industry's share had also been volatile but overall on an increasing trajectory.

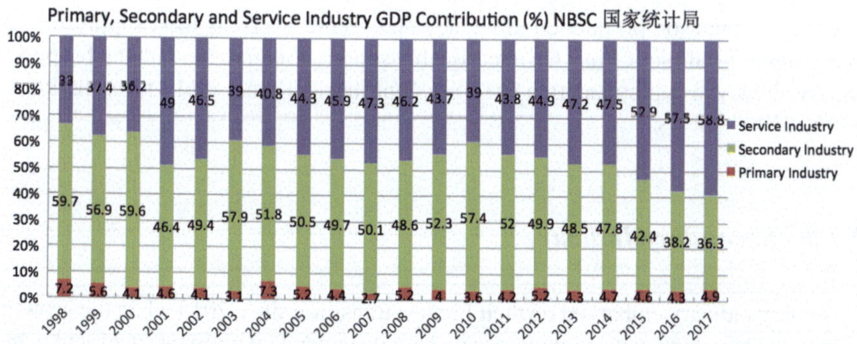

Though diminishing by time, vast employment is still provided by primary industry often acting as labor pool buffer during periods of economic shock. Employment in the secondary industry has held up while its GDP contribution has decreased from

2010 at 57.4% to 2017 at 36.3%, pointing to a difficult macro transition from export-pulled manufacturing industry to more domestic demand-pulled manufacturing industry. Service industry witnessed rising number of employment.

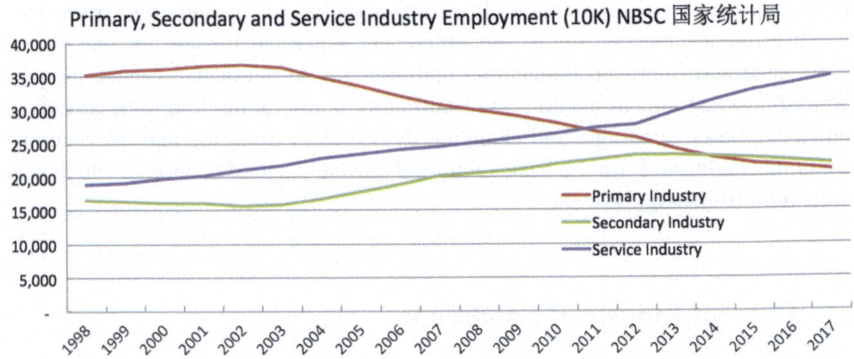

2.3.1 *Primary Industry*

The relative low but stable share of primary industry contribution to GDP is both an economic necessity and the result from careful planning. China has low arable land stock per capita and a large populace at the same time. Stable agricultural output safeguards country's economic security, while large domestic-originated output increase requiring substantial land element input is considered economically impractical. Therefore supplemental import demand in this area is long term in nature. Macro primary industry and specific agricultural industrial investment strategies, designed to enhance domestic production efficiency and secure overseas food supply for an increasingly wealthier China, have reasonably sound economic fundamental support and are already in implementation by some countries richly endowed with agricultural production elements.

2.3.2 *Secondary Industry*

Secondary Industry embarked on their biggest transition since 2015 when the growth of low-end labor-intensive manufacturing heavily dependent upon international markets and energy-intensive steel/real estate segments stagnated, while the high-end manufacturing industries led by communication equipment makers started to emerge.

Careful planning and coordination among various ministries, including NDRC, PBOC, Treasury and local government from provincial to country level, to accommodate large-scale industrial landscape shift with minimal labor and geographical utilization disruption is one of the biggest strength of current China economic management model. The production capacity reduction of coal and steel, accompanied by the increased usage of alternative energy including hydro, wind and solar energy, the nationwide adoption of 5G network infrastructure, are prime examples of those industrial policy coordination and implementation success to help stabilizing the economy.

To pinpoint regional and secondary industrial shift and follow up with a feasible investment plan in an often fast-pacing environment requires persistent effort and a ready solution when opportunity does occur, but they are prerequisites for any possible long term regional and secondary industrial investment success in China.

2.3.3 *Service Industry*

Tertiary industry's garden-variety sector composition is where primary/secondary/tertiary industry classification becomes overstretched for GDP growth contribution source analysis. For example, the continuous expanding software service can be a symbiotic coexistence within a sophisticated hardware manufacturing ecosystem, especially when we enter the rapidly developing AI era, and this traditional classification method that separates two heavily interwined sub-components into two seeming unrelated categories can be misleading during macro analysis. Over time, large number of well-trained engineering students entered labor force with enough employment flexibility in modern industries including software and high-end hardware manufacturing. With that human resource advantage, assuming continuously careful macro policy implementation, service industries related to AI, telecommunication, shipping, railroad transportation and clean energy, will have high probabilities in solid long-term growth. To make some analogies, the age of enterprise software service in US arrived on the success of its chip-making manufacturing industry, and Germany and Japan had some of their successful service companies built on top their auto-centric industrial strength. Other service industries that might see solid growth include health industry and education industry to accommodate a rapidly aging society, and logistics industry to support e-commerce economic component.

2.4 Financial Landscape

Industries are monetarily supported by finance, thus industry landscape has to be structurally matched with and dynamically supported by financial landscape. Within financial landscape, monetary resources are allocated to different industries by different players supplementary to policy initiatives and parallel to fiscal initiatives, and with instruments more based upon loan and bonds, and less upon equities. These characteristics together make China financial landscape very unique when compared with other large economies.

2.4.1 Monetary Liquidity and Money Market

Economic growth, and more specifically industry growth, needs to be funded with monetary resources, which can be quantitatively measured by M0, M1 and M2. In China's monetary system, M0 is defined as cash in circulation; M1 = M0 + enterprise cash deposit, including platform cash deposit, and is under the influence of both loan and foreign currency adjustment; M2 = M1 + term deposit, resident saving deposit and other deposit, and is under the influence of both loan and shadow banking. Accompanying China's economic growth over the years, M1 and M2 grew substantially.

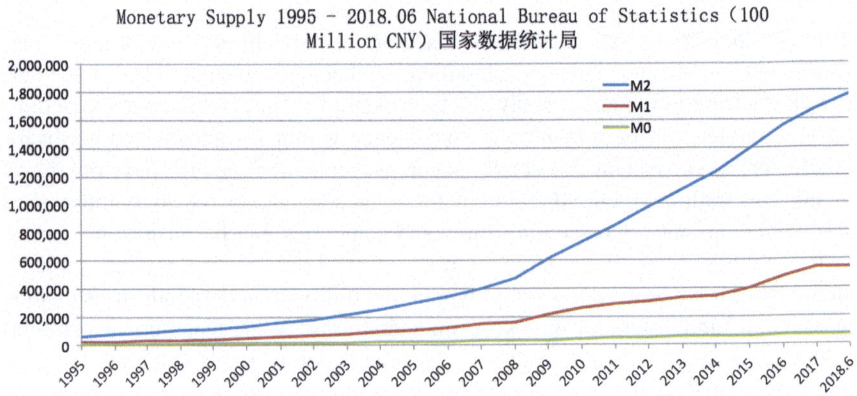

M2's much faster growth over GDP since 2008 credit crisis was partly due to its monetary application in offsetting anemic external demand with more capital allocation to produce internal demand, much of it via real estate development and infrastructure investment, and partly due to its application as a liquidity response to match global central banks' QE monetary measure. To reset the M2 to a more sustainable level, structural remedies to create more capital efficient internal demand, regulatory remedies to improve financial transparency, monetary remedies to drain excess liquidity are needed. An important reason the large M2 was not causing inflation was the real estate asset class's capability in absorbing the excess liquidity, therefore policies to restrict flipping of real estate assets including those in 1st tier and 2nd tier cities are in place to prevent the releasing of excess monetary liquidity from posing a large inflation shock.

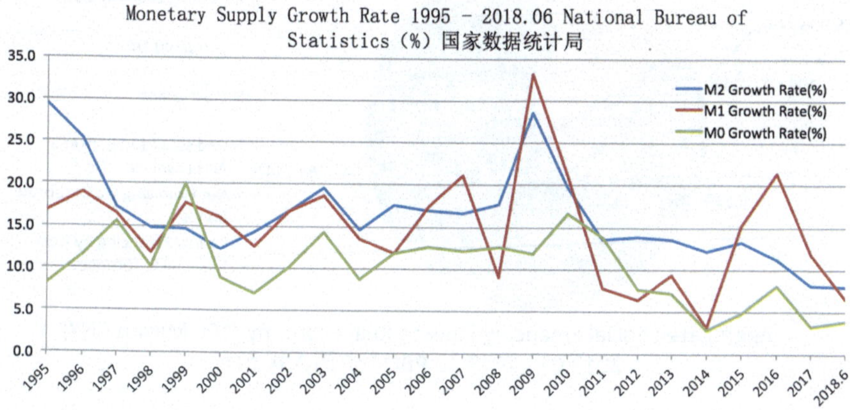

2.4.2 *Loans and Shadow Banking*

Since M1 and M2 are used to measure the liquidity amount from the monetary supply perspective, M1 and M2 alone are not sufficient to explain the level and application of liquidity circulating within the economy, especially regarding the large amount of shadow banking that is mostly in the form of Entrusted Loan and Trust Loan. The aggregated social financing measures the liquidity from the monetary demand side, and its delineation of direct financing, indirect financing and off-balance sheet financing makes it more relevant for explaining liquidity condition within the Chinese economic system versus the M2 number.

From 2012 to 2017, of all the financing activities forming the aggregated social financing, the largest type was bank loans, followed by corporate bonds and entrusted loan. While the capital markets in China had grown substantially over the recent years, it is important to keep in mind that the indirect financing methods remain to be its most important financing venues.

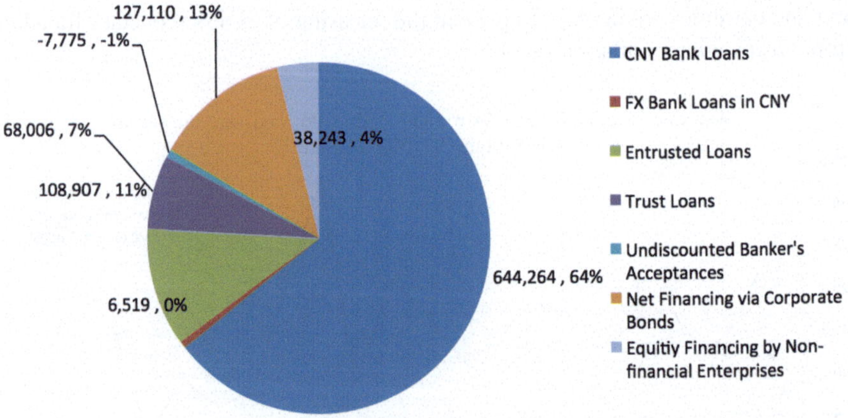

Aggregated Social Financing Flow to Real Economy (100 Million CNY) 2012.01 - 2017.12 PBOC 中国人民银行

Between 2012 and 2017, loan being the most important type of financing venue, its growth had been consistent so was its percentage expansion within the group of activities. Bond issuance had rapid growth both in terms of its amount and percentage except in 2017 due to the central government restraint on local government leverage. Entrusted loan was often tied to local platform hence the local real estate boom and bust cycle. Trust loan was also heavily tied to real estate cycle. Both entrusted loan and trust loan were subject to regulatory push for better financial transparency hence their percentage volatility.

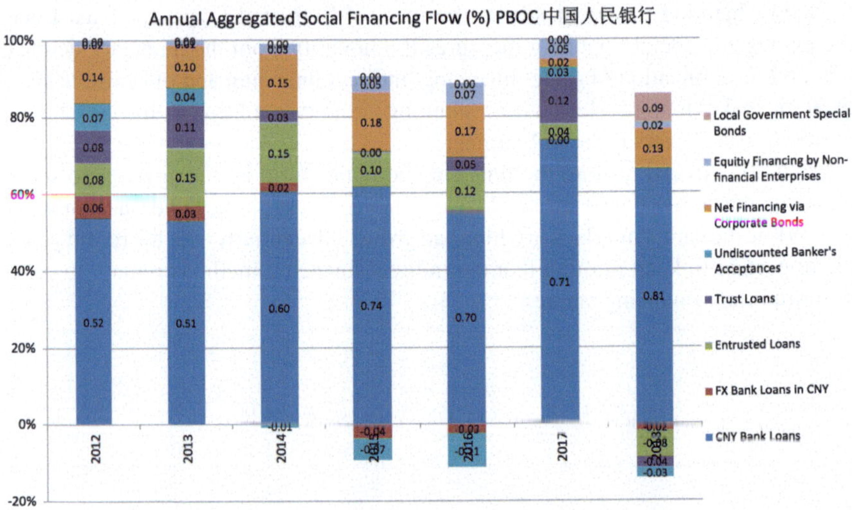

A large percentage of entrusted loans are loans made by one entity to another entity via banks as a conduit. It is the original lender but not the conduit that bears any future default risk. Entrusted loan venue was often used as financing vehicle by local government, to gain financial resources via public listed companies as front that are controlled by local State Asset Regulatory Committee, to support mining, real estate and small enterprises. Trust loan is a loan made by a trust. While bank loan is categorized as indirect financing instrument, trust loan is actually categorized as direct financing instrument. A Trust is a legal entity and trusts together as a specific investment vehicle class exhibit certain economic behaviors.

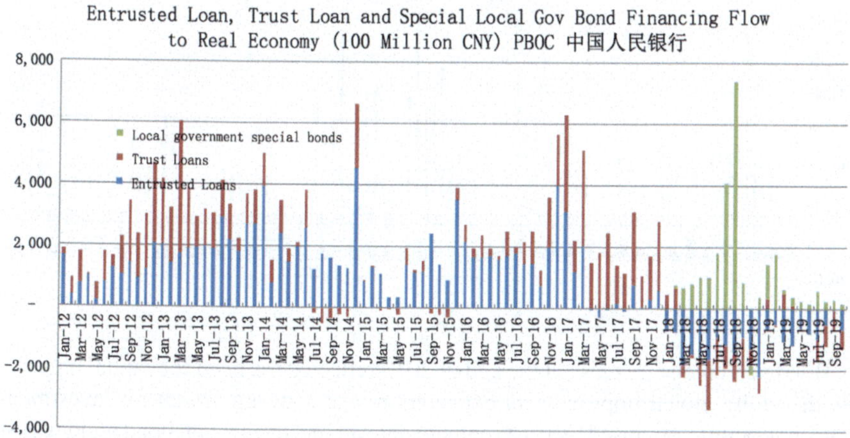

Banks set up trusts to gain access to off-balance sheet higher yield assets without paying the corresponding balance sheet capital charge before 2013. Entrusted loan is another venue to fund large amount of local projects without paying corresponding level of risk charge. The peak of trust loan ended in 2013 when regulatory measures were taken to control banks' off-balance sheet risk. But starting from the end of 2016 regulatory effort was made to clean up borrowing irregularity at local government level, causing a significant fall of entrusted loan activities. The curtailment of entrusted loan caused trust activities to rise the second time in 2017 but only to face scrutiny again in 2018. For borrowers, both trust loan and entrusted loan are expensive and risky financing resources compared to local government bond, but they did serve funding purposes for local government and real estate projects at the time. Since the end of 2017 as both the deleveraging effort and anti-corruption effort were gathering pace, entrusted loan and trust loan activities are under heavy regulatory pressure.

2.4.3 Bonds and Capital Markets

The volatile monthly figure for bonds percentage within the aggregated social financing reflected many factors simultaneously in the play, including bonds offering, demand, liquidity condition, yield expectation and others. Generally more bonds are issued during later half of a year as part of the budgetary cycle. More tax deposit in the later half also drains liquidity and bond investment return could be higher, make issuing expensive but investing opportune.

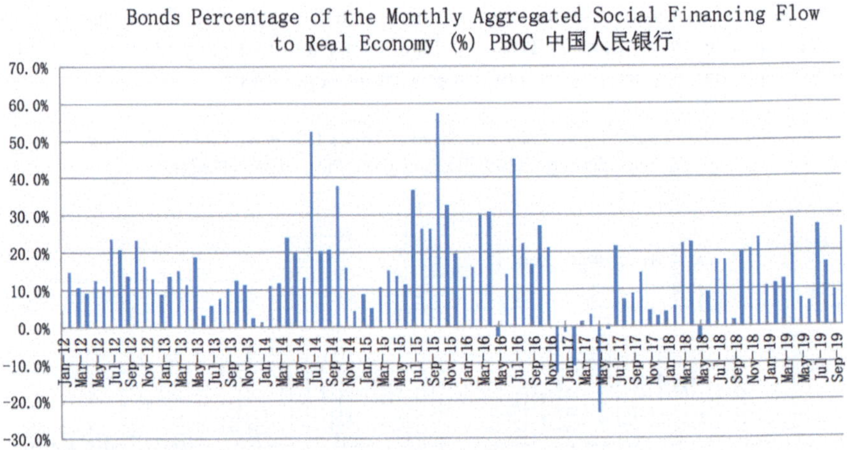

Bond percentage increase at the end of 2013 reflected the need for capital borrowing driven by global improvement expectation, and a strong search for investment amid asset shortage caused by trust segment deleverage, even when bond yield was at a high point making it disadvantageous for bond issuance. Between 2014 and 2015, the strong need to finance via bond market was heavily driven by the bond for loan swap during the economic growth moderation, even though bond yield was at a low point making it less appealing for bond investors. There was also ample amount of liquidity in the system during economic restructuring. Starting at the end of 2016 bond percentage dropped to negative territory. The circumstance could be partially contributed to a regulatory drive to lower financial leverage especially regarding the local government platform borrowing.

The bond market place is composed of three segments: exchanges, interbank market, and retail market. (1) The exchange market has both institutional and individual participants, and thus a mixture of both retail and wholesale market characteristics. (2) The interbank has only institutional players, thus making it an OTC wholesale market. (3) Commercial bank's OTC retail market, which is an extension of OTC wholesale market to reach retail customers. Some bond types could be simultaneously listed on multiple markets, and sold to retail and institutional customers. Based upon data published on China Bond, by the end of 2017, the total value of bonds outstanding was 50,95 trillion CNY. Among issuers, the largest was local government, followed by Treasury department and China Development Bank. Together, national government, local government, and three major policy banks that include CDB, Export-Import Bank of China and ADBC, account for more than three quarters of bonds issued. This has contributed to sufficient liquidity to the interest rate section of the bond market. The development of a liquid interest rate section produces the pricing baseline for the less liquid credit market where a credit premium/spread analysis drives credit market spread/risk trade-off trading activities.

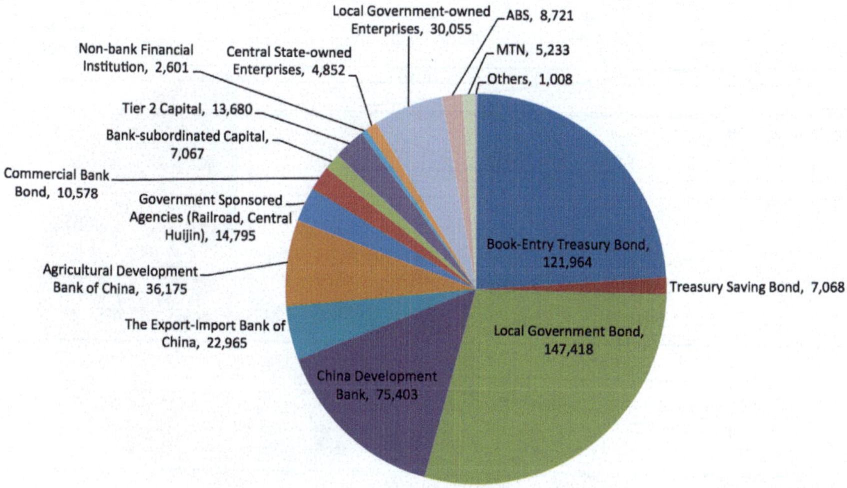

2017.12 Inerbank and Exchange Markets Bond Outstanding Amount by Bond Types (100 Million CNY) China Bond 中债登

The most significant development from 2014 to 2016 was the introduction of local government bond. It was used to reduce the level of local government interest payment by swapping local government loan with local government bond, which had much lower coupon rate. Treasury bond amount was increased to add fiscal stimulus to the economy, while ADBC bond amount increase was a more agriculturally targeted financial stimulus. MTN outstanding amount was reduced partly because of higher issuing cost as interest rate moved up in the last couple of years.

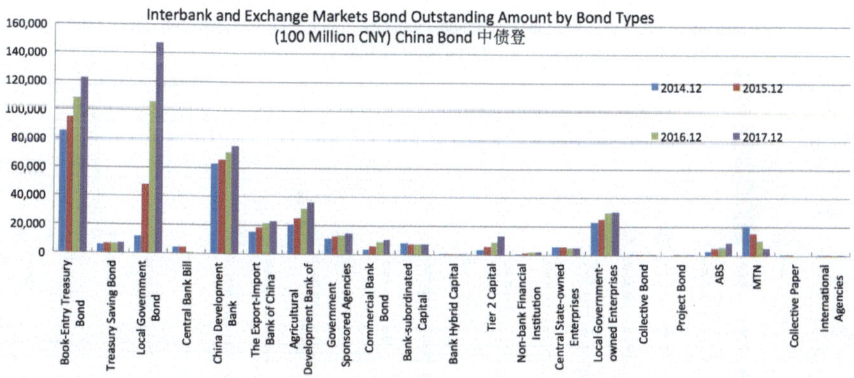

Majority of the bond investments were held by various banks, which include national commercial banks, urban commercial banks and rural commercial banks. Adding insurance companies, the buy-and-hold is still the behavioral norm for bond asset class.

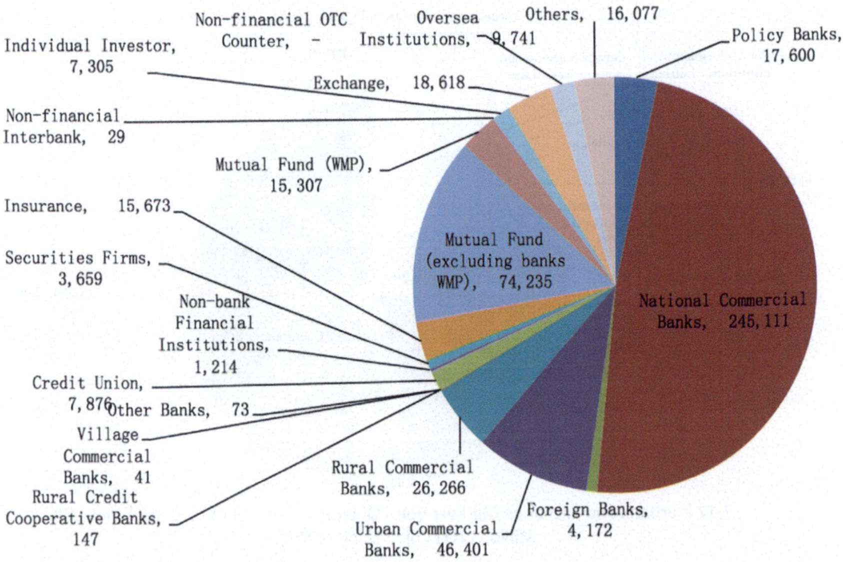

Interbank and Exchange Markets Outstanding Bond Amount by Investor Types (100 Million CNY) 2017.12 (China Bond, 中债登)

While large banks still retained their influence in the fixed income asset class partly due to their increased positions in illiquid local government bonds, mutual funds clearly expanded their presence in the more liquid space. That increased presence was also the case for urban and rural commercial banks. Overall, the bond market has become more dynamic due to more diverse investor types' active participation.

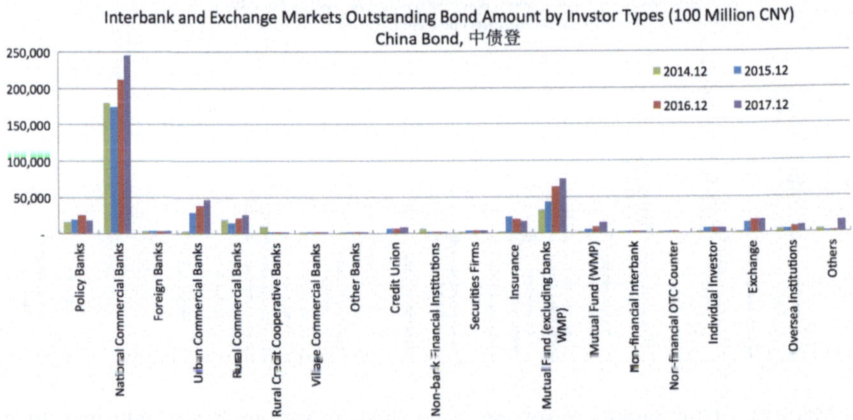

2.4.4 PE and Trusts

Private equities grew by competing in the same space with securities firms' asset management division, mutual fund sub-affiliates and trust with more flexibility. The sector was not as regulated until 2013 when rules specifically targeting PE area were issued. Recent trend was to bring more order and transparency, including regulations issued in 2016 on various leverage ratio limits.

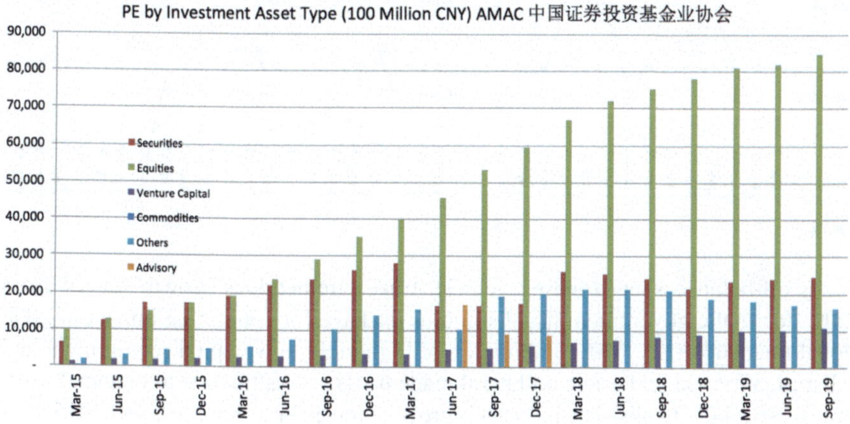

Private equities invest mostly in equities and that sets its limit in a mostly loan lending-based financial landscape. Since China market is very different from US market, the applicable strategies are also quite different. As market evolves and demands more accountability, the so-called Sunshine PE funds that usually specialize in secondary market are gaining wider acceptance. These PE funds are often designed and operated by asset management companies. In practice the asset management teams would reach out to banks and solicit funds via bank-affiliated trusts. Periodical reporting of net asset value brings much desired transparency to the table.

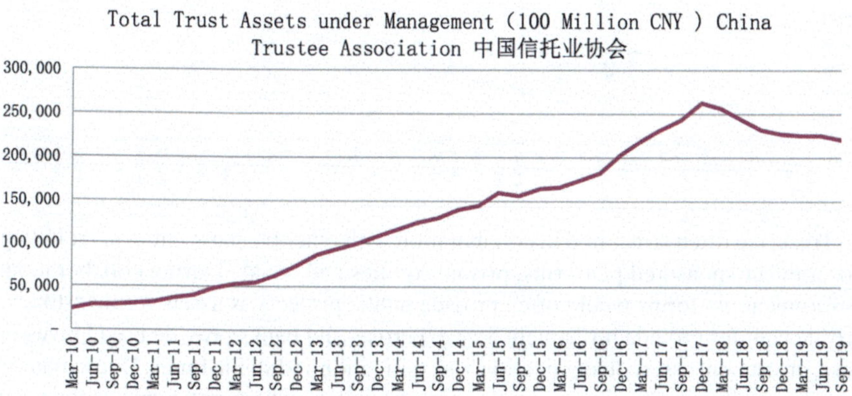

Trust holds much more importance as a financing venue versus PE, both in terms of the size and the breadth of its investment reach. By the end of 2018 the trust industry as a whole managed 22.7 trillion CNY.

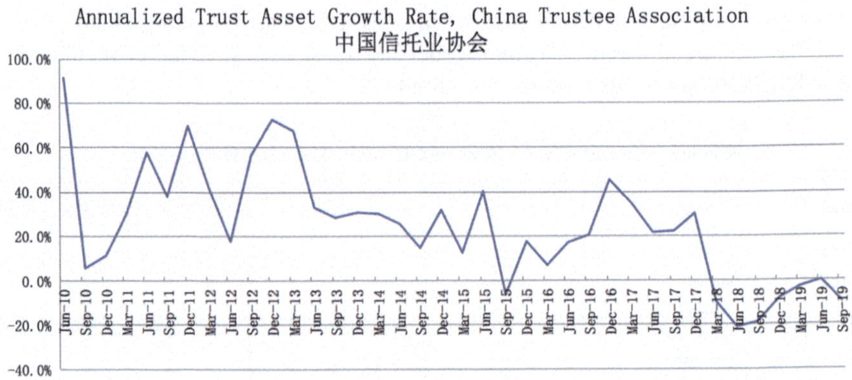

An off-balance sheet funding vehicle, trust's tremendous growth started from 2009, due to the government fiscal stimulus package for countering impact of 2008 global financial crisis. The combination of high yield, low capital requirement and risk mitigation via real estate collateral made trusts very attractive to financial institutions especially banks. The industry's growth slowed between 2013 and 2015 after multiple regulatory policy initiatives, with the most significant one on regulatory capital arbitrage. Trust industry growth resumed in 2016 with continued liquidity release and pressure on entrusted loan after local government leverage control. Starting in 2018, heightened regulatory pressure on shadow banking leverage started to have impact on trust, as well as entrusted loan.

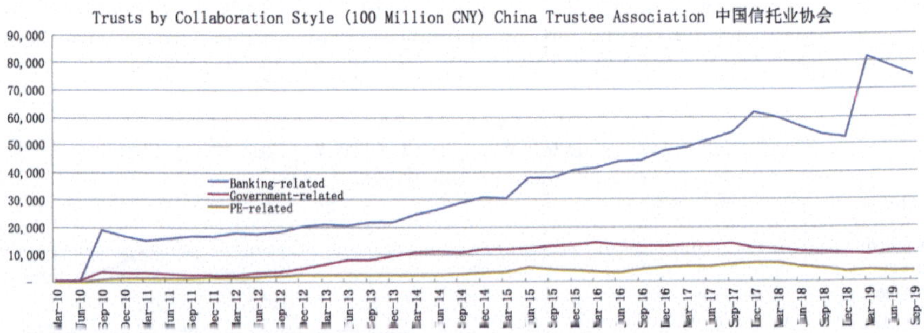

Trusts are often structured in collaboration with other business entities, including government-sponsored platforms, private equities and banks. During collaboration, government platforms would often provide public projects as assets for investment, private equities provide investment area expertise, and banks provide broad investor base, investment assets diversification, risk mitigation and stable funds. Due to banks' strong influence in China's financial area, trust collaboration with banks is the most common form of trust collaboration. Trust classification by origination method again explains banks' influence in the trust business. By the end of 2017, 45.73% of all trusts were single fund trust. Single fund trust is often set up by banks as an off-balance sheet vehicle with underlying loan assets and is structured to meet single institution's investment need. Banks, through single fund trust, either obtain funds via Wealth Management Product and invest in the loan asset; or pool resource to invest in a high priority tranche within a structure and let the trust to solicit additional funds to invest in lower priority equity tranche. A single trust often raises capital for state-owned companies or local government-sponsored development platforms.

2.4.5 Social Security and Insurance

The criticality of the social security and the insurance industry lies in their capabilities and capacities for providing social safety net. There are three types of insurance service providers. The foremost is social security that is administered by the government. The second is the corporate annuity provided by corporations for their employees as supplementary benefits. The third is commercial insurance service provider.

Social security provides coverage on retirement benefits, medical insurance, work-related injury, unemployment benefits and birth insurances. Over the recent years social security expenses increased faster than domestic product growth. The largest allocations went to urban retirement insurance and basic medical insurance.

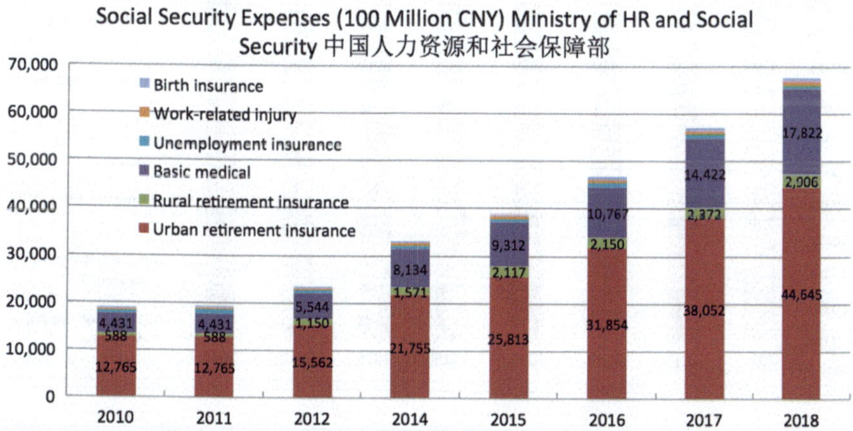

The percentage pattern of expense allocation has been stable. One exception is the rural retirement. While still small, rural retirement expense has increased relatively faster since 2012, reflecting the need for balanced social growth agenda.

Social Security Expenses Allocation (%) Ministry of HR and Social Security 中国人力资源和社会保障部

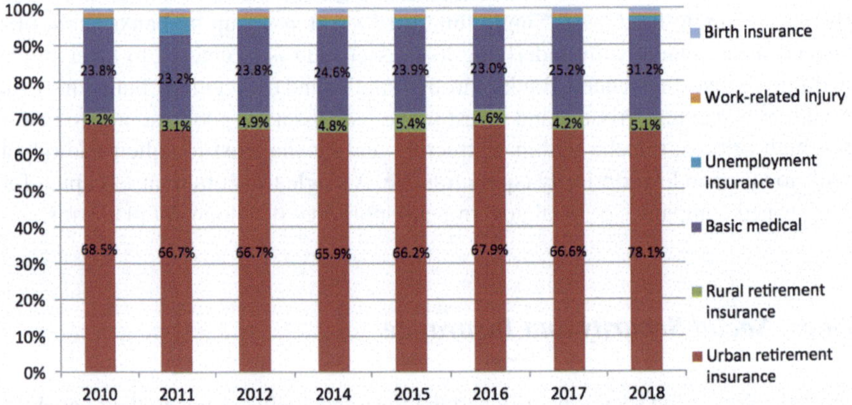

That emphasis on balanced social growth is more pronounced when we look at social security segment balance. A rapid build-up of balance occurred for rural retirement insurance aimed at providing better rural coverage for the country in the future and reducing the living standard inequality between urban and rural areas so as to encourage labor mobility between industrial and agricultural sector, an essential element in successful urbanization.

Social Security Balance Allocation (%) Ministry of HR and Social Security 中国人力资源和社会保障部

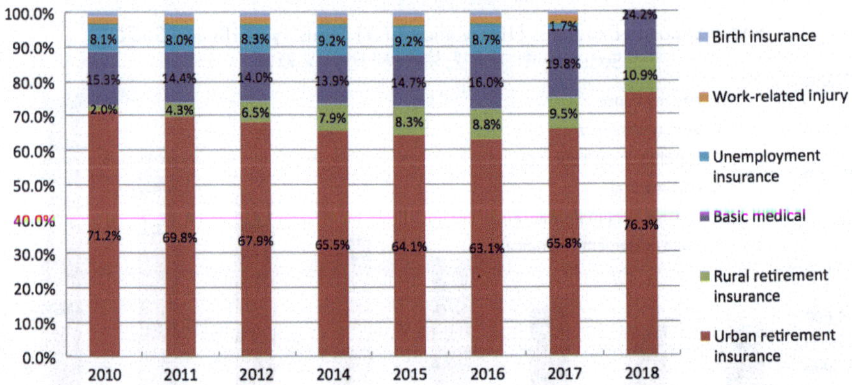

2.4.6 Corporate Annuity

Corporate annuity benefit for employees is supplementary to the mandatory social security coverage. There are 4 roles involved in annuity management, trustee that acts as the legal entity representing the interest of the annuity investor; account manager that manages the cash flows of investment accounts; custodians that are commercial banks offering accounts; investment manager responsible for investment management. While growing fast, annuity total asset size is still small and coverage reach limited to well-funded entity employees.

2.4.7 *Commercial Pensions and Insurance*

Commercial pensions provide coverage for both individuals and groups. Commercial pension funds can be both open-end funds and close-end funds. Commercial insurance business provides coverage on both property and personal insurance. Property insurance tends to be of shorter maturity, typically within 1 year. Personal insurance tends to be of much longer maturity. Personal insurance includes life insurance, health insurance and personal accident insurance. It has long been the case for the industry that more coverage is provided on personal insurance versus property insurance and the majority of personal insurance coverage is for life insurance.

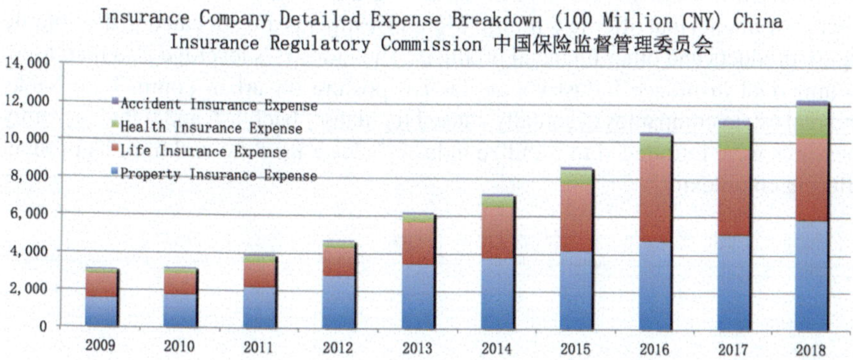

Since more commercial insurance expenses are associated with personal insurance, and personal insurance has longer maturity versus property insurance, the largest portion of accumulated assets to support different business lines belongs to personal insurance business line. Property insurance has less expense coverage and much shorter maturity coverage hence it takes a distant second spot. The domination of life insurance within personal insurance, combined with the domination of personal insurance assets within the industry, have decided the asset allocation for insurance industry investment is long maturity in nature.

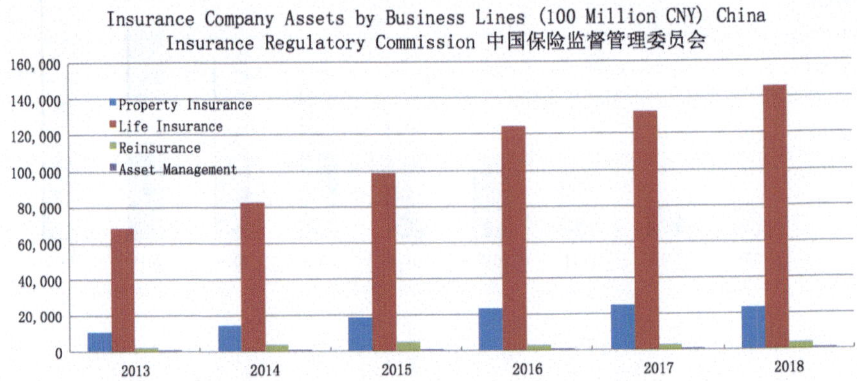

The reduction of bank deposit rate in 1999 as part of the financial market liberalization process caused outflow pressure on life insurance product, which was considered a competing offering. To lessen this pressure, upper limit of life insurance return rate was fixed to 2.5% to prevent insurance companies from competing with each other by offering higher insurance return. As market liberalization progress continued this fixed ceiling rate rendered the insurance industry products even less competitive. In 2013 the upper limit of life insurance rate was raised to 3.5%. Since 2014, both incomes and expenses have risen fast. In 2015, the upper limit was further raised to a company's 5-year average investment yield. At the same time, the investment types allowed are also becoming more complex. Proportionally there is less invested in bank deposit and investment grade bonds, which are simpler and safer instruments that offer less return. More investments are allocated to the volatile equity products and other financial products. The industry's leverage also increased. Commercial insurance industry's aggressive posture on urban commercial banks and real estate companies eventually caused regulatory backlash and tighter scrutiny measures were introduced to stabilize industry's leverage ratio and limit its product offering complexity.

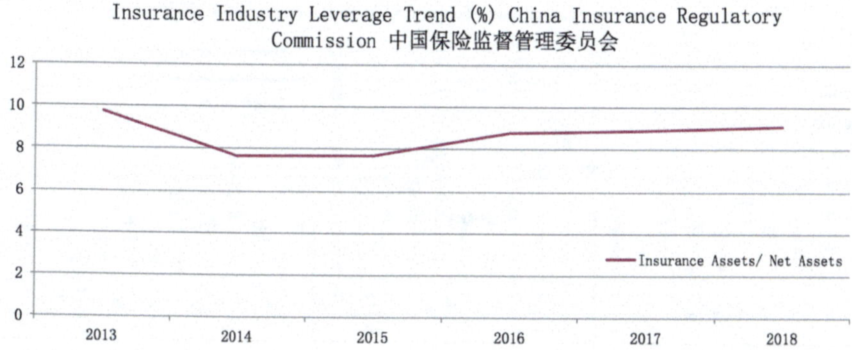

It is important to study social security and commercial insurance business together and a couple of conclusions can be drawn: 1st, the total depth and reach of their coverage have been on the increase to provide a larger and stronger social safety net, a healthy change for more balanced social and economic growth agenda; 2nd, the level of coverage still lags far behind those of advanced economies; 3rd, the coverage for rural area needs to be significantly improved for both retirement and medical benefits.

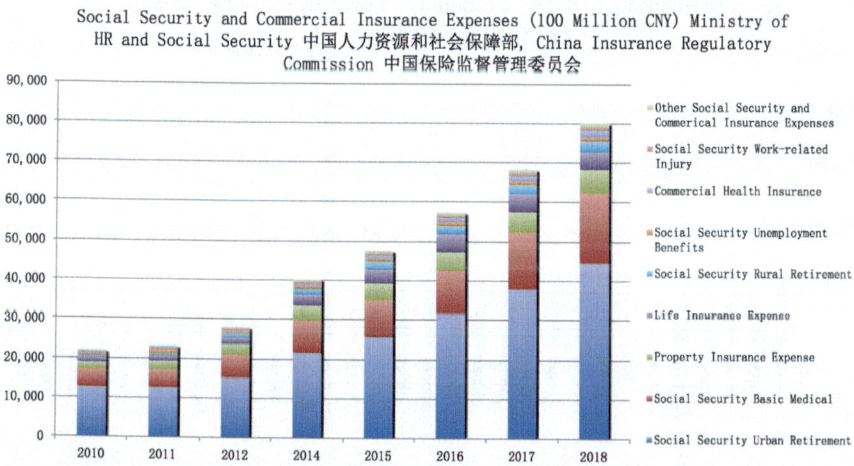

2.5 Geographic Economic Landscape

Regional general budgetary expenditure, which includes government-sponsored retirement benefits and basic medical coverage, forms the baseline financial resource that flows into regional economy. NBSC does not yet provide the large land transfer fee income data at the provincial level.

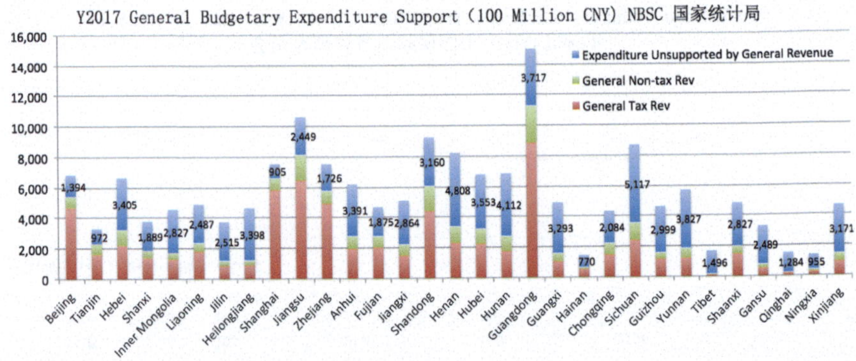

On top of baseline budgetary expenditure, more dynamic financial resources from different providers, including loans from banks, entrusted loans and trust loans from shadow banking, and bonds and equities from capital markets, flow into different regional economies in China and translate into various business and consumption activities. Therefore those different sizes and types of financial resource flows shed light upon the dynamic characteristics of each regional economy.

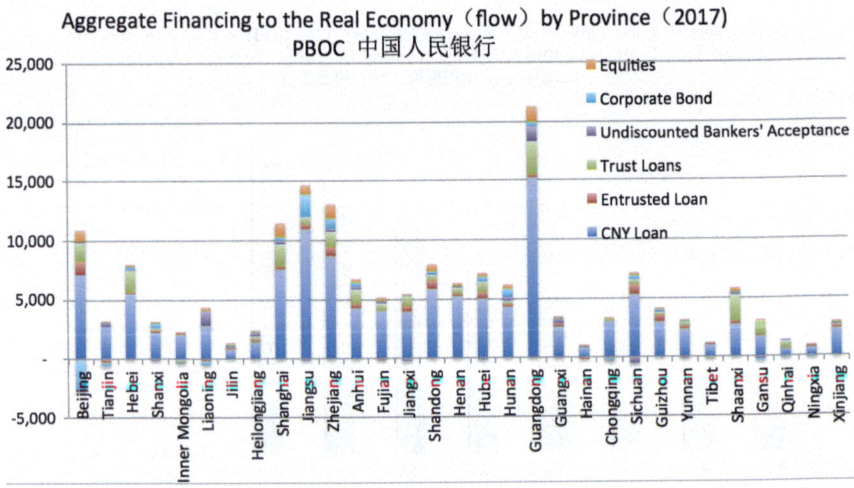

An important piece of data is the total size of aggregated social financing for each region. Past number showed that regions in China with the largest amount of financing activities included Guangdong, Jiangsu, Beijing, Shanghai, Shandong and Zhejiang. They are either coastal provinces or capital city, with vibrant high tech, finance and export industries.

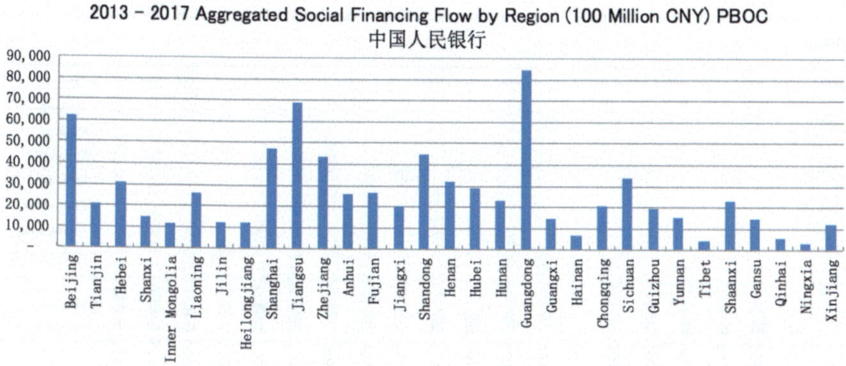

One factor that can greatly impact regional economic stability hence the aggregated social financing data stability is the presence or the lack of commodity resources such as fossil fuel deposit, which can act as growth contributor by producing chemical/energy supplies in a country that has large demand for raw chemical/energy resource. The supply, demand and price of fossil fuel can be quite volatile with international and domestic circumstance change and policy change. Fossil energy is not evenly distributed, with production concentrated in northwest Xinjiang, central Shaanxi, northeast Heilongjiang and east coast Tianjin (Bohai Gulf).

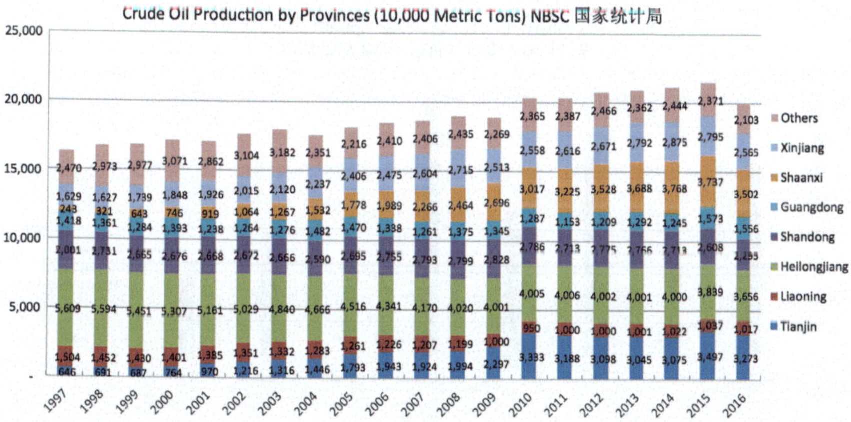

Gas supplements coal. As a clean energy source it has good prospect in the future. Gas production is concentrated in northwest Xinjiang, central Shaanxi and southwest Sichuan.

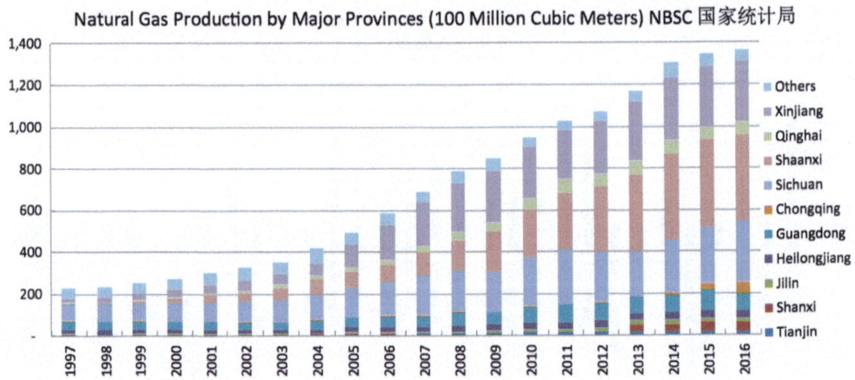

Not only is the level of aggregated social financing, so is the composition of regional aggregated social financing useful in explaining the dynamic characteristic difference of each region. For most of these regions loan is the most important method to obtain financial resources, with Beijing being the exception using large amount of bonds to obtain funding possibly because of heavy concentration of large corporate headquarters. Undiscounted banker acceptance is widely used in regions with export supply chain and small medium enterprise financing, which include Jiangsu, Guangdong and Zhejiang.

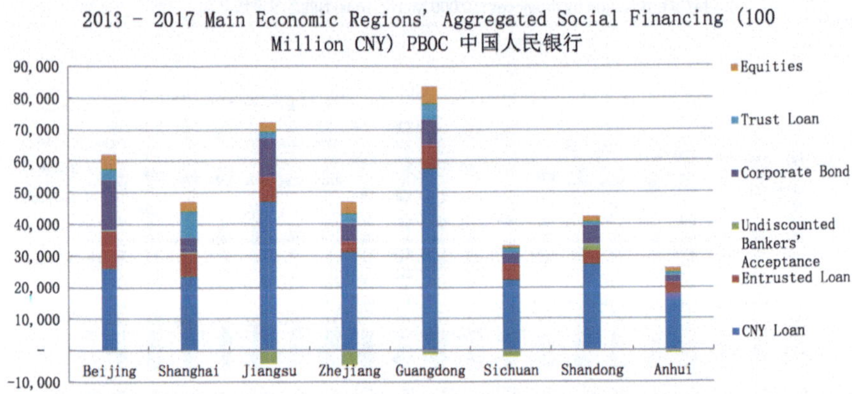

In addition to aggregated social financing, regional electricity consumption amount can also used as a measurement for the state of local economy, but pointing more towards industrial activities. Zhejiang, Jiangsu, Shandong and Guangdong, all provinces on the coast, are low in terms of natural resource availability, but rather active in terms of industrial economic vibrancy.

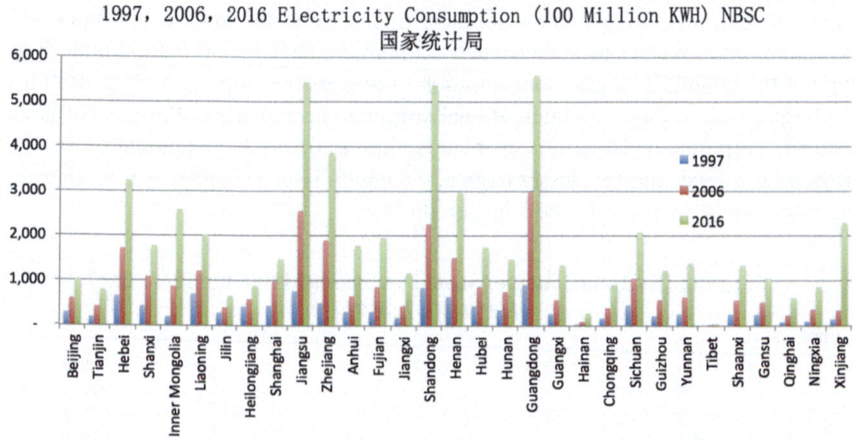

Since not every region enjoys the same level of economic development, revenue transfer from central government plays an important role in the growth of less developed areas, including those agricultural provinces and far-flung regions. Regions with lower tax revenue transfer to aggregated social financing ratio, included Beijing, Shanghai, Tianjin, Zhejiang, Jiangsu and Guangdong that received relatively much less revenue transfer. They were essentially resource providers to rest of the nation via the central government transfer process.

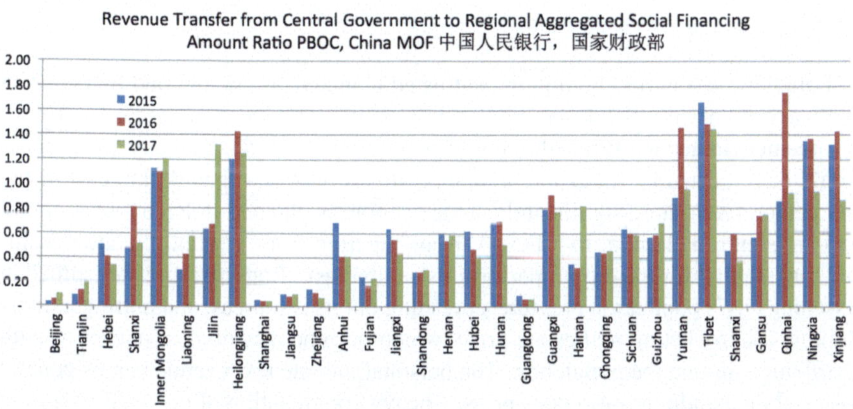

2.5.1 Beijing and Its Adjacent Areas

Geographically Chinese economic system has three main pillars. Beijing is the political and administrative center, while Yangtze Delta (including Shanghai, Zhejiang and Jiangsu), and Pearl River Delta (including Guangdong/Shenzhen), are its two economic engines. This pattern is unlikely to change in the foreseeable future. As the capital city and the most important economic center for northern China, Beijing has the country's largest concentration of universities, top research institutions and hospitals, domestic and international corporate headquarters. Presence of large domestic corporate headquarters enabled Beijing to obtain large amount of finance via bond issuance, and to a lesser degree, via equity issuance and these are cheaper and more liquid sources of funds than credit loan.

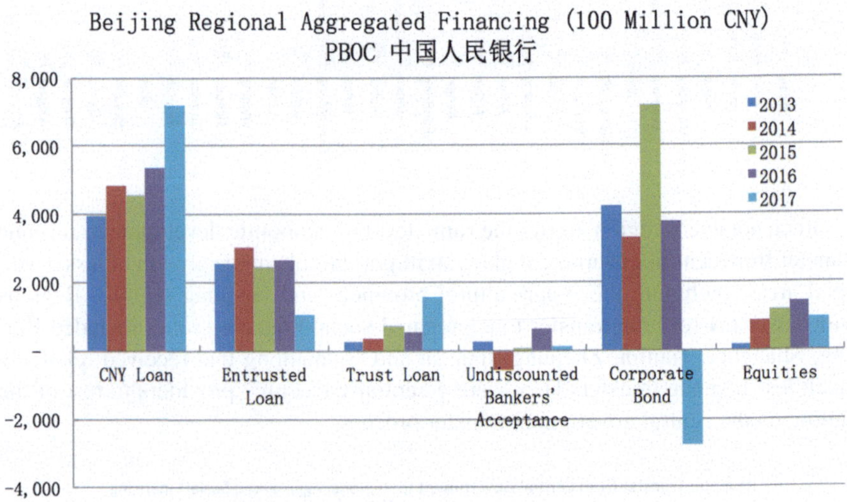

Large drops occurred both in the entrusted loan and corporate bond financing in 2017, a result of overall deleveraging environment and the most strict real estate curb enforcement in history. While the central government is staying put, city government would be relocated to Tongzhou, a municipality a little less than 23 km east of the city center. Even more significantly, a vice capital is planned in Xiong'an, roughly 150 km south of Beijing, to relieve various function from Beijing that are considered unessential for the city to perform its capital task. Both measures are aimed at lessening city's population pressure, spreading out its resources, and putting a lid on Beijing's skyrocketing real estate price, which became a symbol of uneven wealth distribution among the population. The personal income tax revenue versus general budgetary expenditure ratio does prove a heavy congregation of personal wealth in Beijing.

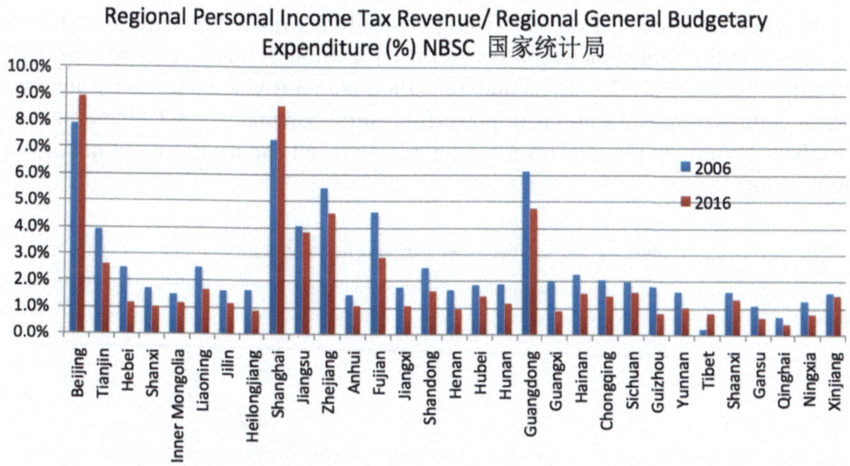

Besides wealth congregation, cumulative effects from many historical factors also contributed to Beijing's high real estate price. In the thirteenth century during the Yuan dynasty, and for hundreds of years since then, Beijing has been chosen as the country's ministerial bureaucracy center to stabilize the vast northern China for political reason, and the city lacks the water resource and sea trade route connection for economic wealth generation. To compensate for the relatively low monetary compensation of the bureaucrats versus their administrative authority over the huge populace, the school and hospital systems in Beijing are traditionally well supported and the best of them have been historically located in the old city center. The city has expanded greatly during that last 30 or so years, but the layout of its core has remained largely unchanged. In the center west, Xicheng is today home to central governing body of the party, the central bank, MOF, NDRC, large policy banks and commercial banks headquarters, hence the very political center of China. Center east Dongcheng and further east Chaoyang host Ministry of Foreign Affairs, some other governmental departments, numerous foreign consulates, international corporate HQs and many wealthy individuals. Further west Haidian is home to some of the best universities in China, including Beijing University and Qinghua University, hence the top echelon of China's educational and technological system. As Chinese living standard improved continuously over the recent years, people are demanding better medical and educational services, and that has increased the attractiveness of Beijing's city core real estate. At the same time, the revenue from large SOEs including the large banks, and the presence of international HQs and business, plus the wealth effect of technology start-ups spawned by the elite technology universities, together have caused trickle-down effect on Beijing's urban environment improvement and job opportunities. Historical layout with concentrated good medical and education services, employment prospect from bureaucracy, presence of many corporate headquarters and start-ups, and recent urban improvement, all have contributed to Beijing's skyrocketing real estate price.

Designed to disperse Beijing existing centrally distributed resources, which as the entrenched establishment can be traced back through many centuries, the two relocation measures to Xiong'an and Tongzhou are no trivial exercises by any historical comparison. Relocations of powerful central bureaucracy in Chinese history have been extremely rare and always required stern and enduring commitment from the very top.

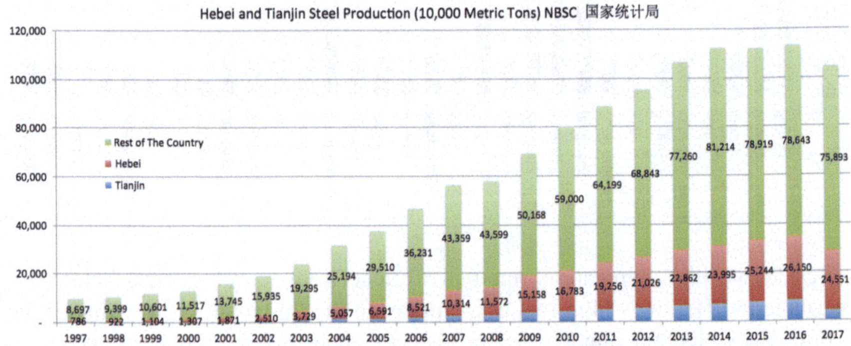

Tianjin as the other major city in northern China, had a prominent presence being the preferred seaport of the north back during colonial days, and that importance has fallen as China's internal transportation system improved and other ports shared the role of the sea route contact points, offering more direct international trade access to manufacturing home bases. Hebei province surrounds both Beijing and Tianjin and it has about a quarter of China's steel production volume. For that reason, the recent supply-side reform to reduce steel overcapacity and the anti-pollution effort to reduce smog over Beijing took heavy tolls on Hebei's GDP. Nevertheless, Beijing, Hebei and Tianjin together form a heavily industrialized area. As Beijing's prominent economic and technological future remains bright, its growth will benefit Tianjin and Hebei for years to come.

2.5.2 *The Northeastern Rusty Belt*

Northeast as a region includes Heilongjiang, Jilin and Liaoning. North of the Great Wall, with fertile land and later oil riches, this region benefited from Russian capital infusion during Czar's era, and Japanese capital infusion before WWII was over, and was the main industrial base for China when the new republic was founded in 1949. Heavily dependent on large SOE in mature industries, and partly slowed down by prolonged lack of progress on regional integration because of North Korea security concern, it gradually lost its industrial edge to the South and coastal region after China entered WTO, illustrated by long declining share of auto production, which was dominated by First Automobile Work in Jilin in the old days. Much effort has been made to rejuvenate the area but the progress is very slow. Area remains as a top spot for mechanized farming practice.

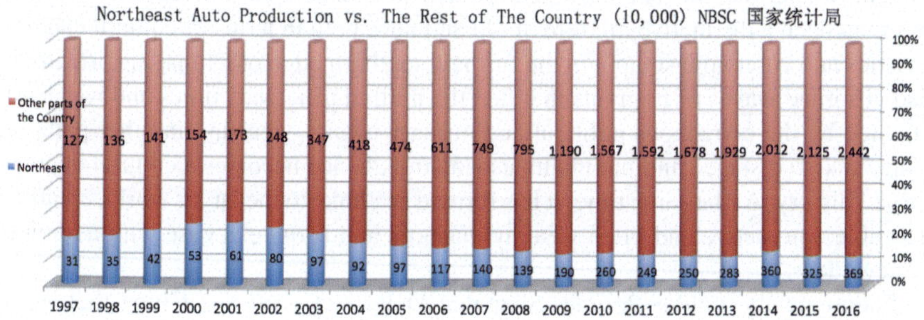

2.5.3 *The Northwestern Frontier*

The northwestern region including Gansu, Qinghai, Tibet, Ningxia and Xinjiang is vast and sparsely populated. The diverse landscape, from the north to the south, includes the Altai Mountain, Junggar Basin, Tianshan Mountain, Tarim Basin, Kunlun Mountain, High Tibetan Plateau and Himalaya Mountain. Too far from the sea to the north and east direction, the area is also blocked by mountains to receive moisture from the south and the west, thus the basins become expansive deserts decorated with oasis on the foothill of the surrounding mountains. Passages such as the Silk Route became the connecting links between China and the Eurasia continent to the west and the India subcontinent to the south. Gas reserve is high and its production as a clean energy source has picked up, but the regional ecosystem is fragile therefore environmental concerns always need to be addressed during the planning stage of any development effort. More recently progress was made to restore the ecosystem back to a healthier state, exemplified by the population of Tibetan antelope bouncing back from 75 thousand in 1995 to an estimated number at more than 150 thousand in 2016.

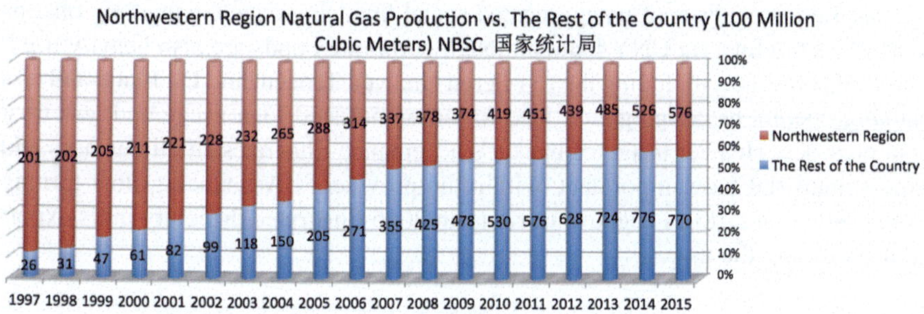

2.5.4 *The Southern Trading Exposure*

Fujian, Guangdong and Hainan together form the southern coastal region. This area has long been a distinctive mixture of old and new, both in terms of cultural characteristics and economic setup. On the furthest southern edge of China, historically it had absorbed waves of migrants that fled the north during wars times and was least affected by the extraneous political and military events occurring in other parts of China due to distance and mountainous isolation, hence becomes a cultural depository of history. At the same time, it has formed sea links to the larger world, creating a sizable, interactive and often wealthy diaspora and is quite at ease with adoption of new ideas.

Economically, unlike Beijing, Shanghai Delta and northeast China that went though heavy industrialization in the early days, this area kept a more dormant and traditional economic backdrop until the country opened up in the 1980s. Hence old economic background coexists with Shenzhen's spectacular rise, and the area becomes home to a list of global tech giants including Tencent, known for its social media Wechat, Huawei, known for its telecom gears, and Dajiang, known for airborne drones. While some other provinces or areas have often grabbed business headlines, Guangdong has been consistently the biggest trade surplus contributing province in China, underlying its industrial capabilities.

Guangdong International Trade Surplus on Goods vs. The Rest of the Country (100 Million USD) NBSC 国家统计局

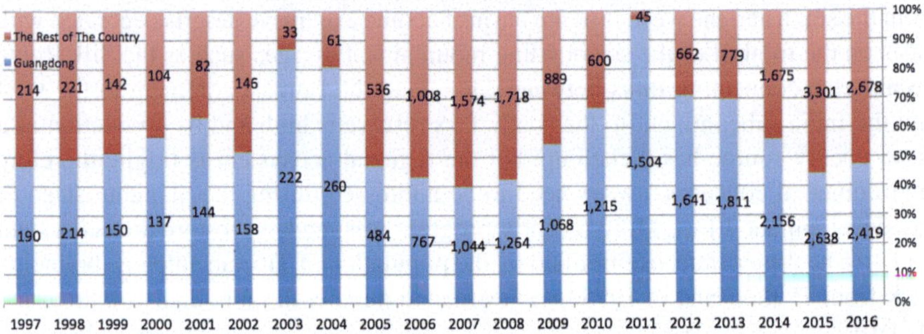

Based upon analysis of its aggregated social financing data, Guangdong obtains most of its funding via CNY loan, although corporate bonds are also heavily used. Large HQ presence, including the top-tiered Huawei, Tencent and Da Jiang, and less banking operations congregation lead to more entrusted loan usage and less trust loan presence. Heavier usage of banker's acceptance illustrates small business and export industrial base importance within the province. BA financing flow turning from positive in 2013 to negative territory in 2016 illustrated difficulty in its export industry during the time.

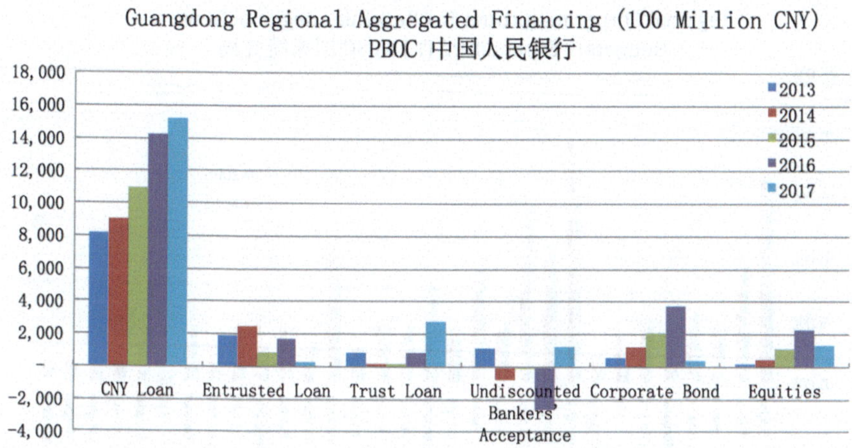

Unlike Guangdong where economic activities congregate on the Pearl River Delta with business intensity rivaling that of Beijing and Shanghai, Fujian's landscape is mountainous except the narrow strip of land located non-continuously along its coastal line, hence it does not possess one particular singular economic center within itself. Hainan province has built up economic momentum as economic integration with ASEAN gains importance, but it has a much smaller economic footprint versus Guangdong.

2.5.5 *The Eastern Prosperity*

Located at the mouth of the Yangtze River, Shanghai, Jiangsu and Zhejiang form the east coastal region and the area is the most important tax revenue source for the country. To help understand the importance of this area, an analogy can be made between the high-speed railroad artery connecting the political/technology center Beijing to revenue center Shanghai, and the Amtrak Northeast Corridor connecting political center DC to innovation center Boston. The importance of Beijing-Yangtze Delta connection remains unchanged since the Tang Dynasty during the first millennium, except the old Grand Canal transport function is being provided by the high-speed train instead. Relatively larger than Beijing or Guangdong when combined in terms of both landmass size and population, with multiplying freewheeling private enterprises, wealth creation has made this delta the most prosperous area in China. Shanghai's towering corporate wealth presence over the rest of the countries, side by side with Beijing, can be illustrated by the regional corporate income tax revenue versus regional budgetary general expenditure ratio. Its relative strength was further increased during the 2006–2016 decade.

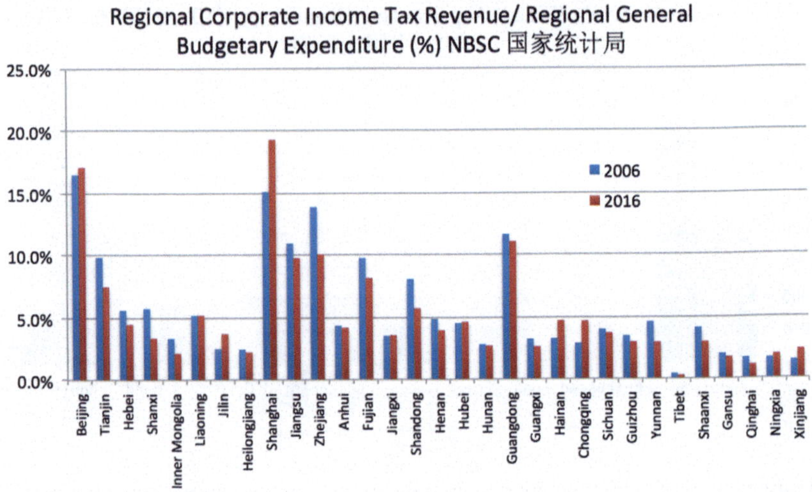

With a strong corporate economic presence, Shanghai relies heavily on direct financing that includes corporate bonds and equities, but to less extent than Beijing. The internationally perceived top position of Shanghai in China's capital markets is not that clear if investment strategy decision process is taken into consideration. Different from markets in the West where portfolio managers and traders in New York and London wield ultimate influence with their collective trading strategy formulation and execution, traders and portfolio managers in Shanghai often need to follow headquarters directives, many of which are issued from Beijing. Trading execution becomes more processing in nature and higher number of processing does not necessarily translate into more market influence. Besides less direct financing and less capital markets influence, less HQ concentration in Shanghai also leads to less entrusted loan usage since those loans have been historically linked to local government projects financed with public-listed companies acting as conduit. On the other hand, there is larger usage of trust loan than Beijing by banks to provide financing to those less established economic entities that are more vibrant in Shanghai Delta area.

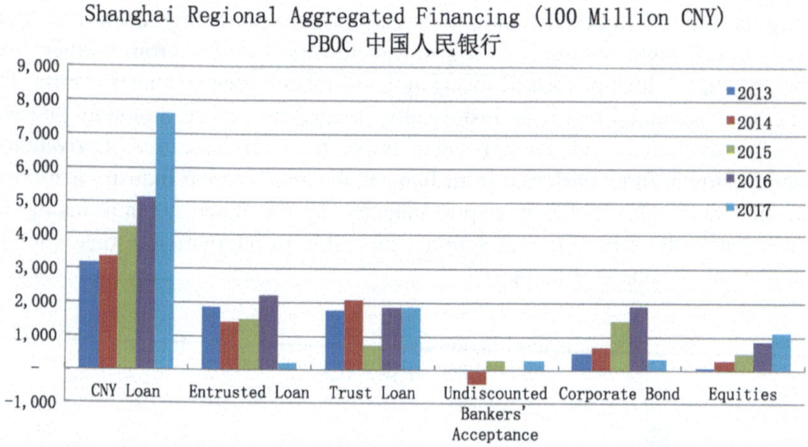

Geographically located north of Shanghai, Jiangsu's economic model is to certain extent comparable to that of Guangdong in terms of having a large export segment, although its export industry is composed more of international versus indigenous corporations. The rising land, labor cost and domestic competition created difficulties for its export industries and private industries, and this was reflected by the drop of BA financing activities. There had been a continuous pullout by existing international corporations, which had created pressure for Jiangsu to make its business environment more attractive and to simultaneously upgrade its manufacturing capability.

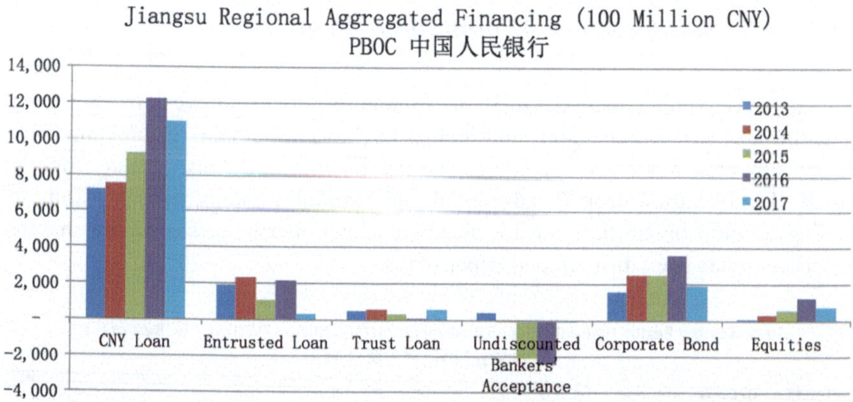

Zhejiang is one of the most vibrant economic regions in China. It lacks the banking and HQ resources enjoyed by Beijing, Shanghai or Guangdong, with the exception of the omnipresent Alibaba and a couple of others, and has to compensate for that lack of resources with self-driven entrepreneurship. With a high population density and only the small northern strip of the province being flat and fertile, the willingness for enduring hardship and maintaining flexibility could go back for hundred of years.

During the time of Imperial Exam, the area produced many high achievers. More recently, many high ranking central government officials came from northern part of the province, which possessed strong agricultural and private industrial base. The southeast coastal area had been historically isolated by rugged mountain and was known for sea-bound trade lately became associated with the source of private real estate investment fund. Different from Jiangsu, the area's export industry is more of domestic origin. This makes its export industry more competitive in terms of cost control, but at the same time also more vulnerable to international trade conflict. Loan is its main source of financing.

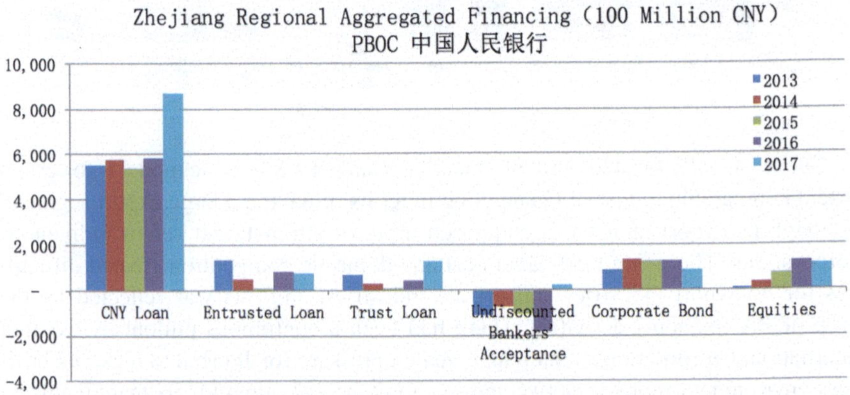

2.5.6 *The Southwestern Mountainous Regions*

Sichuan, Chongqing, Guangxi, Guizhou, Yunnan form the southwestern region. Far from the northern frontier and land-locked by large mountain systems and high plateau, the area was often considered the last bastion in defense during imperial tumult. The elevation drop is substantial and hydraulic energy reserve is ample. Finding a compromise between the need for clean energy versus natural habitat preservation has been difficult and expensive.

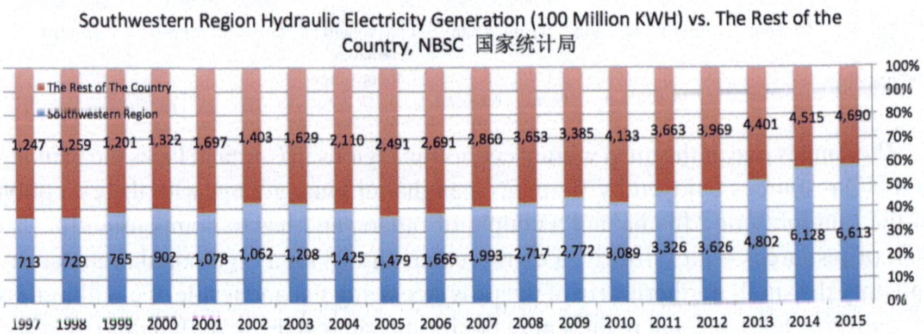

Sichuan is the most important provincial economy in this area. It is one of the largest provinces in China. Being populous with fertile plain in the center, it has strong agricultural and industrial capacities, especially regarding electronics, partly due to a good educational base. Similar to Shandong, it has low cost of living, hence a relatively small aggregated social financing for its large economic output. The province is also an important natural gas provider. Loan is its main source of financing and equity venue hardly used.

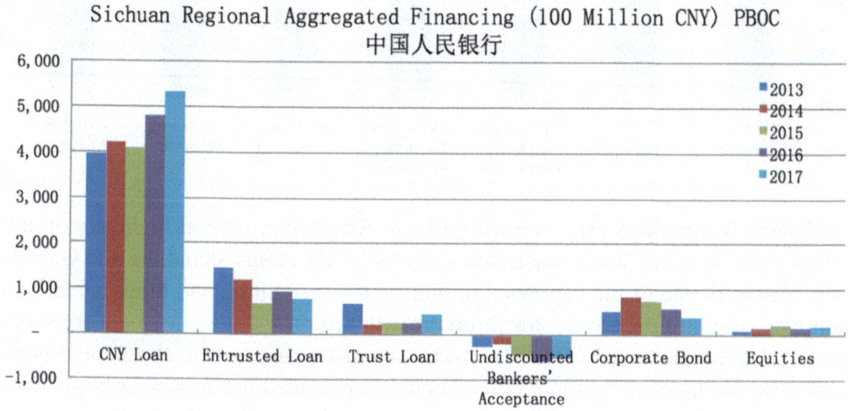

2.5.7 *The Central Heartland*

The central heartland was the origin of China's civilization. Regional and national dynasties before Yuan chose their bases in these areas, before Beijing became the national capital. In modern days, these areas provide both industrial and agricultural output backed by large workforce of different educational levels.

[Shandong] With a long coastal line and fertile landscape, Shandong has been an important industrial and agricultural base, producing many of the traditional industrial products that include yarn, paper, sodium hydroxide and others. It also has a large export industrial base, led by companies such as Haier. Since the traditional industries are often energy intensive and reside in relatively saturated product sectors, in an environment-conscious era with more emphasis on value-added technology improvement, its recent growth paled against those regions booming with high tech industries and it has made substantial effort in upgrading its industry composition to spur growth and reduce pollution.

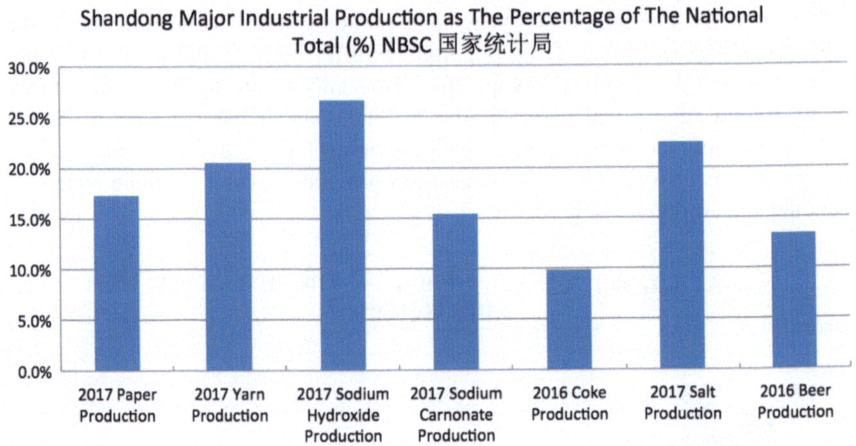

[Henan] A populous province with a large workforce, both at high school and college graduate level, and a much lower cost of living versus Shandong and Guangdong, Henan is one of the backbone provinces for agriculture and more recently, a manufacturing hub positioned for future growth. To provide employment for large provincial population and offset the rising manufacturing cost of the Yangtze and Pearl River Delta areas, national government has provided incentives for large manufacturing companies to move there, the most significant of which is the continuous expansion of Zhengzhou Rail Yard. Transportation capacity in quantity, low development cost and large size of educated workforce help Henan to further its growth potential.

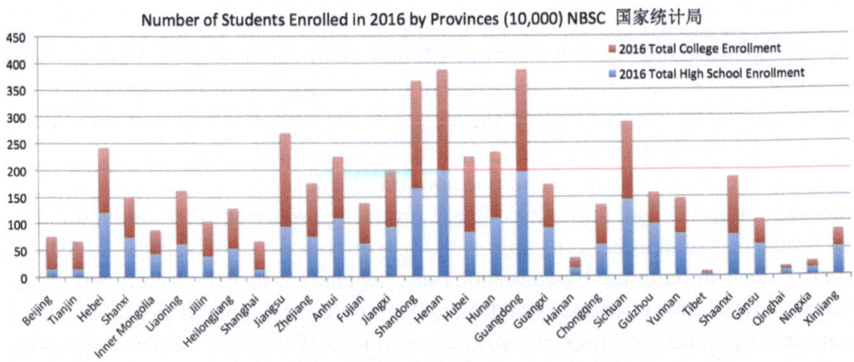

Being an important part of China's central region, Henan's education data change actually coincides with China's progress towards industrialization. Critical resources were first provided to increase the education level of general population resulting in a large increase of HS enrollment. Later in the mid of first decade of this century, college enrollment increase started to gather speed, reflecting higher level of modernization in need of a better educated workforce.

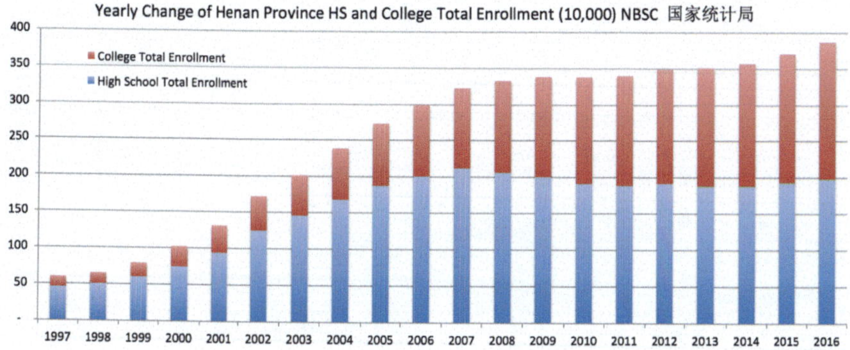

[Anhui] Anhui had enjoyed good growth over the recent years, represented by its increase in aggregated social financing. The powerful presence of the elite University of Science and Technology of China has made its provincial capital, Hefei, one of the top four AI innovation zones, beside Beijing, Shenzhen and Hangzhou, underlying the important role played by leading high tech education institute in changing fate of a city, much in similarity with what Carnegie Mellon University has done to Pittsburgh in the US. iFLYTEK in Hefei and the more established Baidu in Beijing were all started by USTC graduates.

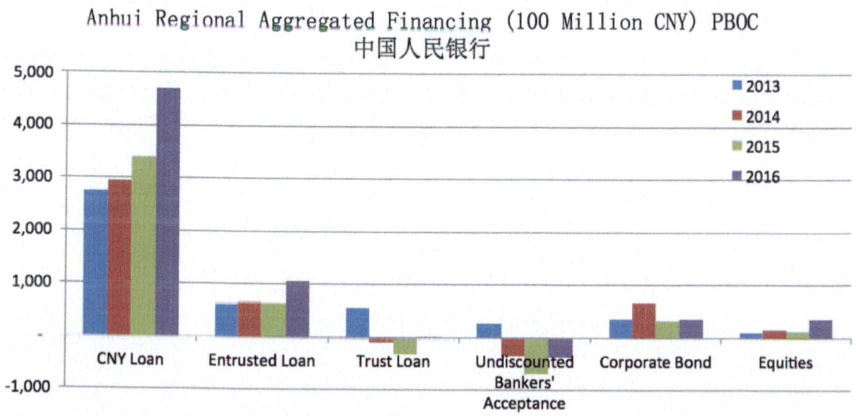

Chapter 3
Economic Structure Management Settings

3.1 Economic Policy Management Structure

The flows of financial and other economic resources breathe life into industrial and regional economic structure. These resource flows can either be pushed by exogenous policy initiatives, originated from central and regional government, or be pulled by endogenous business and consumption activities, originated from domestic or international, big or small corporations, and individual consumers.

3.1.1 Four Pillars of Governance

When economic resources are pushed by policy initiatives, the formation of most fundamental economic policy initiatives starts at the top of central government. There are four pillars at the core of central Chinese government, including the Party, the executive branch State Council, People's Congress and the Political Consultative Conference (PCC). Though each part plays a different role and not everyone is directly involved at each procedural stage, they together are responsible for the iterative budgetary formation and execution process at the core of economic policy. In broad terms, PCC provides consultation, Ministry of Finance would put forward budgetary proposal for a vote, to be approved by National People's Congress (NPC), and carried out by the executive branch upon NPC approval and revision, all under the Party's leadership.

3.1.2 The Executive Branch and Governance

Central government in stricter definition refers to the executive branch under the State Council headed by the prime minister, which includes Ministry of Finance, NDRC, Ministry of Foreign Affairs, Ministry of Civil Affairs, among many others. The executive branch, from central top to its most basic level, forms the largest part of

X. Zhang, *Mechanical Analysis of China's Macro Economic Structure*,
https://doi.org/10.1007/978-981-15-3840-7_3

the governance, much so versus the NPC and PCC, which also have multiple levels, illustrated by the difference on the size of their budgetary expenditure.

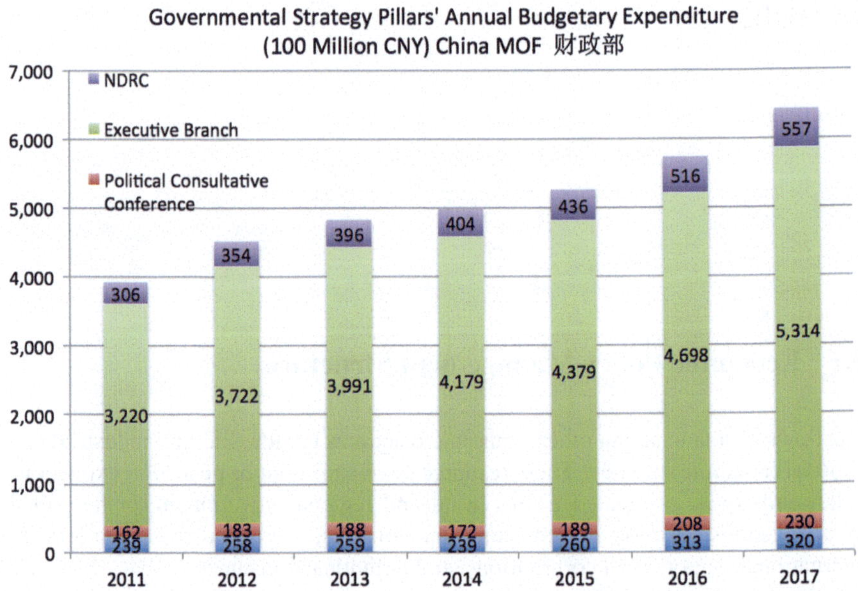

3.1.3 Economic Coordination Sub-committee

In the last couple of years, some high level cross-departmental structures were created or reorganized to strengthen governmental capability in pushing forward various reform agenda. Foremost new structure was the Central Finance and Economics Committee, leading and supervising economic work of both the CPC Central Committee and the State Council, and is headed by CPC General Secretary and Premier of the State Council. Another important structure was the Financial Stability and Development Committee under the State Council to oversee financial stability and development with the central bank expected to play a stronger role in macro management and guarding against system risks. Those structures could provide important guideline level input into the budget proposal mainly drafted by MOF.

3.1.4 Think Tanks

Think thanks hold an important role in the process of China economic policy formulation. The leading think tank was China Academy of Social Science. The academy also has regional branches that are heavily involved in 5-year planning process.

3.2 Economic Planning Management Structure

Bureaucrats are deeply involved in the economic planning and plan implementation of China's macro economy. For their influential handling in sometimes quite specific and critical economic activities, their absence in analysis might render any study on China economic management lacking substantiation.

3.2.1 NDRC and Infrastructure Marvels

Being the most prominent economic planning agency within the administrative branch in China, National Development and Reform Committee (NDRC) was instrumental in delivering economic transformation that took place in China over the last 30–40 years. It usually works with other department to create regulatory and policy framework. Its work is organized around a series of 5-year economic development planning.

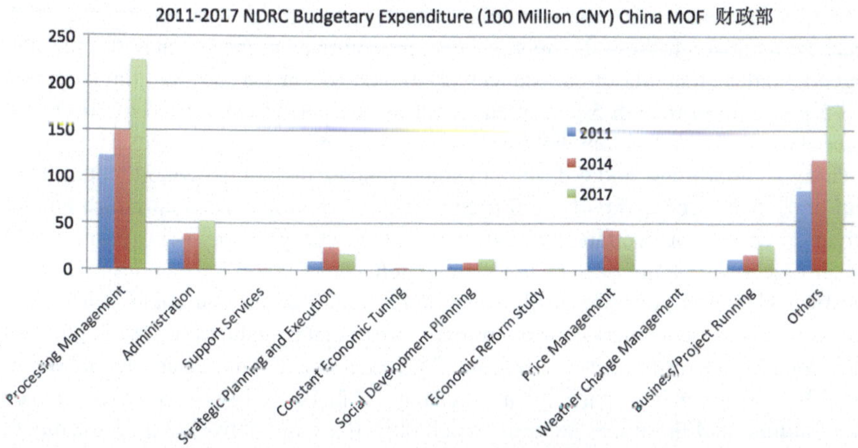

The formation process of a typical 5-year plan is rather methodical. First, it needs to reflect the need of social improvement in its draft; 2nd, it has to reach overall consensus before being accepted; 3rd, it needs to able to produce an expected cohesive outcome at different governmental levels and across different governmental regions; 4th, it needs to be practical with implementation details. There also has to be mid-term deliverable assessment and end-period assessment with predefined benchmark.

Based upon regulation published by the State Council in 2005, the plan has 3 different levels, including national, provincial and county levels. The plan is also categorized into 3 sub-types: comprehensive planning, which is coordinated by a corresponding level of government and drafted by NDRC of the same level; specific planning, which is handled by government of the same level; and cross-regional planning, which is coordinated by national NDRC in collaboration with relevant regional government. Specific planning is a specific extension of comprehensive planning and therefore has to conform to the comprehensive planning result.

The planning process includes bidding by domestic and sometimes international institutions for plan proposal; soliciting public input and input from government of lower levels; debating confirmation by specialist committee; consultation with People's Congress and Political Consultative Conference of relevant levels. Specific planning that requires national NDRC approval can only be implemented after NDRC approval; regional planning that requires national NDRC approval can only be implemented after national NDRC and provincial government coordination. For a plan proposal to be approved, it needs to have sufficient explanation for proposal drafting process, accompanied by public feedback, debating confirmation result, and is then sent to the appropriate level of government, which then sends the proposal to People's Congress of the same level for approval. Important projects that require State Council approval can only be implemented after State Council approval. There is a lot left in the plan process for possible improvement, including more transparency in proposal drafting process, transparency in coordination decision making process, but it was this system that had produced the China infrastructure wonder of the past 30 years.

China has had a series of 5-year plans since the founding of the republic in 1949, each being different from the previous one, reflecting evolving social and economic agenda under changing circumstances. The most recent 5-year plan, the so called 13-5 plan, the thirteenth 5-year plan, covering the period from 2016 to 2020, had set out to achieve 5 development themes, including innovation, greenness, openness, sharing and harmony, and 6 developmental agendas, including economic, political, cultural, social, eco and party, and tried to strike a more balanced approach among green environment, welfare, infrastructure, economic growth, social fairness and other objectives. Many of the agenda items reflected general societal improvement desire and would not have easily quantifiable outcome measurement, while others were given benchmarks for quantified performance evaluation. Developmental benchmarks are further categorized into 2 types, those that are desirable and delivered by various market participants and may be facilitated by government, hence not binding, and those that are must-reach objectives and delivered by government agencies. This categorization is adopted since 11-5 planning and a common practice among national and regional NDRC offices.

3.2.2 *Ministry of Finance*

After planning, funding with financial resources is the next step for economic policy implementation. The Ministry of Finance and its local bureaus have more responsibilities compared with their western peers, due to larger social and economic roles played by different levels of government entities through the SOE and non-SOE channels. Budget is proposed by the executive branch and requires approval from people's congress at the same level. Coordination required with other agencies is substantial, especially after the more recent deleveraging process. Local budget now requires sign-off from Ministry of Finance.

Within the list of budgetary charts published by the Ministry of Finance, 3 types are the most important for detailing governmental revenue sources. 1st type explains general revenue that is funded mostly by taxes and eventually used for general governmental purposes, and this category of charts includes National General Public Budget Revenue, Central Government's General Public Budget Revenue and Local Government's General Public Budget Revenue; 2nd category explains fund revenue that is sourced from income generated by special projects and eventually used for specific purposes, and this category of charts includes National Government-managed Fund Revenue, Central Government-managed Fund Revenue and Local Government-managed Fund Revenue; 3rd category is state capital revenue, and this category of charts includes National State Capital Operations Revenue, Central Government's State Capital Operations Revenue and Local Government's State Capital Operations Revenue.

Within the first category of MOF reports, National General Public Budget Revenue report combines both central and local general public revenue data. The largest reported revenue sources include VAT, corporate and personal income tax. China's tax is largely based upon indirect tax, and less so on direct tax that is directly levied upon entities, which include corporate and individuals, and personal income tax takes a rather small portion in the total revenue source. The relative small portion of direct tax and personal tax is common among developing countries where tax infrastructure is less mature and personal income is at relatively low level.

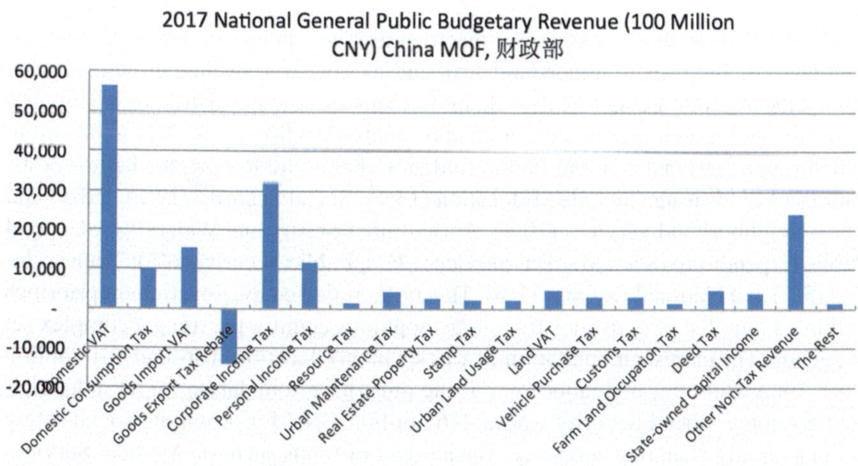

Central Government General Public Budget Revenue and Local Government General Public Budget Revenue reports explain revenue data at central and local government levels respectively. Combining data from two levels does not automatically lead to the result on the national revenue report, since a large portion of central government revenue is transferred to local government, in addition to other adjustments. While the large central to local government transfer may introduce some degree of bureaucratic inefficiency into tax collection and expenditure administration processes, on top of better balancing regional inequality and supporting national initiatives, the importance of this transfer mechanism was taken down from history book, for local government's greater self-sufficiency often led to regional instability with insubordinate warlords fighting each other, which was the direct cause of ending for Tang dynasty and Qing dynasty.

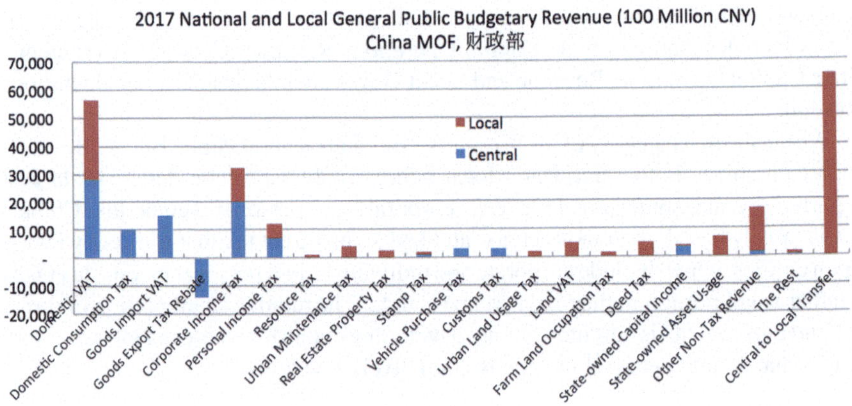

During high-level fiscal study for macro assessment purposes, while the revenue data analysis helps us to understand segment tax cost and revenue growth sustainability, the expenditure data analysis helps us to understand the distribution pattern of governmental spending demand. Based upon analysis of fiscal year 2017 expenditure data through National General Public Budget Expenditure Report, the largest destinations of funds usage included Education (15%), Social Security (12%), Urban and Rural Neighborhood Services (10%), Agriculture Forestry and Water (9%), General Public Expenditure (8%), Medical Services (7%), Public Security (6%), Transportation (5%) and National Defense (5%). This order reflected the government priorities within its long list of mandates for a large populous country pursuing a complex set of agenda. The largest amount of funds was spent on education at around 3015 billion CNY, for a well-educated labor force is the must-have foundation for an industrialized economy. Social Security was at 2461 billion CNY for providing social safety net in a rapidly changing economy. The amount of funds spent on Medical Services was 1445 billion CNY.

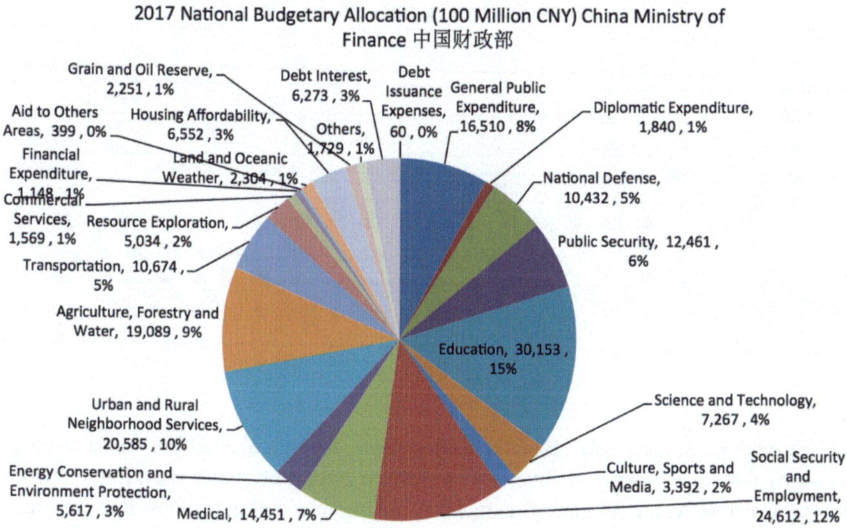

While absolute spending amount maps to the size and relative importance of each categorical governmental final demand, the annual growth pattern of each categorical spending amount reveals China's domestic initiative shifting focus. From 2011 to 2017, the growth of general public expenditure, which supports a large amount of administrative functions, was subdued underlying government effort in reining in bureaucratic cost and corruption. On the other hand, education, social security, urban and rural neighborhood services, agriculture and housing affordability received much larger increases. High spending growth creates macro conditions for potential investment opportunities in respective segments. For example, consistent social security expansion correlates to the need for taking care of an increasingly aging society and the rising governmental geriatric service demand, hence pointing to related business opportunity. Similarly, in educational category, driven by 5-year plan objectives on increasing compulsory 9-year education rate and average number of years of education for labor force, large educational spending increases suggest continuous effort on human resource quality improvement and therefore possibly instill a higher level of confidence in China's future manufacturing growth, since a large and well-educated workforce had been the bedrock of China's advancing manufacturing capability.

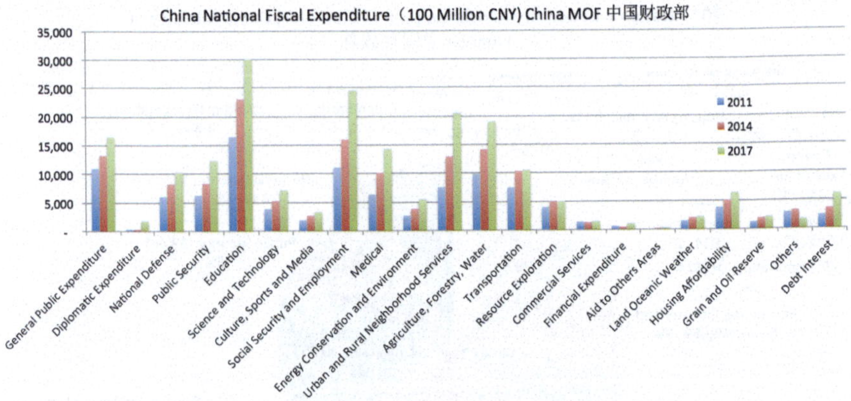

National General Public Budget Expenditure Report also offers more detailed spending data at subcategory level. From 2011 to 2017, budgetary spending on pollution prevention, water-related projects and housing renovation projects had increased substantially, pointing to a more balanced development approach. Increased road construction spending and maintained railroad transportation spending had broad ramification on regional economic integration and industrial growth assessment. Affordable housing expenditure came down, partially reflecting difficulty in administer eligibility assessment. At the same time, housing renovation had became important driver in delivering real estate-fueled GDP growth in many 3rd and 4th tier cities when residents moved into better residential dwellings, hence its spending level was an important leading economic indicator during the time period. These levels of detailed spending data are important for creating segment and regional economic forecasting and compiling a corresponding investment strategy.

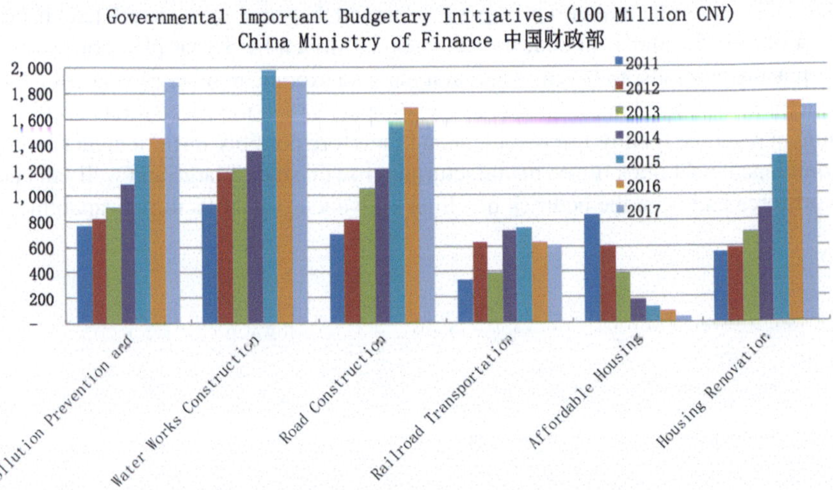

The 2nd category of MOF reports provide details on fund revenue received from specific sources unrelated to general tax collection and designated for specific purpose usage. Different from the general budgetary revenue, within which overall collected amount is somewhat evenly split between central and local level government, the vast majority of funds revenue is collected from and spent at local government level, and vast majority of those local funds revenue, for example at 86.7% for fiscal year 2017, is collected from land usage right transfer fee, hence the large local government dependency on real estate industry.

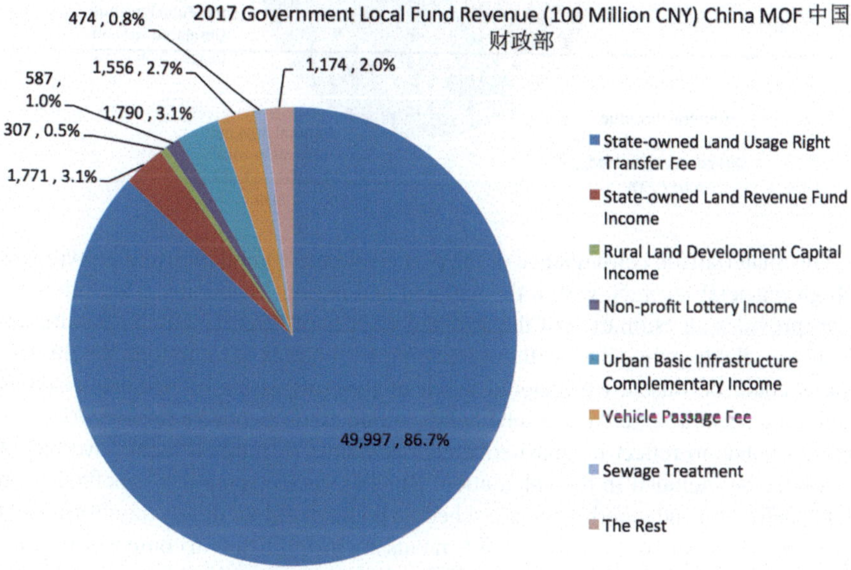

The large real estate-dependent local funds revenue was the result of 1994 tax reform and fierce regional development competition. In that tax reform, by changing the tax collection method from business tax to a new VAT system, with 75% of the VAT tax collected going to central government and 25% going to local government, the central government strengthened its fiscal control over regional government for better balancing regional inequalities and supporting national initiatives. Still, vast majorities of governmental responsibilities remained local government assignment. In 2017, National General Budget Expenditure was 20.3 trillion CNY, and 17.3 trillion CNY out of those was Local General Budget Expenditure. This was only made possible by a large 6.5 trillion CNY central government to local government transfer. Since much of the general expenditure funded by general revenue was restricted to predetermined usage, and in the several decades of heated regional economic development competition, local government needs to acquire funds that can be used at their own discretion. As a result, large amount of land usage right transfer fee was collected when constructions were carried out around the country, and those collected fee was then fed into local funds revenue to power the astonishing regional growth around the country.

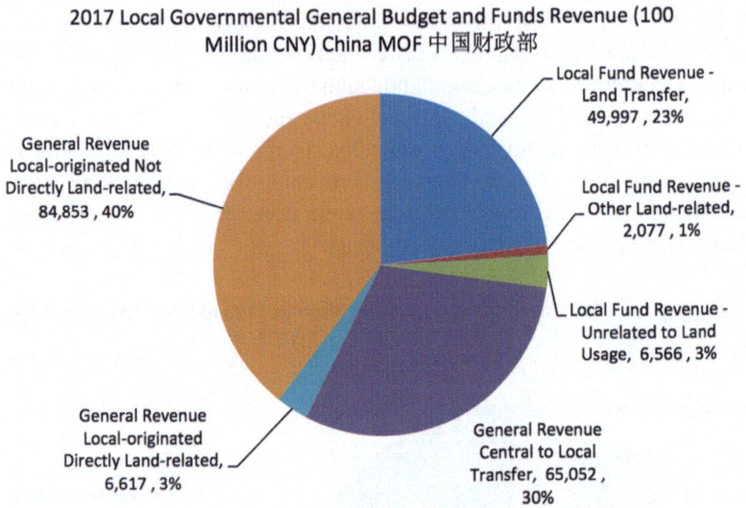

One materialistic consequence of the past economic competition and growth was a high financial leverage within the national and regional economy. The following chart provides an estimation of the size and sources of leverage based upon immediately available public data without resorting to complex assumptions. Legitimate points could be raised, e.g., should much of the trust assets be re-categorized as banking assets, or large bank-issued bonds within credit bonds be re-categorized as interest bonds to reflect its quasi-sovereign standing, or implicit local government guarantee be included in the calculation. But this data schema has benefited from stable definition and monthly release schedule both critical for timely monitoring and time series comparison, and those adjustments are insignificant in comparison hence the presence of ambiguity does not defeat the usefulness of this chart in analyzing the leverage within China's economic system.

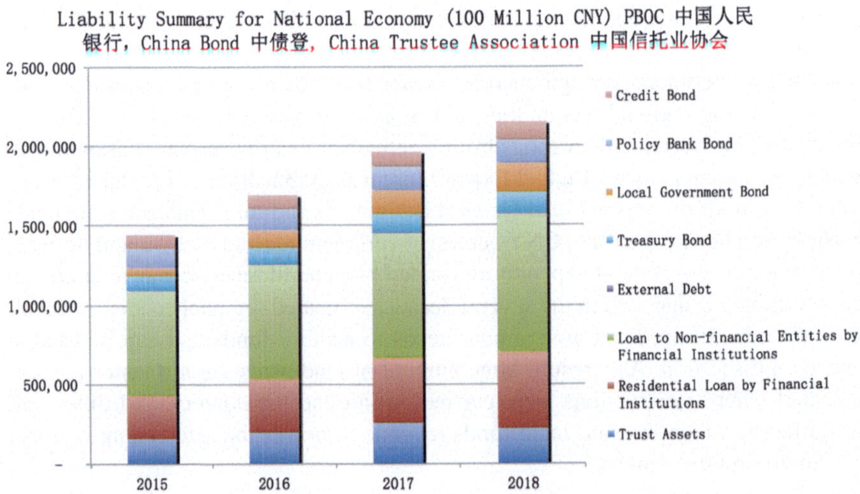

The chart showed liability sum at 144.4, 169.6, 196.7 and 215.5 trillion CNY, with corresponding GDP at 68.9, 74.4, 82.1 and 90.0 trillion CNY for the year 2015, 2016, 2017 and 2018 respectively. This translated into a leverage measure in terms of total liability/GDP at 2.10, 2.28, 2.40 and 2.39 respectively for the year 2015, 2016, 2017 and 2018. The largest three leverage contributors were loan to non-financial entities, residential loan and trust assets. Trust assets as part of shadow banking activities have been under heavy deleveraging pressure for their inherent lack of regulatory transparency penetration. Local government bond, loan to local government buried within loan to non-financial entities, and implicit guarantee made by local government are under scrutiny and resulted in strengthened administrative power to MOF over local government borrowing.

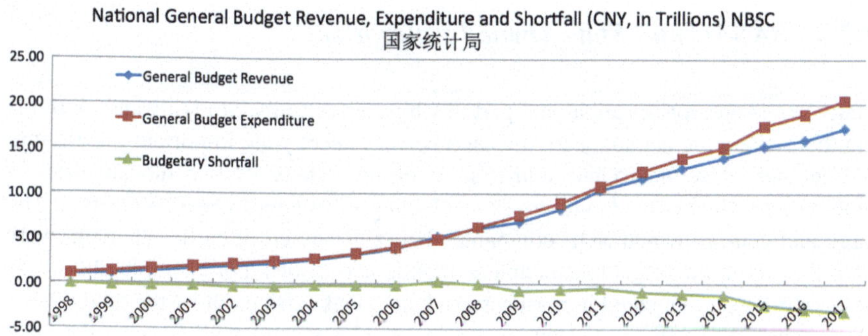

Another important leverage contributing source was the national debt accumulated by the central government amid its effort to stimulate the economy while the country is trying to reorient its supply side away from international export demand to more domestic-originated demand. The gap between annual budget revenue and expenditure, though not an exact measure of fiscal balance because of the existence of various adjustments, had changed from 150 billion CNY in the black in 2008, to −3076 billion CNY in the red in 2017. If we consider the bonds outstanding by the Treasury and three policy banks as the main accumulative debt incurred by the central government, those bonds' combined amount rose from 21.7 trillion CNY in 2015 to 24.5 trillion in 2016 and 27.1 trillion in 2017, a 2.8 trillion increase from 2015 to 2016 and 2.6 trillion increase from 2016 to 2017.

Central government debt, when strictly defined, would only be financed by Treasury bonds. Ministry of Finance creates annual fiscal budget plan estimating the amount of surplus or deficit for each coming year hence the fiscal deficit forecast is available for macro analysis. In the case when the amount of Treasury bond issuance needs to be estimated and progress be continuously monitored, the surplus/deficit amount from the budget plan, combined with the amount of Treasury bonds maturing next year, is the total estimated issuing amount of Treasury bond for next year. Local government and policy bank bonds to be issued can also be estimated from various announced directives.

Credit bonds make only small presence in the total leverage amount. China's bond market is largely an interest rate instrument play, with Treasury bonds, local government bonds and policy bank bonds taking the vast majority share. Credit bonds are often issued by big name corporations, many of them state-owned, and are also often issued with short maturity with good liquidity and low spread. Because of limited credit risk exposure, bond market is an overall safe place for investment and hence the yield is generally much lower versus rate on credit loan obtained by private institutions in loan market.

3.2.3 SASAC and State-Owned Enterprises

State-owned enterprises are a vital part of Chinese economy. Studying and monitoring their economic agenda, activities and performance, yield important insight into present and future macro and industrial conditions. There are two subcategories of SOE, central state-owned enterprises and local government-owned enterprises. The large and central-owned SOE companies being discussed in earlier chapters were born from both historical reason and economic necessities. For example, discovery of large oil reserve located in northeastern China was carried out by the predecessor of current central state-owned enterprises in oil industry, and made China self-reliant on crude oil until economy took off much later on. Central state-owned enterprise, when strictly defined, refers to those enterprises that are directly under the management of State-owned Assets Supervision and Administration Commission of the State Council (SASAC). When broadly defined, central state-owned enterprises can also include large banks and policy banks that are under the supervision of CBRC and CSRC. As far as revenue contribution on MOF general revenue report is concerned, strict definition for state ownership is applied. By December 2017, they were 96 SOEs listed on official SASAC site.

In the past these large companies produced considerable amount of revenues and have committed large amount of resources to the development of China. The revenue data shown below are from General Public Budget Revenue Report published by Ministry of Finance compiled at both central and local level. The revenue number does not include all contribution by state-owned enterprises, as taxes including VAT and business income tax are not classified specifically for state-owned enterprises in these general revenue reports.

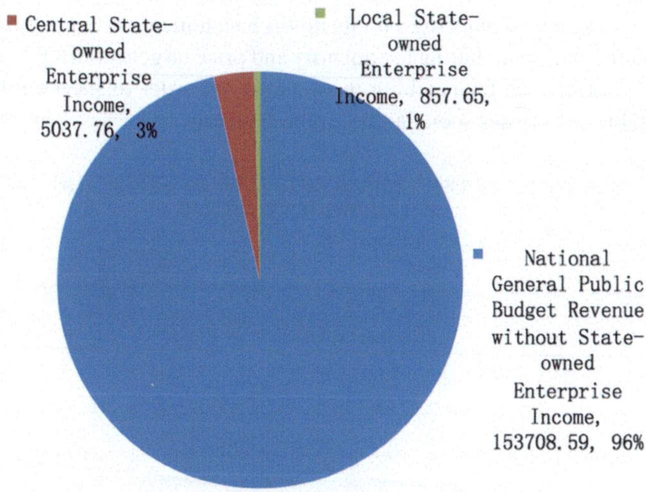

2016 State-owned Enterprises Revenue Contribution (100 Million CNY) China Ministry of Finance 中国财政部

Some of the companies within the 96 listed by SASAC are industry leaders in their respective area, and can be grouped into the following industries:

(1) Oil industry: PetroChina, Sinopec, CNOOC;
(2) Airline industry: Air China, China Eastern, China Southern;
(3) Metals: Aluminum Corporation of China, Baowu Group, An Steel, SinoSteel, China Minmetals Corporation;
(4) Automobiles: FAW, Dongfeng Motor Corp;
(5) Telecommunications: China Telecom, China Unicom, China Mobile;
(6) Food: COFCO;
(7) Train: China Railway Rolling Stock Corporation (CRRC), China Railway Signal and Communication (CRSC), China Railway Construction Corporation (CRCC), China Railway Group (CREG);
(8) Aviation: Commercial Aircraft Corporation of China (COMAC), China Aerospace Science and Industry Corp (CASIC), Aero Engine Corp of China (AECC);
(9) Shipbuilding: China State Shipbuilding Corp (CSSC), China Shipbuilding Industry Corp (CSIC).

3.2.4 Central Bank and Monetary Policies

MOF manages financial revenue flow to support governmental expenditure demand, while central bank PBOC manages monetary liquidity to support banking credit flow and fiscal deficit-financing bond flow underwriting much wider economic demand.

PBOC has a long list of objectives on its mission statement, with the most followed policy implementation including the quantity and price targets of PBOC, and its main operational tool actions for reaching those targets in order to successfully manage financial stability to foster social and economic growth.

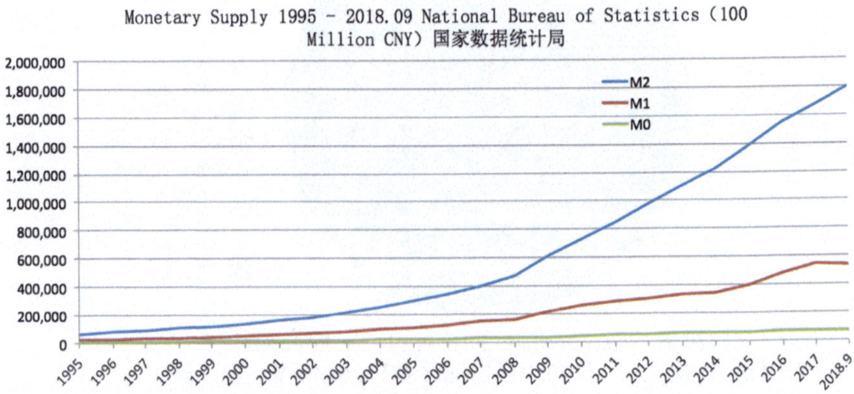

One set of quantitative monetary targets includes M0, M1 and M2. The monetary quantity change, when all else staying constant, leads to price change, which is interest rate on money, therefore important for credit creation, financial assets purchasing and leverage. M0 is defined as cash in circulation. M1 = M0 + enterprise cash deposit, including platform cash deposit, and is influenced by loan and foreign currency adjustment. M2 = M1 + term deposit, resident saving deposit and other deposit, and is influenced by loan and shadow banking. M1 and M2 are often used together to explain the level of liquidity that actually circulating within the economy. Their divergence or convergence is often related to activity change from shadow banking.

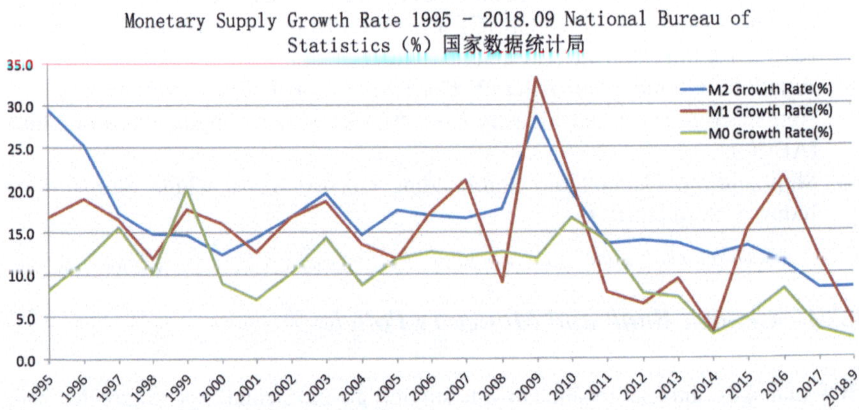

M2's faster growth divergence from M1 started in 2005 and was highly related to shadow banking for local government platform development and real estate. The argument for sustained M2 growth to support a certain level of GDP growth dissipated in 2018, as more moderate GDP growth rate became acceptable and the negative consequence of high real estate dependency and high financial leverage became clear. The focal point has been more on whether an M2 growth deceleration too fast could lead to a dearth of liquidity to local government and private industries, many of which were financed via shadow banking in the form of entrusted loan and trust loan.

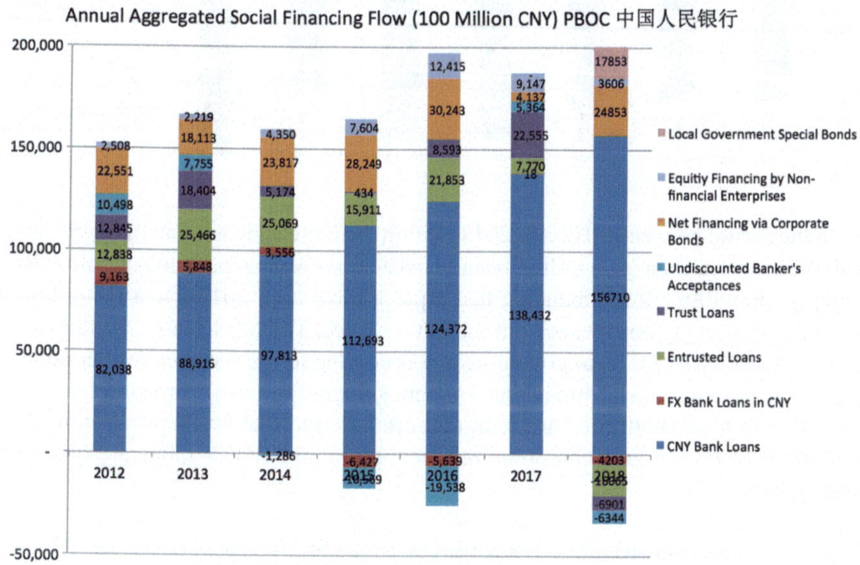

While M0, M1 and M2 measure the monetary liquidity from the supply side, aggregated social financing measures monetary liquidity from the demand side that includes direct financing (equities, bonds and BA), indirect financing (loans) and off-balance sheet financing (entrusted loan and trust loan). With the financial system still mostly relying on indirect-financing venue to function, and shadow banking cure being a working progress, the aggregated social financing becomes just as useful if not more useful for monitoring liquidity condition versus M2.

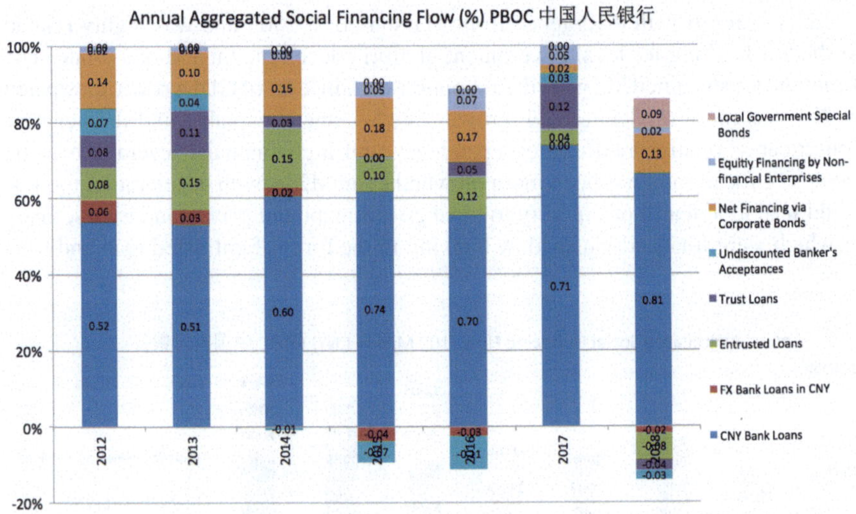

In the period between 2012 and 2017, within the increasing amount of aggregated social financing, loan growth had been consistent so was its percentage within the group of activities. Bond financing had rapid growth until 2017 when rising bond yield deterred many borrowers from market issuance. The other reason was in 2017 bond for debt swap for local government was coming to the end thus further reducing issuance requirement. Financing via banks, including loan, entrusted loan that often tied to local platform, trust loan that often tied to real estate projects, makes banking industry the most important recipient group of PBOC's monetary quantity management.

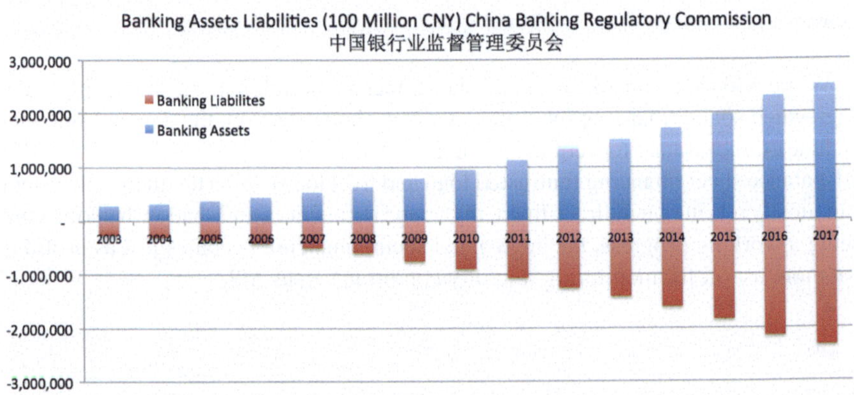

Regulators increase or decrease the deposit reserve ratio to decrease or increase the amount of funds available from the balance sheet that banks can use to issue loan credits. This is an effective tool to manage the total monetary quantity since China's banking industry is the main actor in aggregated social financing and has a large balance sheet. PBOC increased the reserve ratio since 2006, roughly the same time FX reserve became materialistic and inflationary pressure started to emerge as a result of USD-CNY currency conversion. Deposit reserve ratio was increased to reduce price inflation. Since 2016, it became clear China's export growth was stagnant, economic growth moderated, and rising US interest rate was leading to a capital outflow. To provide liquidity support to counter economic slowdown and a reverse CNY-USD conversion drain, deposit reserve ratio has been reduced multiple times. Each 0.5% reduction was more than 1 trillion CNY released from balance sheet before multiplication factor is taken into account.

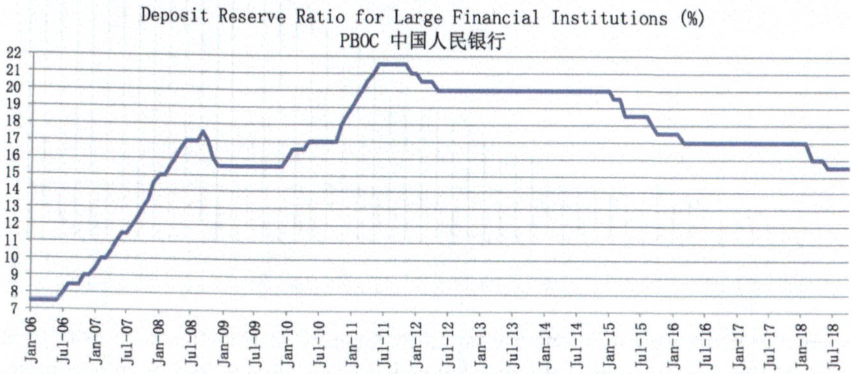

Besides deposit reserve ratio, PBOC also applies SLO (Short-term Liquidity Operations) to meet the temporary capital demand requirement in the market. SLF (Standing Lending Facility), MLF (Mid-term Lending Facility), and PSL (Pledged Supplementary Lending) were later added into the central bank toolbox by taking various assets as collaterals to release liquidity more specifically into targeted segment of monetary system.

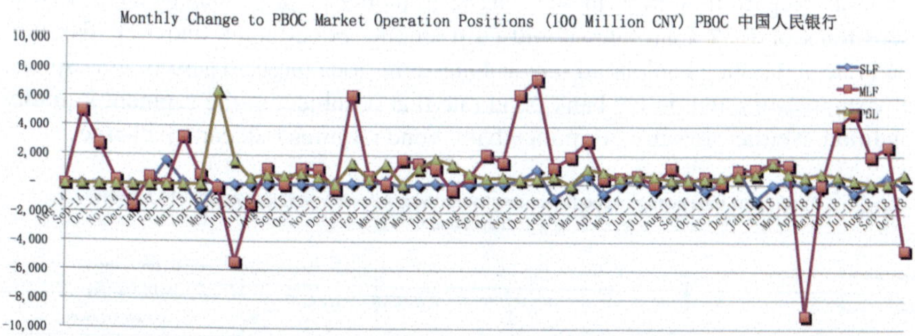

To map some of the PBOC market operations to macro economic circumstances, in the first half of 2015 MLF and PSL actions were taken during a severe equity bubble burst. The beginning of 2016 and beginning of 2017 MLF actions were taken to counter the Fed interest rate increase and subsequent capital drain event. In the beginning of 2018 great effort was introduced to reduce overall financial leverage, and in June of 2018, emphasis was given to encourage MLF liquidity release towards small business and farmers. The following chart of outstanding SLF, MLF and PSL amount illustrated PBOC's accumulative monetary liquidity release to specifically targeted economic segments to encourage more balanced growth.

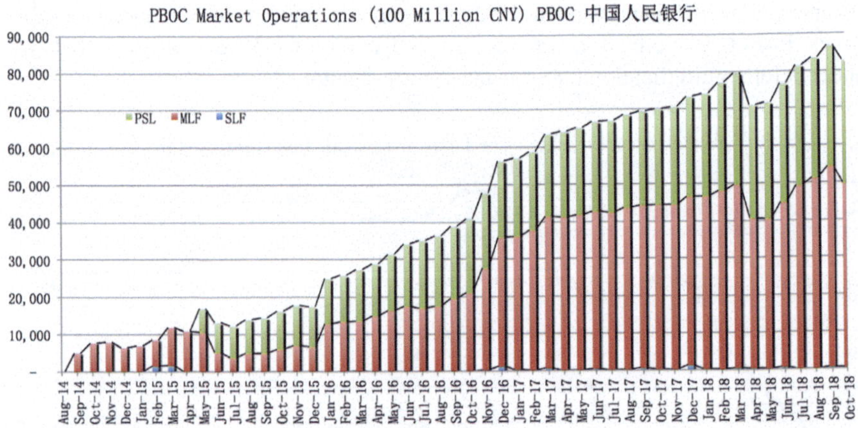

For PBOC to regulate monetary liquidity, quantity instruments such as deposit ratio and PSL are considered effective but lack result accuracy. As Chinese economy and financial markets evolve, PBOC is also applying a set of price target tools to manage monetary condition. For short maturity open market operations, PBOC deals with a list of selected counterparties including some large banks and some non-banking institutions. Via those open market operations, interbank repo based upon Treasury bond collateral becomes the most liquid trade on the short end term structure and the benchmark 7D average repo rate is comparable to Fed Fund overnight rate in signaling the change of short-term liquidity condition. Repo is relatively liquid up to 3 months. Regarding mid-term and long-term monetary price management, PBOC keeps track of 1-3Y loan rate as mid-term lending price target, and 10Y Treasury bond rate and policy bank bond rate as long-term price target. There is a tax spread between treasury and policy bank bond rate that is subject to the segment liquidity condition. Neither treasury nor policy bank bond requires risk capital charge.

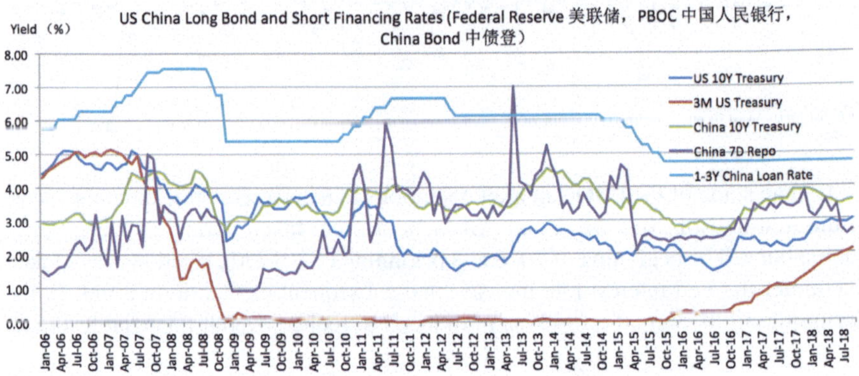

At micro level PBOC's short-term price stability management improved significantly and repo execution effect on the mid-to-long term monetary price targets had been in sync with PBOC's macro assessment and objective. Starting from the end of 2010, repo rate's upward and downward movement supported the stable spread formation between US and China long bond yield, a risk premium roughly equivalent to global capital risk charge. This relative market-oriented funding mechanism was part of large picture of PBOC-instituted interest rate liberalization reform. As the difficulties within China's economic reform became more apparent and resolves to tackle those difficulties more determined in the last couple of years, the country's economic growth moderation is expected to persist, while the US growth prospect remains solid. The two diverging growth paths and resulting volatile capital movement across the border eventually led to capital control measure put in place since 2017, and the stable spread pattern between USD CNY long bond yield all but disappeared. Since then the repo rate sets tone for domestic mid-to-long term monetary price that no longer hinges upon any international monetary price anchor.

Stable 7-D repo rate helps the price target formation of 1-3Y loan rate and 10Y long bond yield price target as the macro monetary price anchor, with credit risk spread added to 10Y T-bond/10Y CDB bond yield to form corporate bond yield, with loan risk premium added to 1-3Y loan rate to form differently rated loan rate, entrusted loan rate and trust loan rate. Bond, loan, entrusted loan and trust loan combined form the vast majority of China's aggregated social financing volume, around 90%. The pricing transmission mechanism is more complex in action, with funding costs in different rating segments, industry segments, small business deviating from PBOC expected price target results, and hence the liquidity action of MLF and PSL taken for targeted funding relief, and Ministry of Finance intervention to rein in local governmental borrowings that are less responsive to changing market borrowing cost.

While on the domestic monetary management PBOC has created a complex set of working mechanism pursing a list of monetary quantity and pricing targets, it has also defined a mechanism on the cross border monetary management centered on USD-CNY exchange rate management.

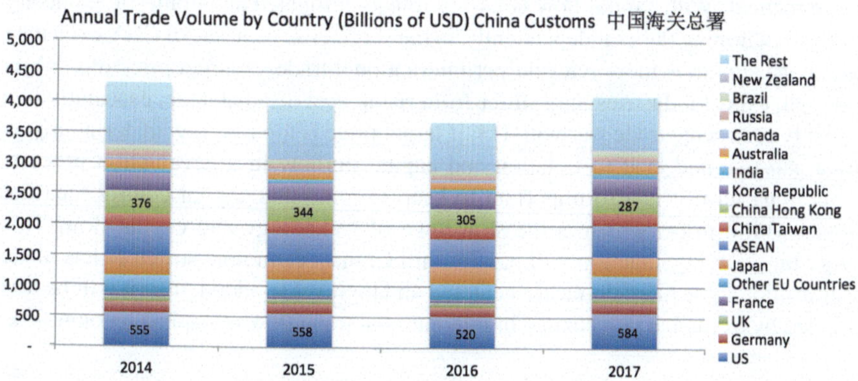

Managing CNY exchange rate is a complicated task. When a country's currency does not have reserve currency status, that country needs to choose a set of criteria to anchor the value of its currency against other major currencies, e.g., USD, EUR, for settling international trade. That runs the risk of compromising domestic interest rate policy due to currency flow across the border. The risk is less so for smaller countries or territories, but much larger for sizable economies. In the case of China, its international trade with US, even after taking into account transit trade via China Hong Kong, is less than a quarter of its total international trade volume. On the other hand, due to the reserve currency status of USD, China's FX Spot trading activities, international commerce-driven since most of the trading is centered on CNY, are executed disproportionally in USD-CNY pair. When settle in international trading accounts, surplus currency has to be converted to domestic currency for domestic circulation. Even with a rising exchange rate from 2008 to 2015, and a high deposit reserve ratio, past China trade surplus and global QE led to a large quantity of monetary inflow eventually producing a real estate bubble and high leverage ratio.

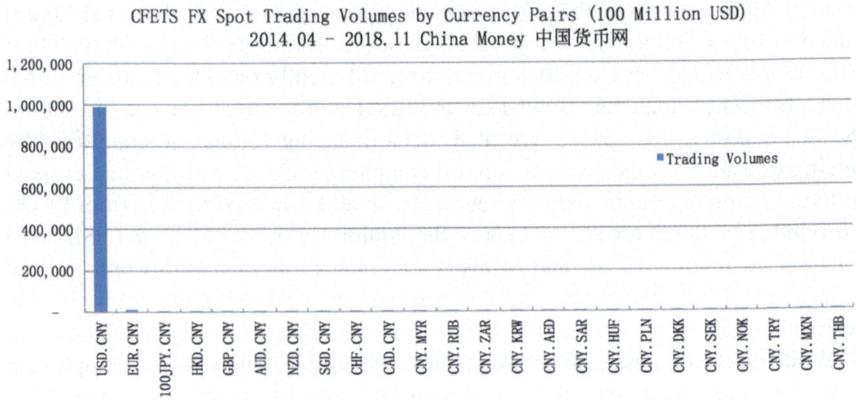

To insulate China's domestic monetary policy from the US dollar cycle, capital control measures are put into place even though complete control of capital flow is impractical. With capital flow volatility impact mitigated and domestic monetary policy functioning rather independently, in the short term, the issue of CNY exchange rate management is more relevant per international trade. If target price of CNY is too high, export industries may suffer from rising cost disadvantage, especially in a possibly protracted trade war with US; if target price is too low, raw material import price can rise and lead to inflation and capital outflow in a devaluation process. In the long term it is also important to keep in mind that capital control measure comes with a price, which is the slowdown of technology and capital flow. This rather unsatisfying situation will persist until China's economic structure has made its transition to be more domestic-centered and high value-added, then it will be less affected by exchange rate change in international trade flow or capital account flow.

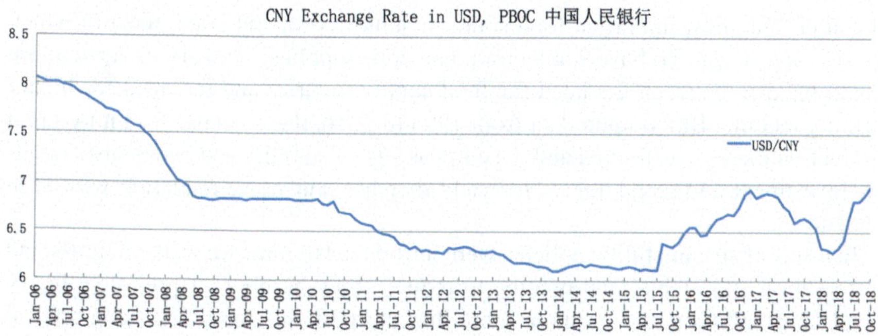

3.2.5 *Ministry of Agriculture*

Within China's central government, Ministry of Agriculture is responsible for managing and coordinating a vast array of sometimes competing tasks for the agricultural industry including but not limited to stable crop and protein output, arable land stock maintenance, improved plantation planning, efficient energy usage, safe equipment usage, new technology application and improvement, waste and pesticide pollution management.

Agricultural business is in essence an energy-intensive business since it requires large amount of fossil fuel input for powering fertilizer production, irrigation, mechanized field work and transportation. With China's industrialization, this industry has gained both output quantity and quality. Different from North America and European farmland including Russian southwest, where arable land resource is in abundance and population density is comparatively low, China has rather limited amount of land stock to supply a large population, therefore the main priorities are to protect food security, maintain industry sustainability and agricultural employment at national level, and promote fine-tuned plantation planning tailored to regions at local level.

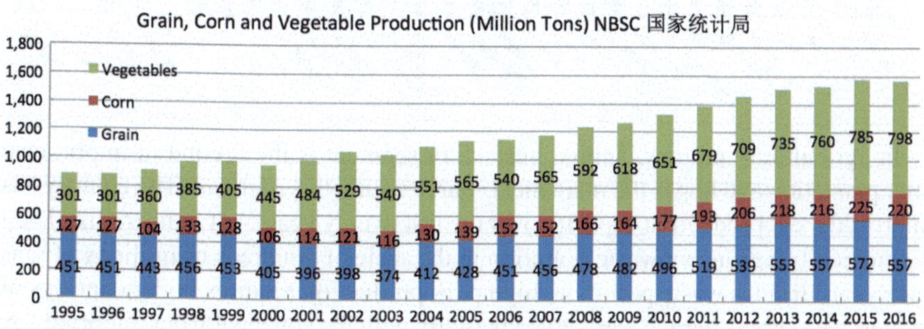

The paramount objective is to grow and stabilize food supply as a national security issue, and this is fundamental to understand the big picture of agricultural business in China. The most important food sources include corn, and grain, most of which are rice and wheat. To have stable grain and corn supplies, Ministry of Agriculture has to balance between the need for food supply security and the need for higher farming income. Based upon data from 1995 to 2016, the potential for future grain production increase is limited and the emphasis is on stability and better sustainability. Investment and technologies for yield increase and waste reduction will be in demand.

In terms of sustainability, policies were introduced to improve wetland, grassland preservation and arable land quality, to reduce straw burning air pollution, heavy metal land pollution and promote more discrete pesticide usage. At geographical level, the northeastern region has long cold winter and fertile land, hence the focuses are upon preventing land degradation using crop rotation and possibly introducing spring crops to increase land productivity; the northwestern area is dry with ample sunshine and the focuses are upon expanding irrigation infrastructure, introducing vegetation with drought endurance quality and more efficient cotton production; the northern area is low on water supply and the focus is upon aqua efficiency with better crop and irrigation technology; the eastern area has high population density and good weather, the focuses are on organic water pollution control and multiple cropping application for land productivity gain; the south is heavy with electronic industry and the focus is on polluted soil restoration. To fulfill each region's different sustainability growth objective, respectively different technologies and investment solutions are in demand.

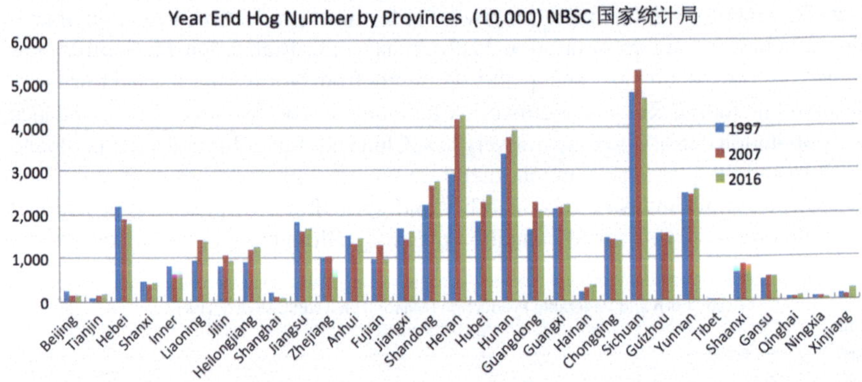

In agricultural industry, animal husbandry segment is the second in importance after plantation and hog is the main meat source within this segment. The country has improved meat production capacity over the last twenty years, but industrialized hog production brings heavy waste pollution in the scale of hundreds of millions of tons each year. Besides waste pollution, high pork production requires high quantities of protein feed supply, which was solved partially with the soy meal from imported soy seeds after soy oil extraction. The possible investment opportunities here include scaled production capabilities and pollution management, especially in Sichuan, Henan and Hunan where the hog numbers were the highest.

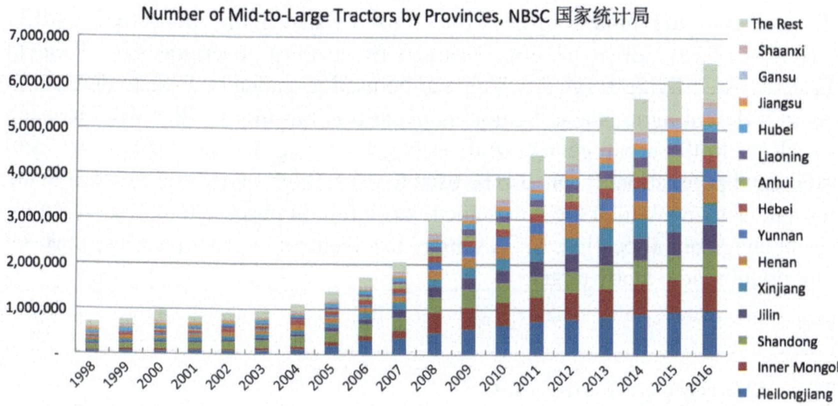

Technological innovation and improvement are fundamental to agricultural industry growth. Advancements in big data and AI have opened new possible frontiers on plantation, aquaculture and pest control management. Biotech application in plant seeds remains controversial. Machinery usage gains importance due to population aging and labor cost increase, and where the machineries are more heavily used, which include Heilongjiang, Inner Mongolia, Shandong and other regions, there is possibly more willingness to commit additional investment for yield gain, hence suggesting more technology-related investment opportunities.

3.2.6 Ministry of Civil Affairs

MCA provides social safety net for the disabled, needy children and elderlies, as well as other important functions that include administrative zoning regulation and social organization management. A few benchmarks can be created based upon ministry accomplishment report data to measure macro economic progress stage, government coverage effectiveness on the general society that can be helpful in identifying related investment opportunities.

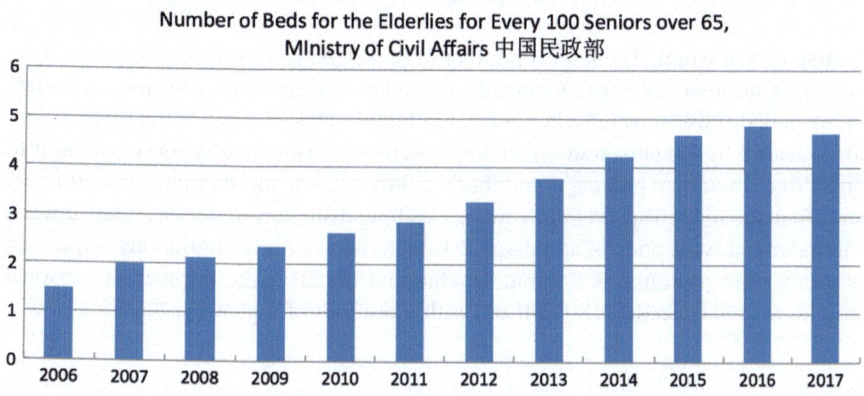

For example, the number of beds for senior assisted living sponsored by MCA per 100 over 65 senior population illustrates the level of government involvement in basic assisted living service, which can be used to gauge real estate demand in areas in different aging stage. Seniors demand tilts towards smaller-sized housing stock closer to the urban center, while strongest buying demand tends to be from middle-aged population. It can also be used to gauge high-end senior assisted living real estate demand, which the government has left it on purpose to market force for efficient budgetary allocation. MCA's broad involvement in general society makes it an important macro study target.

3.2.7 *Ministry of Transport*

Transportation is one of the most important modern industries. Ministry of Transport is responsible for this industry's developmental planning, regulatory oversight, standard setting, safety measure enforcement and cross-departmental coordination. It manages National Railway Administration, Civil Aviation Administration, Water Transport Bureau and Highway Administration for transportation via railway, air, waterway and highway.

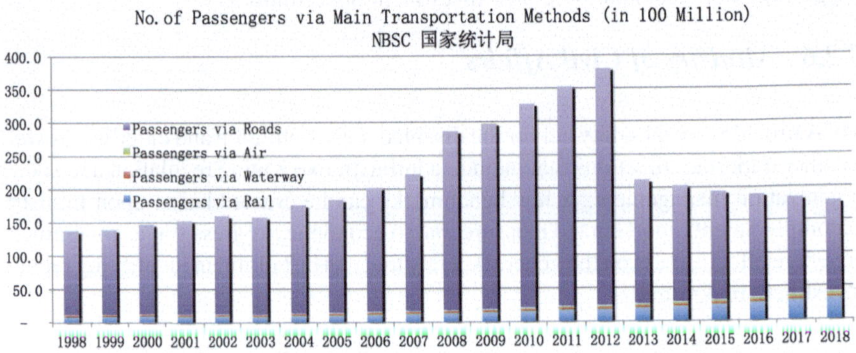

Transport via Road The largest number of passengers still traveled by roads. That passenger number collected included both inter-city and intra-city road travelers but excluded those traveled via personal vehicles. This number had a large fall in 2013, caused by the appearance of Didi, which offers ride hailing service similar to Uber. Since then road passenger number's falling became more gradual nevertheless persistent due to high speed train's impact on long distance bus service, and subway, ride hailing service and rising personal vehicle ownership's continuous impact on inter-city road passenger's volume. By the end of 2018, the number of personal vehicles owned exceeded 180 million, with more room for growth.

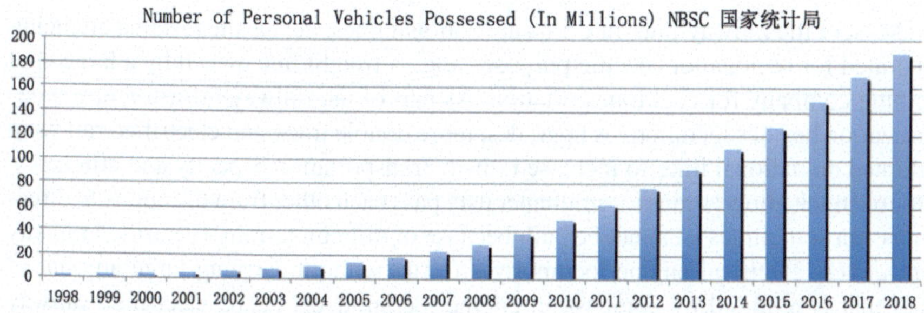

Transport via Railway After road, the railway is the second most important way for traveling. While traveling via waterway number had been stable, traveling via air number increased from 60 million in 1998 to 610 million in 2018, traveling via rail number was still many times the traveling via air and waterway number combined, at 3370 million in 2018.

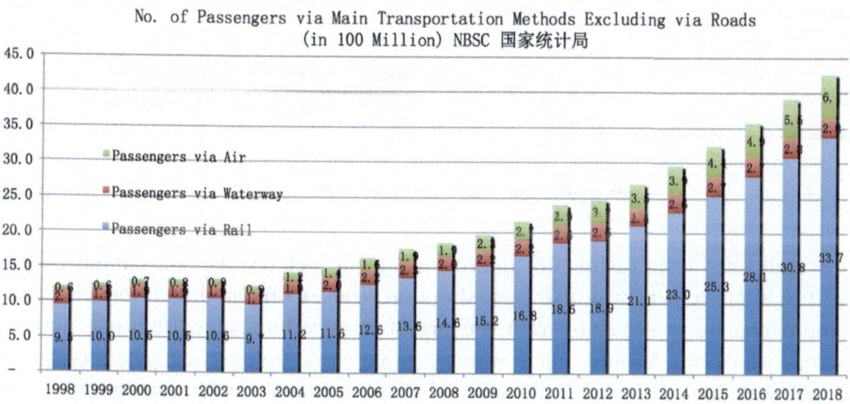

The large increase for the number of traveling via rail was supported by continuous technology upgrade. Steam engine locomotives were retired and combustion engine locomotives were gradually replaced with cleaner electrical engine locomotives.

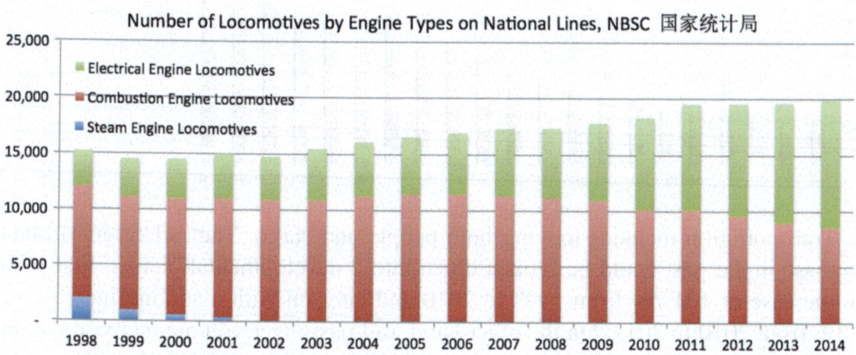

Most of the railway lines in China are national lines, versus the rest that are being operated for regional or specific purposes, e.g., a freight line owned by a large coal mining company for coal transportation. As part of the railway infrastructure modernization besides locomotives upgrades, more double track and electrified rail were adopted on national lines to increase railway transportation capacity and efficiency. Double track allows trains to simultaneously pass each other from the opposite directions, but sometimes it cannot be built because of difficult terrain. Electrified railway lines allow electrical engine locomotives to run without carrying large amount of fuel that is required by combustion engine locomotives, hence electrified railway lines are more efficient but can not be adopted universally due to complex logistic infrastructure support required.

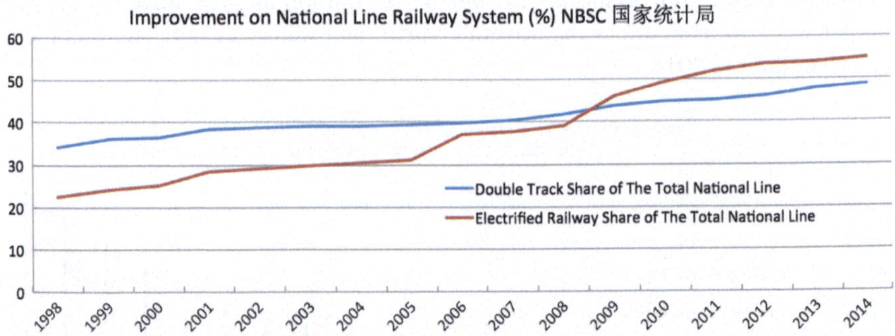

To put railway infrastructure improvement into perspective, substantial infrastructure improvement was also carried out on roads. Compared with modest cargo volume increase produced by train, the largest cargo volume increase was generated by road transport. Another place where sizable cargo volume increase took place was the waterway segment. Rail cargo volume is in much smaller percentage within total cargo volume, versus rail passenger volume within total passenger volume.

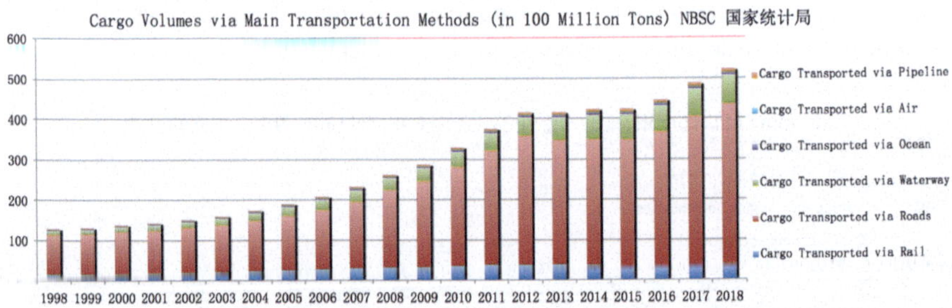

Transportation includes moving both people and cargo. The rail cargo volume increase in the past could be broken down into 2 developmental phases, first with an increase of 121.7% from 1998 to 2010 and later on with a stalling increase of 1.3% from 2010 to 2017. On the other hand, rail passenger volume increase was at 76.3% from 1998 to 2010 and later on at 84.0% from 2010 to 2017. This diverging growth pattern was created by economic mode change. Before 2010 China's largely export-driven economy was growing broadly with rapid rail cargo volume increase. From 2010 after the global credit crisis, China made huge effort to stimulate domestic demand by investing in the high speed train system, the most important of which was the line connecting Beijing to Shanghai that officially came into service in 2011, though some less prominent lines were put into services as early as 2009. These newly-added high-speed train services led to rail passenger volume increase without corresponding rail cargo volume increase that could be more related to export-related long distance cargo transport. Road cargo volume with shorter carrying distance still had healthy growth.

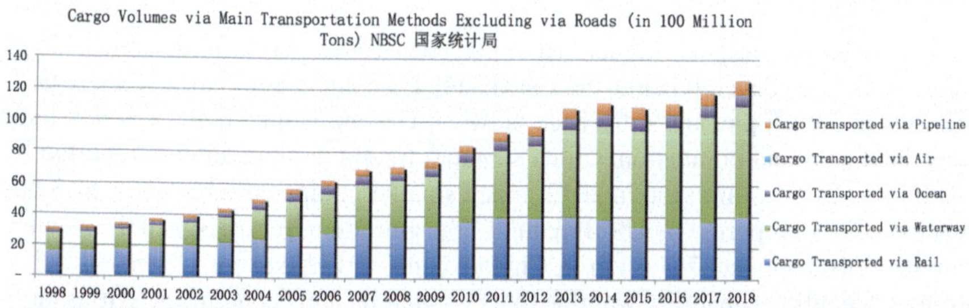

Often used benchmark for measuring railway service quality is the on-time rate. Passenger train operating on-time rate had been steadily improved and freight train rate was a little lower. Still they pointed to real accomplishment considering the length of newly added rail lines into services, the cargo volume increase up to 2010, and the large passenger volume increase since 2010.

Benchmarks to measure the freight train operating efficiency include the average amount of time a single transfer and a single handling will take, both of which are difficult to minimize. In terms of operating performance, there is an important distinction between the passenger lines versus the freight lines, with the first emphasizing speed and punctuality, and the second emphasizing hauling efficiency, i.e., the ton-km per dollar.

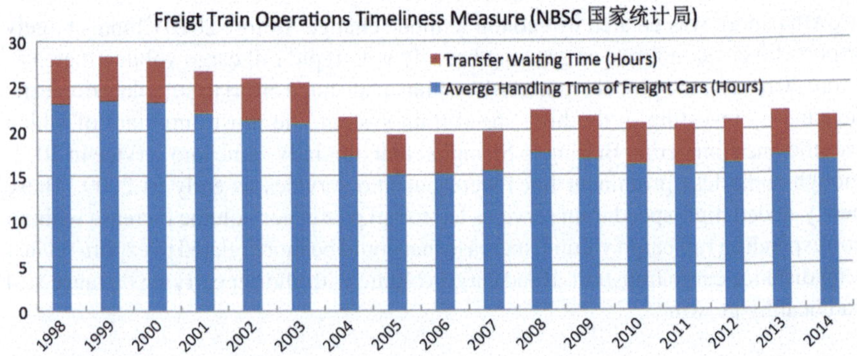

The unique geographic characteristics played no trivial part in influencing China's railway services' developmental plan and result. If a comparison is to be made regarding railway developmental difference between US and China, both of which have large landmass and population, China's annual freight hauling amount reported by NBSC was 3.904 billion ton in 2012, much smaller compared with US at 11.3 billion ton in 2012 reported by US Bureau of Transportation Statistics, and the average shipment distance was 747.6 km in China, versus 1013.9 km for US in 2012. The strong US hauling capability was due to its population and economic activities more disbursed across a large expanse of accommodating landscape, versus China's population and economy more concentrated on the eastern side hence the need and capacity for freight hauling in terms of both amount and distance are comparatively smaller. On the other hand, China's long eastern corridor with high population density makes it economically feasible for high speed passenger train development, and that development in turn facilitates more balanced economic development across regions rich and poor, which is politically important for a large developing nation. That need and feasibility condition are somewhat lacking for US Amtrak passenger service, with a car-centric developmental history hampering the need for more passenger rail line services, limited rail line ownership constraining Amtrak capability for on-time rate improvement and expensive land-acquiring funding requirement prohibiting a straightened rail line outcome that is a prerequisite for high-speed train movement.

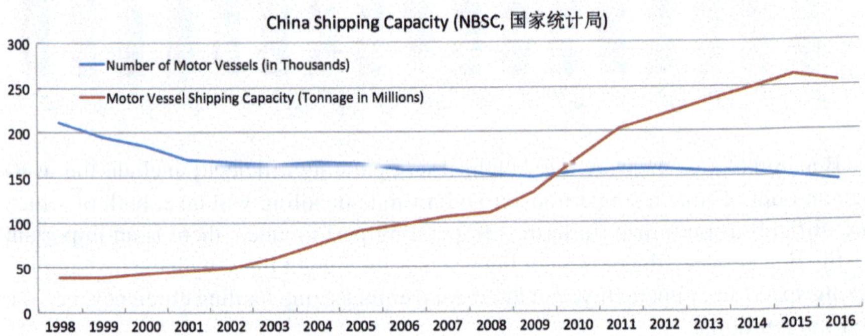

Transport via Ship Ship transportation can be divided into 3 following sub-segments, 1st ocean transport, 2nd coastal transport and 3rd inland waterway transport. NBSC data showed that the percentage of passengers transported via ship among total passenger transported was rather small, at 1.53% for the year 2017, versus the percentage of cargo transported via ship was much bigger among total cargo transported, at 13.9% for the year 2017. Cargo volume via ship increased from 1096 million tons in 1998 to 6678 million tons in 2017. Fleet had been modernized with less number of ships and larger shipping capacity as average ship size increased.

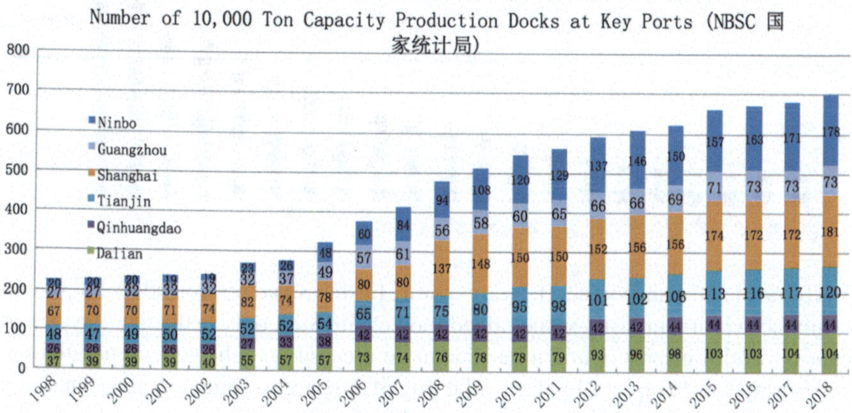

As important as the modernization on fleet quality, was the infrastructure improvement on ports, illustrated by increasing number of large docks at some of the most important coastal locations. As China shifts its demand away from external trade and more towards internal consumption, inland waterway infrastructure effort would gain further traction and worthy of extra attention for both regional and industrial investment opportunity identification.

The inland waterway fleet and infrastructure expansion is complicated by the uneven distribution of precipitation between seasons and among geographies. China's land mass is locked by high plateau to the southwest and far away from the sea moisture to the north. The gradual and substantial rise of landscape from east to west, with the Pacific Ocean on the east, created seasonal precipitation that is rich in the southeast and decreases towards north and west. For example, Beijing in the inland north has small annual precipitation amount that is also heavily concentrated in the summer months. Shanghai on the east coast has ample precipitation amount throughout the year and even more during the summer season. Therefore northern China has had less usage of inland waterway transportation, and usage in the southeast is seasonal and often requires canal and elevated dam application especially for waterway further inland or during the dry seasons when water level is low. Industrialized countries such as Germany have high percentage of waterway in the form of canals to improve waterway connection, and US waterway ship tonnage is higher due to standardized fleet and infrastructure implementation across waterway systems. Therefore to expand the usage of inland waterway, more dams, canals, standardized dock and larger ships need to be built, and extensive low cost waterway transportation should in turn improve investment condition where transportation cost is an important part of the production cost. Larger ships would travel further upstream on the Yangtze River and the Pearl River and connections between two large rivers via canals should be expected.

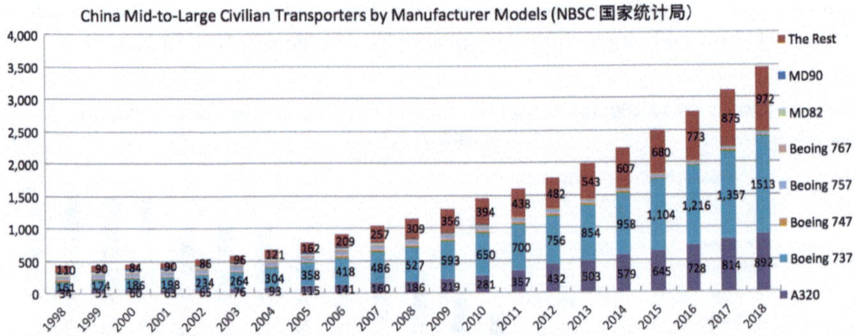

Air travel and transport services are mature business and not considered high-end within the aviation industry value-added food chain. Still, only in the last 20 years or so, as a travel/transport option it became more accessible to the general population. Profitability was hampered by the availability of airspace to commercial airlines, and strong competition from high-speed train within short-to-medium range. Also, unlike vehicles used in travel/transport via road, railway or shipping, majority of the vessels used in air travel/transport are large airplanes provided by foreign suppliers. This high vessel cost further limits air travel/transport room for profitability improvement.

3.2.8 *Provincial Government*

China has four forms of provincial level government, province, autonomous region, central-administered municipality and special administrative region. Each provincial level region has its own rationale in history for coming into existence. Some were created due to domestic geopolitical history, while others were due to much broader history, economic or legacy reasons.

Domestic geopolitics history from dynasty era offers the main explanation for provincial making. In the case of the landlocked Sichuan province that is surrounded by mountains on three sides, Hanzhong area to its north was carved out to Shaanxi province. Loss of Hanzhong deprived Sichuan province the natural geographical defense line for potential separatist movement in the old time. In another case, Jiangsu province and Anhui province are set up to split the Huai River region into half, an area dense with waterway hence a natural defense parameter against northern tribal cavaliers for the south. Separation of Anhui and Jiangsu along a north to south line will prevent any southern separatist movement from forming a cohesive west to east defense line north of the Yangtze River.

The autonomous region was a Soviet era idea designed to give large ethnic minority groups a greater say in their social and economic life. Inner Mongolia Autonomous Region was in that case designed with the need of Mongolian minorities in mind. Special administrative region (SAR) includes Hong Kong and Macau, both colonial era's trading outpost nowadays acting as free port on Chinese periphery under Chinese sovereignty.

Central administered cities are metropolitan areas being managed directly by central government for their specific importance. In the particularly complicated case of Beijing, since many ministries and central-owned SOE HQs are located there, a normal municipal level government would often not wield enough authority for municipal coordination or enforcement. Separately managing the capital city in China went long way back to Song Dynasty, and in the case of Beijing, back to Ming Dynasty.

Provincial party secretaries and governors are powerful administrators. They take general guidelines from the party center and developmental objectives/benchmark from national ministries under the State Council, then study and delegate tasks to county level administrators and provincial SOEs, and deliver final result with their own perceived priority and practicality in mind. The task objectives and results are mapped out in provincial 5-year plans and result assessment.

3.2.9 City and County Government

There are 5 main layers of governance in China, central, provincial, city, county and township. City is one level lower than province and one level above county. Township structure is at the lowest level for social and economic activity coordination and implementation.

As the most basic governance layer with systematic economic planning and implementation capabilities, county was created in Qin dynasty more than 2000 years ago and nowadays updated with complete set of modern bureaucratic details. County has its corresponding level of People's Congress, party chief, county chief, bureau of finance, bureau of medicine and bureau of transport, etc. Party chief is the number one person in a county, county chief is responsible for executive branch implementation, hence a bureaucratic check and balance. Each county usually has at least one urban center where the county administration office is often located. There were 2851 counties in 2017 based upon NBSC data. In the past, since county party chief was rather physically and administratively remote from national political center, therefore the number one person often had a lot of autonomous authority. That autonomy was partially responsible for past China economic growth as county from county competed in a nationwide GDP growth race, but was also partially responsible for widespread corruption duo to lack of organizational check and balance. How to improve county management by fine-tuning balance between autonomy and top-down disciplinary check is therefore very critical for China's future social and economic growth. For example, on top of anti-corruption measure implementation, modern day separation of enforcing municipal responsibility and providing municipal services has been gradually rolled out to offer more county governance transparency, lessen rule ambiguity, reduce room for corruption and introduce better services.

3.2.10 *Village and Rural Governance*

For rural area governance, township, which totaled at 39,888 in 2017, has two subcategory, Xiang that is more agricultural in nature and numbered 10,529 in 2017, and Zhen that is more urban in nature and numbered 21,116 in 2017. Though sometimes perceived as chaotic and mundane for scholastic studies, this level is where actually developmental tasks are implemented and agenda outcome delivered.

3.3 Economic Entities

China is a quite unique place for economic entities categorization. The types discussed here include listed companies, local governmental platform, small and micro companies, and consumers, all of which are outside the realm of direct fiscal governance.

3.3.1 *Layers of Listed Companies*

There are multiple places where companies can get listed and have their shares traded: 1st, the main board market, which includes Shanghai Stock Exchange and Shenzhen Stock Exchange for large cap companies; 2nd, Small and Medium Enterprise Board, which was intended for companies in a transitional state from being a start-up to main board listing; 3rd, Growth Enterprise Market, which was intended for start-up companies, many of them in the high tech area. For OTC trading, there is New Over-the-counter Market where small and micro-sized companies ownership can be traded. There are also various local exchanges to supplement the above 4 markets. More recently a new board called Sci.-Tech Innovation Board was created for small technology firms.

The tiered market structure was designed as such so companies can migrate upward on the listing ladders when their business grow and migrate downward when their business weaken. But the transition mechanism in practice has been a working progress at best and tiered structure perceived static. Shanghai Stock Exchange is the main place for large SOEs and other well-known companies and Shenzhen Stock Exchange for relatively smaller companies. Small and Medium Enterprise Board provides a financing venue for technology companies and some non-SOEs that are leaders within their respective sectors and often geographically originated from the southeast coastal area.

Some of the large cap names listed on Shanghai Stock Exchange include Industrial and Commercial Bank of China (ICBC), Chinese National Petroleum Corp (CNPC), Agricultural Bank of China (ABC), Bank of China (BOC), Sino Petroleum Corp and China Yangtze Power. Some of the large cap names listed on Shenzhen Stock Exchange, though generally smaller versus those listed on Shanghai Stock Exchange, include Beijing Oriental Electronics (BOE), Shenwan Hongyuan (SWS) Securities, Pingan Bank, TCL Group and Wanke (Real Estate). Large cap names listed on Small and Medium Enterprise Board include Suning.com and Hikvision. By December 2018, Shanghai Stock Exchange reported listed market cap at 26.95 trillion CNY, Shenzhen Stock exchange at 16.54 trillion CNY, Small and Medium Enterprise Board at 7.01 trillion CNY and Growth Enterprise Market at 4.05 trillion.

The equity bubble burst in 2015 was a clear signal that the market did not price adequately the equity investment risk given the underlying general macro and sector economic condition. That weakness in properly pricing equity investment risk made it the focal point of many investors' complaints and much of the recent reform was to inject better regulation and fair practice into this part of the capital market. Still, equity market provides a place for identifying industry leaders, the specific studying of which can shed light on macro and industrial condition and investment opportunity within Chinese economy.

3.3.2 Local Governmental Platform

With some exceptions, most of the so-called platform companies were started as proxies by local government to provide legal entity status for credit borrowing and direct local development and are never listed. Tax reform in 1994 split the most important part of tax revenue between central and local government at a preset ratio so the central government could reassert itself in setting national social and economic development agenda. For VAT, the split ratio is 50% for central government, 50% for local government (75% for central vs. 25% for local before VAT reform). For corporate and personal income tax, the ratio is 60% for central and 40% for local. While tax revenue ratio to local government was decreased, majority of civil responsibilities still fell upon local government thus the substantial need for local financing was created.

Platform companies together are an important economic force since they are the development arms of local government, which are responsible for majority of the governmental budgetary expenditure. In 2017, National General Budget Expenditure was at 20.3 trillion CNY, and 17.3 trillion CNY out of those was for Local General Budget Expenditure. Not market-oriented, local government platform funding capability and revenue expectation are highly linked to local government willingness and capacity in terms of level and duration of resource support. Investor might view a platform company more creditworthy when its largest owner is a local bureau of finance, which is more capable of coordinating and providing various resources versus owner being a local SASAC or just another platform. What platforms do is often straight construction and land development hence income is often generated from real estate transfer fee for local government fund revenue. More transparently run platform companies with more diversified revenue sources often suggest strong local economy and better regional investment environment.

One example is Shanghai Municipal Investment (Chengtou) Group Corporation, which is completely owned by Shanghai SASAC. It finished investing 58.7 billion CNY in year 2017 with its total assets amounted to 547.6 billion CNY at the end of 2017. Its main lines of business include tap water supply, flood control, sewage treatment, real estate development, highway, and subway construction. Its social responsibility report showed the amount of tap water supplied barely changed from 2.305 billion m^3 in 2013 to 2.283 m^3 in 2018, but sewage treatment capacity was greatly expanded. Another example is Beijing Infrastructure Investment Co that is funded by Beijing SASAC. Its main lines of business include rail transportation and real estate development. Its total assets amounted to 483 billion CNY at the end of 2017 and finished investing 54.6 billion CNY in year 2017.

Real estate development powered the growth of local government platforms in the past. Loan origination, land development, real estate sale, land transfer fee income and loan repayment formed a development cycle that pushed forward nationwide municipal development with astonishing success. With real estate dependency coming to an end and deleverageing process continuing, local government platforms are under increasing financial stress. But with the ratio of government spending to GDP remaining at high level and local government still being responsible for above 80% of final government expenditure (in 2017), plus platform companies being important venue for local discretionary spending, analyzing platform company performance will remain useful in shedding light on macro and investment condition of both national and each specific regional economy.

3.3.3 Small and Micro Companies

SMEs as a whole are an important part of local economy. SMEs are less likely to be congregated based upon population geographical distribution vis-à-vis the economic vitality at regional level. Large numbers of them were to be found in economically prosperous provinces/cities, which included Guangdong, Jiangsu, Zhejiang, Shandong and Shanghai. One fact worth noting is the smaller number of SME being set up in Shanghai versus Beijing, which illustrated the rather different economic posture taken by the twin powerful cities. In comparison to Beijing, Shanghai's industries tended to be more mature of large scale, and there were more tech start-ups in Beijing on the other hand.

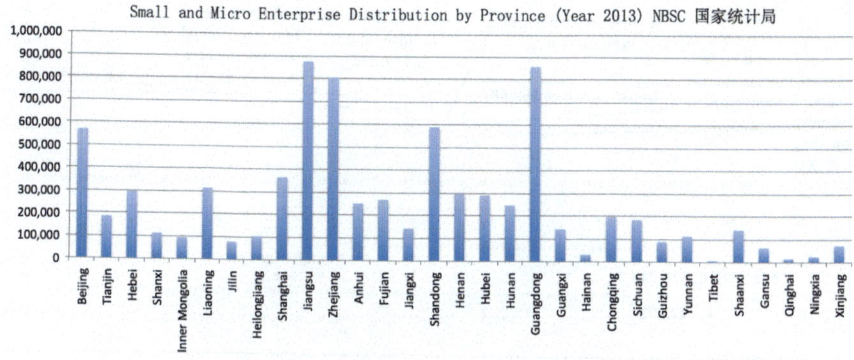

That distinction was even more pronounced when SME employment data was analyzed. The average number of employees per SME in Beijing was less than 8 and the average number in Shanghai was close to 15. In fact, Beijing having the smallest average number of employees per SME among large regional economies illustrated the dynamic presence of start-ups in the capital city, hence likely relevance for venture capitals to look for potential investment recipients. On the other hand, Shanghai often provided high-end manufacturing ecosystem orchestrated by large companies, some of them multi-nationals, hence became a suitable place for more scaled industrial investment.

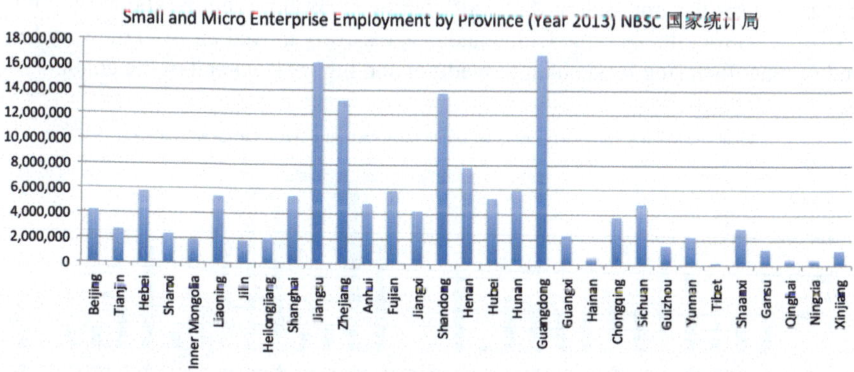

In terms of industry distribution, most of SME resided within retailing, manufacturing and leasing segments. Given the importance of real estate industry, the number of SMEs within that was rather small.

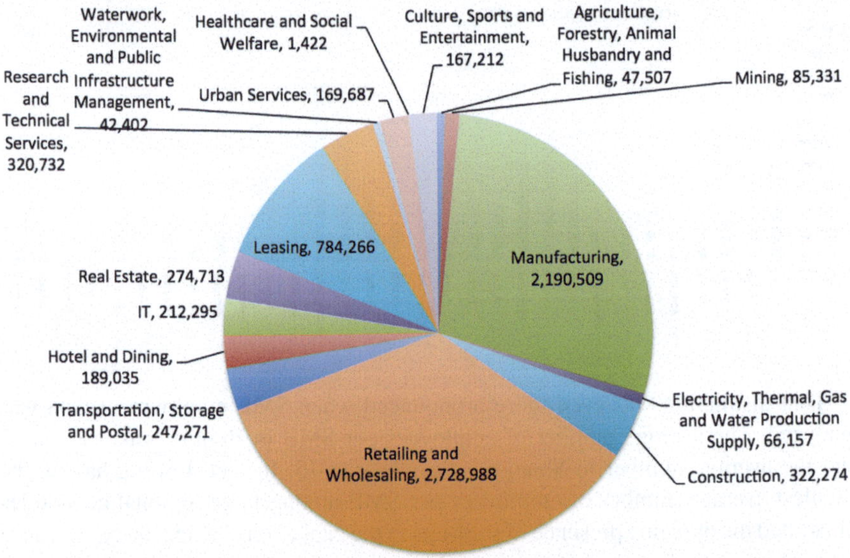

Small and Micro Enterprise Distribution by Industry (2013) NBSC 国家统计局

Within the important manufacturing sector, rubber/plastic product, metal product, general/specialized equipment and electrical equipment took the lion share of the sector, against the impression that textile/garment forming the backbone of China SMEs, reflecting the fact that China had progressively moved on from the very low end of manufacturing food chain to medium and higher level end of the chain.

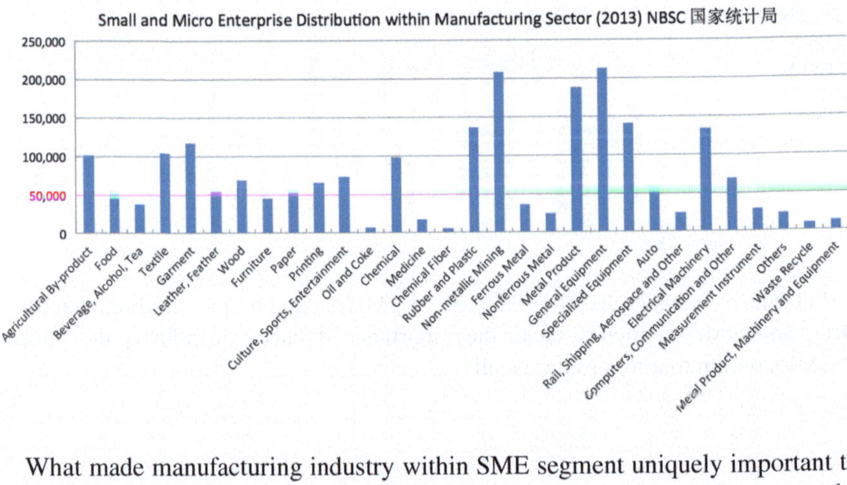

What made manufacturing industry within SME segment uniquely important to the broad national and local economy was its disproportional contribution to the labor employment. Being at around 30% of the total SMEs standing, manufacturing SMEs provided about half of the employment within the total SME employment.

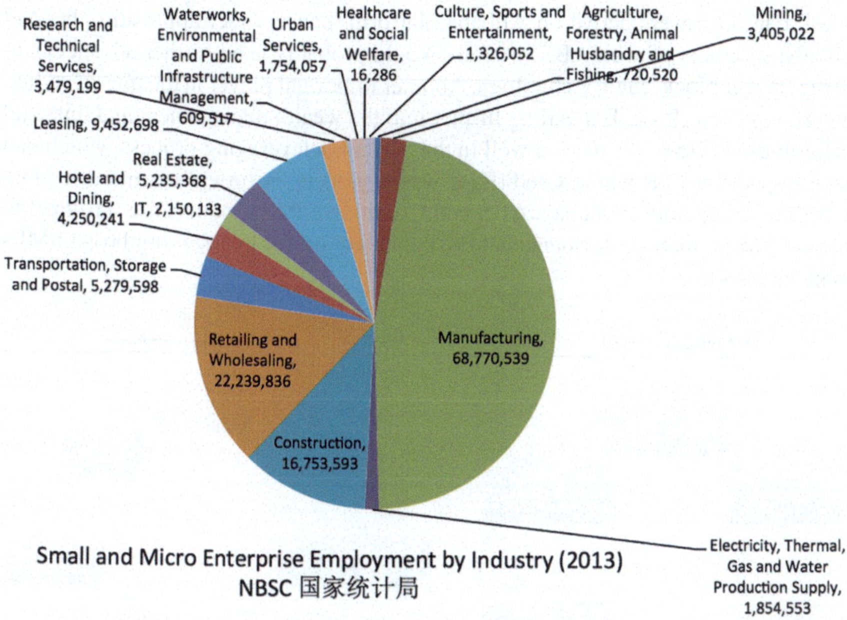

The sub-segment SME employment data pattern within manufacturing segment was consistent with the sub-segment SMEs enterprise number pattern within manufacturing segment.

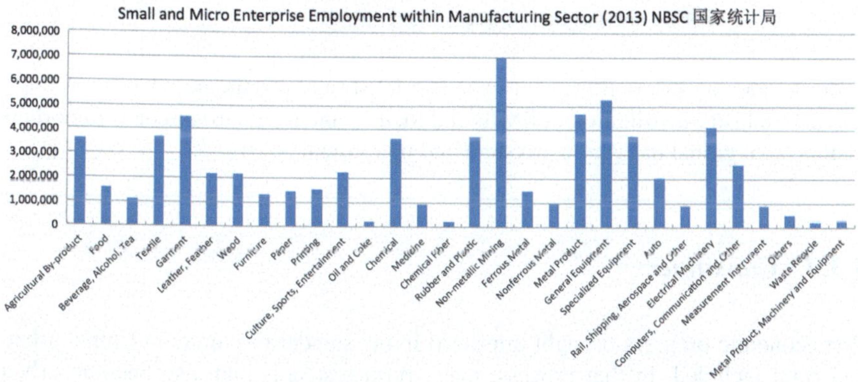

Broad financial health of SMEs may be gauged by looking into Alibaba ABS and CreditEase's P2P investment product data. Administering credit loan to SMEs is a difficult issue worldwide and a good solution is difficult to come by. Alibaba designed an asset-backed security structure specifically for small business loan. Issued by Ant Financial, this structure recycled loan payback to the ABS to invest in new micro lending for the first 12-month period, and gradually paid down ABS principal in the second 12-month period. The pooling of loans diversified risk exposure for credit lenders. Additional risk mitigation came from Alibaba's big data knowledge of those small loan borrowers active on Alibaba platform, hence wider application beyond Alibaba suppliers of such ABS structure would probably need further advancement on big data or block-chain technology. Another important player in the micro lending business is CreditEase. Expanding further into the wealth management and financial technology services, it survived well in the current deleveraging process, which had huge impact on P2P where CreditEase was a pioneer in providing micro lending to SMEs. Since both Alibaba's ABS and CreditEase P2P products are designed to support SMEs, their performance and risk data are useful in assessing broad SMEs financial health.

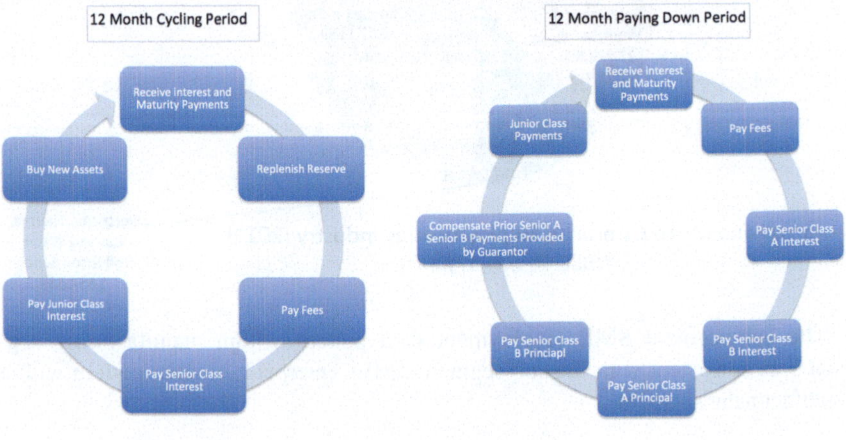

Alibaba Ant Financial Micro Loan Enterprise ABS

In the end, an external investor or industrialist may use the population, average size and industry distribution of SMEs and their financing environment as important factors for regional industry ecosystem and investment assessment.

3.3.4 Consumers

Past economic progress brought improved living standard to many in China, urban and rural included. In that process, many rural residents had also become urban residents, which was part of urbanization. Urban residents in average spend more than twice rural residents spend, and have higher social mobility and awareness. Before urbanization reaches its full potential, China macro economy still has substantial room for relatively fast growth.

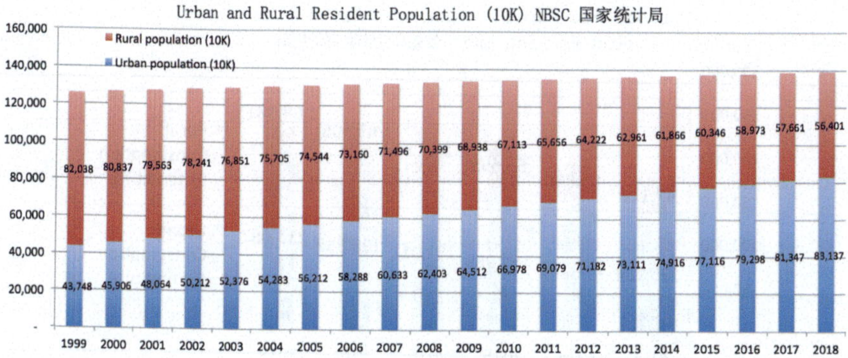

Though under the current leadership's mandate for more balanced growth, rural residents income had improved, large inequality still exists, illustrating that the road to well balanced social and economic growth, including reducing urban and rural wealth gap will be a long journey ahead. Many of the those causes for inequality are difficult to eradicate within short period of time, which include the lack of financial service penetration at reasonable cost, lack of scale in agricultural production and relatively low level of education.

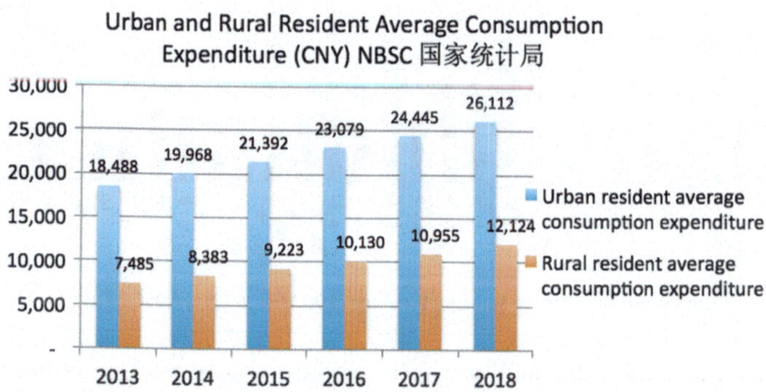

The total amount of resident consumption expenditure was a large number, from 18.2 trillion CNY in 2013 to around 28.5 trillion CNY in 2018. This will keep growing at a healthy pace amid further urbanization and improved manufacturing sophistication.

Urban and Rural Consumption Expenditure
(100 Million CNY) NBSC 国家统计局

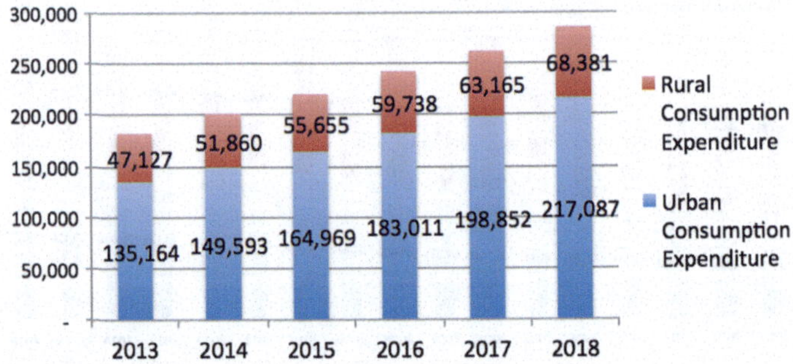

The spending power inequality not only existed among urban and rural residents, it also existed among different regions. An important proxy for different regional spending power is the consumption of commercial real estate properties.

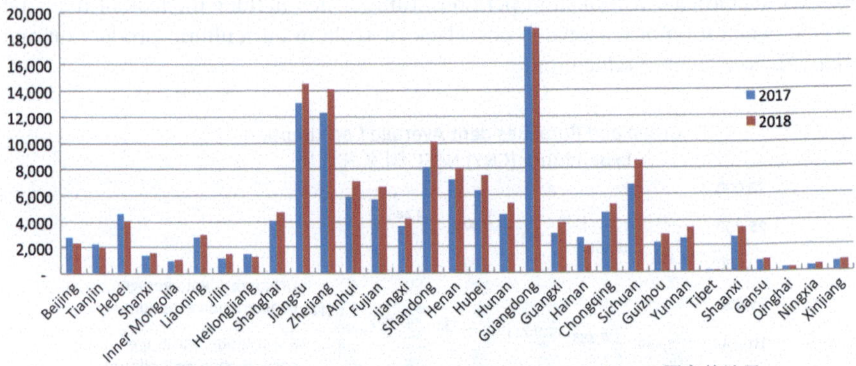

Commercial Real Estate Sales by Province (100 Million CNY) NBSC 国家统计局

This spending power inequality can be partially traced back to regional wealth difference. To measure regional personal wealth differences, we might use regional personal income tax revenue/regional budgetary expenditure ratio. The region with the highest ratio therefore possibly the wealthiest region in China was Beijing, followed by Shanghai, Guangdong, Zhejiang and Jiangsu. As was discussed before, three metro clusters, Beijing and its surrounding areas, Yangtze Delta and Pearl River Delta formed three vibrant cores of the Chinese economy. Other areas had to balance their fiscal budget with considerable amount of tax transfer from central government. Hence their resident spending power strength also heavily relied upon support and wellbeing of the wealthier regions. Since any growth slowdown in those core areas has broad ramification through the national economy, it is important to measure and forecast resident spending change of that three regions for macro and investment assessment.

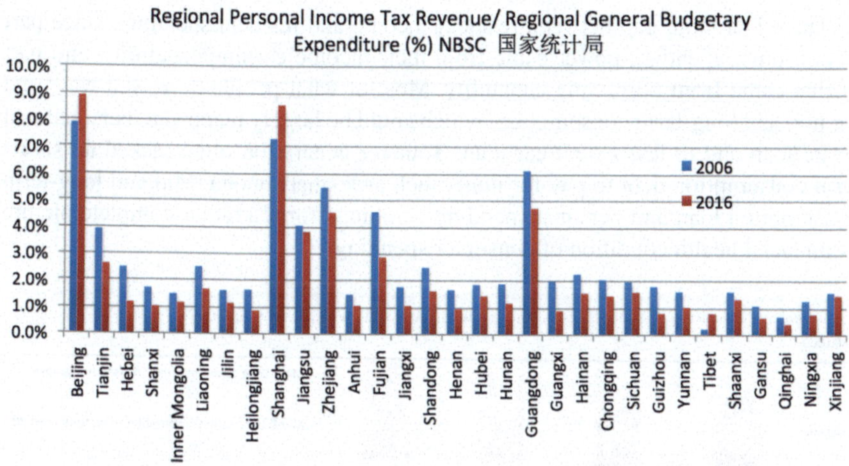

Spending inequality also existed among different industries/sectors employment. Manufacturing sector was the largest contributor to urban resident income, followed by construction, public management and education. Large income streams coming from manufacturing and education sectors feed into higher spending on education and manufactured goods, the producers of which often cluster in more developed economic regions. Those advantages and higher spending mutually reinforce each other making it difficult to reduce long-term regional spending gap.

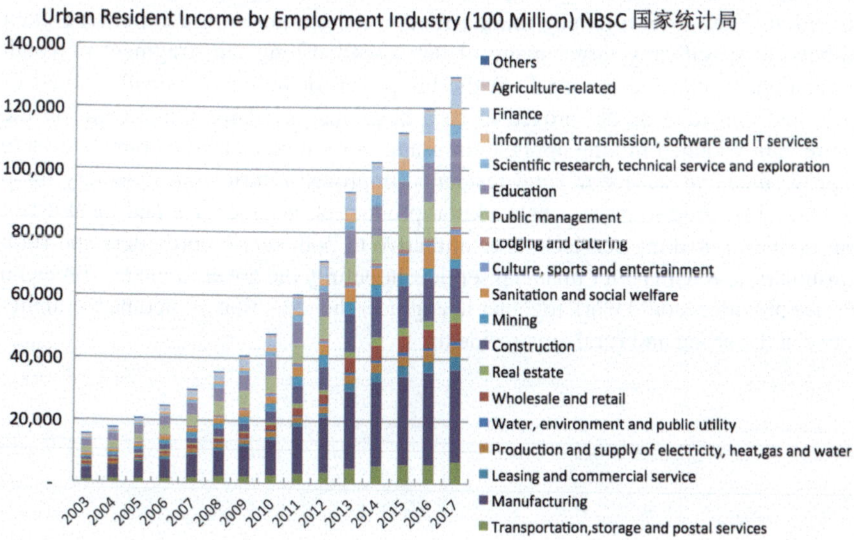

There is a large gap between resident income and resident spending, since part of consumer spending power came from their income earning capability, and part of that came from borrowing capability. Most of what people borrowed was used for mid and long-term consumption, which could be largely mapped to personal real estate loan and to less extent car loan. Younger generation often racked up short-term consumption debt to pay for items such as a smart phone. Mid and long-term consumption loan and personal spending combined form a rather complete picture of financial health condition of consumer spending.

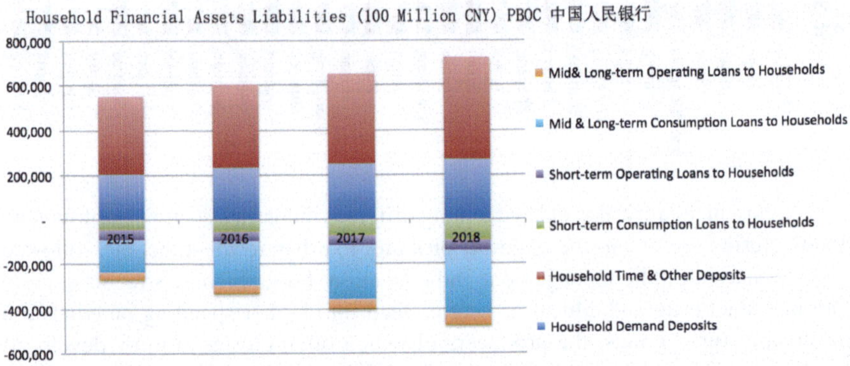

For those people who do not engage in standard bank saving and loan borrowing activities, YueBao may be a good place to analyze their aggregated financial health condition. YueBao is a money market fund collaborating with e-commerce giant Alibaba to specifically target many of the so-called long tail, fragment of youth population, to generate return from the lump sum of individual small amount of cash, and that fund model proved to be a huge success. This model could in the future gain widened mobile application usage in rural areas as the country tries to improve financial service to rural residents. Improved return from monetary lump sum could be used to pay for agricultural production weather risk and local credit risk premium, making services more attractive to both service providers and rural consumers, and with better financial service, hopefully the government and financial service providers could work together to engineer the reduction of income inequality between the urban and rural area residents.

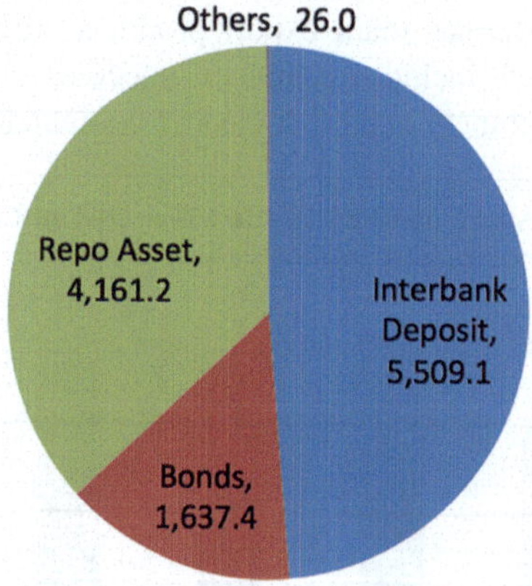

YueBao Money Market Fund Asset Allocation (100 Million CNY) 2018 Year End Fund Annual Filing

3.3.5 MNCs

Multinational Corporations are the key driver behind the current global supply chain formation, and the past several decades witnessed their astounding success in shaping the economic and political landscape of the world, including China. Foreign-owned enterprises are responsible for close to half of China's import and export in value.

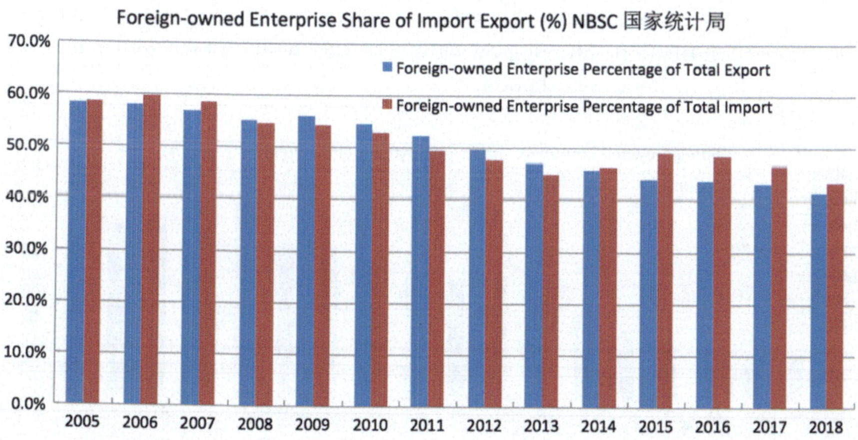

Foreign-owned enterprises main export products are in the high tech manufacturing category, which includes computer, telecommunication, other electronic equipment, electric machinery and other electric equipment.

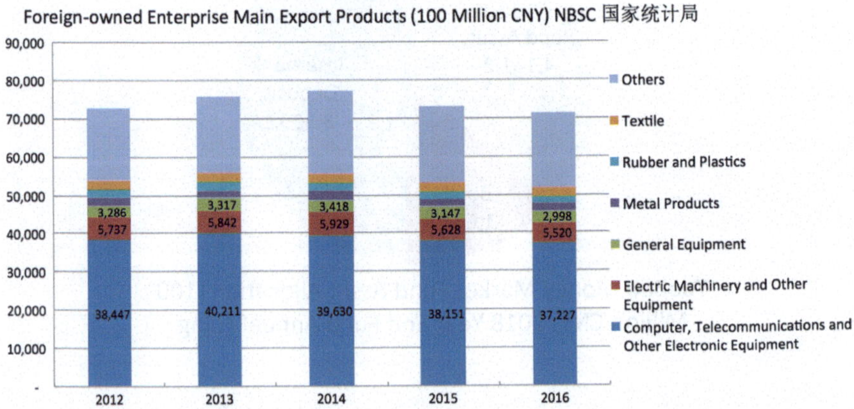

Besides aiding export, foreign-owned enterprises also contribute to tax revenue and employment income. Excluding those originated from China HK and China Macau, foreign-owned enterprises figure showed their employment number peaked in 2013, the time when US recovered from the 2008 financial crisis but the global trade started to enter stagnation phase, and global QE's inflationary effect on China cost lingered on, causing labor resource diversion towards domestic demand. China resident expenditure for 2018, urban and rural combined, was 28.5 trillion CNY combined. The average annual salary for foreign-owned enterprises was about 100k CNY, not substantially higher than the average salary in enterprises of other ownership types. The income contribution of foreign-owned enterprises, while not insignificant, is not as significant as its trade contribution.

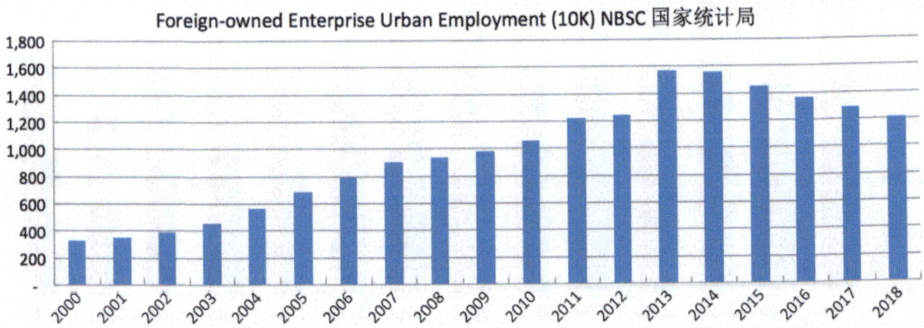

3.4 The Economic Flow Events Within the Structure

Economic flow events pass through economic structure, generate economic activities, and produce industrial and regional growth. Structural components listed in earlier sections include central government, various ministries, provincial and other levels of local government, local governmental platforms, small and micro companies, consumers, and MNCs. Flow events include central government initiatives, provincial Initiatives, local Initiatives, corporate Initiatives, individual consumer demand, and international trade.

3.4.1 5-Year Plan and Central Government Initiatives

Earlier discussions upon the drafting and approval of the national 5-year plan showed the top-level plan being an aggregation of lower regional and different industrial plans. While analyzing a national 5-year plan as a starting point is useful for China macro economic assessment and forecast, it is important to remember that the essence of that national plan for a country of China's size, is a complex combination of regional, specific (industrial) and cross-regional plans and it acts more as a general guideline for regional government and involved ministries to follow versus detailed economic execution plan. Therefore specific economic agendas can be analyzed with more clarity when we take a deep look at some of the major regional 5-year plans, which often present more specific quantified objectives.

3.4.2 Provincial Initiatives

A good starting place to understand China's regional economic planning might be Shanghai's recent 5-year plans published by Shanghai Municipal Development and Reform Commission. The order of the listed plan objectives would not exactly be equivalent to the priority assigned by the local MDRC, but it broadly reflected government priorities when we looked at various regional plans across different time periods. For the top 5 desirable objectives, Shanghai has evolved from pursuing GDP growth with more private and service industry presence implying higher employment growth, to more GDP and revenue/productivity growth, and top 5 must-reach objectives evolved from energy saving, city renovation, welfare coverage to continuous city renovation but with more strict population and pollution control. City renovation pulls steel and other upstream industries demand, improves existing living condition, without using land resource to accommodate more people. This reflected the desire for stable economic growth after replacing some of the heavy industries with service industries, while providing a more livable urban environment, with less population growth to ease the soaring demand for real estate in this first tier city.

Shanghai 11-5	Shanghai 12-5	Shanghai 13-5
Top 5 desirable objectives		
GDP growth	GDP growth	GDP growth
Tertiary industry % of GDP	Fiscal revenue growth	Fiscal general revenue annual growth
Center city 3rd industry % of GDP	Tertiary industry % of GDP	Service industry % of GDP
Private industry % of GDP	Resident consumption % of GDP	Labor productivity (10,000 CNY per person)
Fiscal revenue	Private industry % of GDP	R&D expenditure % of GDP
Top 5 must reach objectives		
Energy consumption to GDP ratio reduction	Affordable housing supply	Center city shanty area renovation
Social welfare coverage	Educational expenditure % of local budget	Permanent resident population
Urban shanty area renovation	Social retirement service beneficiary	Work-related accidental death reduction
Social retirement service coverage ratio	Energy consumption reduction per unit of GDP	Energy consumption reduction per unit of GDP
Social safety index	CO_2 emission reduction per unit of GDP	Major pollutants emission reduction

The only other area in China that rivals Shanghai in terms of a large and complicated economic footprint within a relatively small administrative boundary is Beijing. Confident of its growth prospect and propelled by the desire to address air pollution and water shortage concerns, the city implemented the most stringent population density and environment must-reach targets in its 13-5 planning and its top 5 desirable objectives are all related to the well-being agenda. The very top objectives listed here, all focusing on green, pollution control, population limit, life expectancy, water and energy consumption, do not preclude the income and economic growth as fundamental concerns, on the opposite, the city's economic foundation of growth was seen as solid enough for the top issues to zero in on improving its environment and spreading city's vast resource to surrounding areas for more balanced regional economic growth.

Beijing 12-5	Beijing 13-5
Top 5 desirable objectives	
GDP growth	Center city green commute ratio
Service industry % of GDP	Personal disposable income annual growth
Final consumption rate	Average number of years of education of newly-added labor force

(continued)

(continued)

Beijing 12-5	Beijing 13-5
Fiscal general revenue growth rate	Urban registered unemployment
Personal disposable income growth rate	Average life expectancy
Top 5 must reach objectives	
Retirement plan, medical plan participation rate	Permanent resident population
Urban employment 5 insurance items participation rate	Urban construction land usage (km^2)
Work-related accidental death reduction	Total water usage (100 million m^3)
Food safety inspection passing ratio	Total energy consumption (10,000 standard coal tonnage)
Medicine inspection passing ratio	PM2.5 concentration reduction

Guangdong is one of the three major growth engines, besides Beijing and Yangtze River Delta, for China's economic growth. By further improving the infrastructure condition for its extensive private industrial base, its recent regional planning was set to address some of its major developmental concerns: pushing further urbanization to integrate various city centers on the Pearl Delta including Shenzhen, Guangzhou, Hong Kong and Macau for improved regional specialization and productivity, better education, and maintain arable land stock level at the same time.

Guangdong 12-5	Guangdong 13-5
Top 5 desirable objectives	
GDP growth rate	GDP (100 million CNY)
GDP growth per capita	Per capita GDP (CNY)
Resident CPI	All-in labor productivity (10,000 CNY per person)
Service industry % of GDP	Urbanization for permanent resident population
Consumption % of GDP	Service industry % of GDP
Top 5 must reach objectives	
Population growth	Average number of years of education for working-age labor
9-year compulsory education coverage rate	Rural poverty reduction
Urban workers basic retirement plan coverage (10k)	Urban shanty area renovation
Urban basic medical insurance coverage (%)	Arable land stock (10,000 ha)
Urban and rural basis retirement plan participation (10k)	Reduction of water consumption per unit of GDP

Shandong is a province on the east coast with a more traditional industrial composition, a large agricultural sector and a large rural population. Its must-reach objectives focus on better education with its implementation goal fine-tuned from compulsory education rate to number of years of education, and arable land stock level control. Urban shanty area renovation was also used as a tool to pull final demand and promote growth thus minimizing side effects from land usage or real estate over expansion. Fixed asset investment target was replaced by productivity goal.

Shandong 12-5	Shandong 13-5
Top 5 desirable objectives	
GDP	GDP
Service industry % of GDP	Labor productivity per capita (10k CNY)
Urbanization rate (%)	Permanent resident urbanization
Fiscal revenue (100 million CNY)	Registered resident urbanization
Fixed asset investment (100 million CNY)	Service industry % of GDP
Top 5 must reach objectives	
9-year compulsory education rate (%)	Labor force average number of years of education
Arable land stock (100 million ha)	Rural poverty reduction (10k)
Water consumption reduction versus GDP (%)	Urban shanty area renovation (units, 10k)
Non-fossil percentage of energy consumption	Arable land stock (100 million ha)
Energy consumption reduction versus GDP (%)	Newly-added construction (10k ha)

Sichuan is a landlocked province in the southwest region also with a large agricultural sector, hence its mandate as well as focus on rural poverty reduction. FDI is a more effective economic tool here in attracting business and investment from international markets, as the province is far away from the coast area and still enjoys a competitive cost advantage over its more developed coastal competitors.

Sichuan 13-5
Top 5 desirable objectives
GDP
All labor productivity
Permanent resident urbanization
Service industry % of GDP
Actual FDI usage
Top 5 must reach objectives

(continued)

(continued)

Sichuan 13-5
Labor force average number of years of education
Urban newly-added employment (10k)
Rural poverty reduction (10k)
Basic retirement plan coverage (%)
Urban shanty area renovation (10k units)

Top provincial objectives set the tone of regional growth and regional industrial growth. But no matter what each region's top objectives are and how those objective priorities may change over the time, the most important long term consideration behind individual regional planning is still economic growth trajectory, without which other objectives, including social fairness, are difficult to be met. This implies objective change and priority shift when economic growth circumstance changes within a plan period, therefore keeping track of and forecasting regional economic growth are very important. For plotting economic growth trajectory, the commonly used GDP growth number has quite a few data components that can be subject to vague interpretation. On the other hand, corporate and personal income tax changes are clear signals for economic growth change, and since any tax policy change has to be gradual and careful for it possible social ramification, tax data are stable statistics for economic analysis regarding regional economic planning forecast. As an example, past corporate tax revenue data showed that Guangdong, Shanghai, Beijing, Zhejiang and Jiangsu had strong growth record and suggested future growth speed potential, far outpacing the rest of the country, giving a strong argument for regional balancing act at the national economic planning level, and that rebalancing mandate filters through to regional planning level, translating into must-reach local immigration population target and industrial environment requirement at Beijing and Shanghai so as to divert population and industrial capacity to other areas with more distributed growth result.

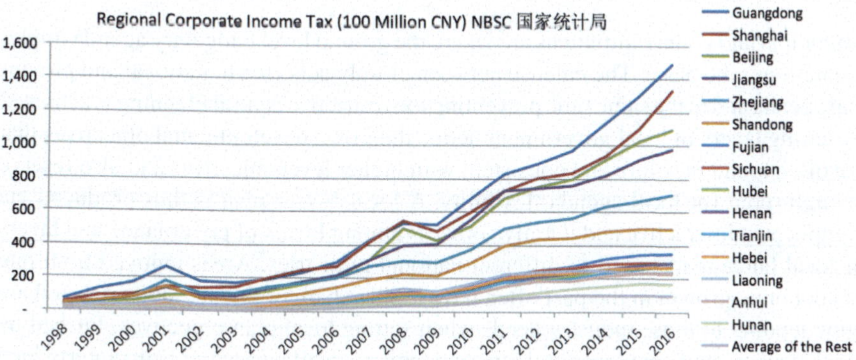

Different from fast but relatively stable corporate income tax growth, personal income tax showed accelerated growth pattern in Guangdong, Beijing and Shanghai. These regional personal income tax revenue diverging paths led to further urgency for balanced economic growth among different regions. The urgency translated into regional economic planning objectives for 13-5 in terms of population limit in first-tier cities to put a stop on rising real estate demand and price, an important source for perceived social wealth inequality.

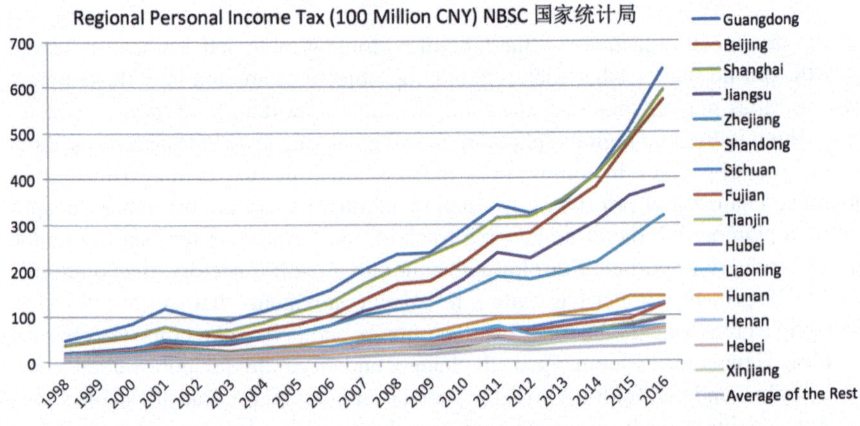

Analogous to central 5-year plan being an aggregation of provincial 5-year plan for implementation, provincial 5-year plan is an aggregation of municipal and county 5-year plans, and has to be translated into municipal and county budget to get final implementation. With better governance transparency, a lot of details can be found in local budgetary release and local NDRC release.

3.4.3 *Local Initiatives*

Municipal and county initiatives are where the ground level budgetary agenda implementations take place. The balance between closely adhering to national and provincial agenda and at the same time preventing too restrictive central planning is achieved by letting layers of local government define their own developmental objectives that are often broad in nature and consistent with higher level objectives and also reserve enough room for local agenda flexibility. A local 5-year plan is thus produced via complicated interactive and iterative process among layers of governance and layers of local bureaus matrixed to different national ministries. Areas enjoyed high rate of economic growth in the past often have higher share of private industries and are quite tending to those industry needs when setting local plan objectives. Pushed by local business and populace for delivering region-specific growth results intertwined with more general developmental agenda that includes education, infrastructure, etc., those regional local government are quite assiduous and meticulous in driving this highly complicated process and the results can be seen from their published plan that also includes prior plan implementation result.

A good place to study local 5-year plan example is Hangzhou, the provincial capital of Zhejiang province. Zhejiang is one of the most affluent coastal provinces with an extensive private industry base and President Xi was its provincial head from 2002 and 2007. The city itself is also home to Alibaba, one of the largest e-commerce corporate. Being acknowledged for and confident in both their bureaucratic flexibility and economic astuteness, city government worked meticulous on their developmental plan and plan implementation often with uncommon audacity.

Hangzhou 12-5	
Top 5 desirable objectives	
GDP growth rate	10%
GDP per capita (CNY)	102,500
Tertiary industry share of GDP (%)	54
R&D share of GDP (%)	>3
Urban registered unemployment (%)	<4%
Top 5 must reach objectives	
Education share of general fiscal expenditure	0.19
Urban employment increase (10k)	28.79
Urban basic annuity participation rate (%)	>95
Arable land stock (10k ha)	22.1
Energy consumption per unit GDP (Coal tonnage/10k CNY)	0.55

Looking into Hangzhou's 12-5 and 13-5 5-year plans, economic growth and to encourage growth through more R&D input had been consistently top objectives. In 12-5, the must reach objectives focused more on broadening educational and retirement coverage for the general population. Once that was largely accomplished, in 13-5 plan the attention was turned to environmental conservation, with land usage efficiency and air quality improvement being top objectives to reflect population concern over environmental condition that had steadily worsened during the previous fast growth years. The fact that Hangzhou city government would published a long list of must reach objectives, boxing itself in for delivering specified progress on education, employment, social safety net, energy efficiency, pollution control, forest coverage, all difficult items, is itself a sign of confidence from local bureaucrats in their capability in delivering planned results.

Hangzhou 13-5	
Top 5 desirable objectives	
GDP growth rate	≥7.5%
Tertiary industry share of GDP (%)	62

(continued)

(continued)

Hangzhou 13-5	
R&D contribution to GDP growth	≥65
R&D share of GDP (%)	3.5
Resident disposable income (CNY)	63,000
Top 5 must reach objectives	
Avg. years of education of newly-added labor force	14
Arable land stock (10k ha)	21.1
Square meter usage per 10k CNY GDP	18.1
Forest coverage (%)	>65
Number of days with good air quality each year (%)	76.7

Another interesting local example is Zhuji, a county located south of Hangzhou, also in Zhejiang province. The county is historically low on arable land stock amount and high on population density. Its relative lacking of resources through out history had pushed many locals to strive for things beyond what local resource could offer and has had a larger than average business and political presence at both provincial and even national level. That aggressive pursuit by the locals had propelled Zhuji to be one of the top 10 counties in terms of economic output among the 3000 or so counties in China, helped at least partially by a string of well-defined and executed 5-year county plans.

Zhuji 12-5	
Top objectives	
GDP growth rate	>10%
GDP per capita (CNY)	93,000
Tertiary industry share of GDP (%)	40
R&D share of GDP (%)	2.3
Urban resident average disposable income (CNY)	50,000
Rural resident average net income (CNY)	24,000
Standing timber volume (10k m^3)	400
Energy consumption per unit GDP (coal tonnage/10k CNY)	−0.18

Similar to Hangzhou, Zhuji also published a list of difficult objectives for delivery. What makes its plan content different from Hangzhou is its additional focuses on rural resident average income, standing timber volume and forest coverage, which are important local issues for this county with much higher rural population presence and a mountainous landscape. Though being at different administrative levels, both

Hangzhou city and Zhuji county belong to Zhejiang province, and each of the local government would identify issues particularly relevant to its own region and publish a list of objectives, some of them quantitatively defined and set as must-reach targets, which make local governments being held more or less accountable for their delivery. The administrative skillfulness and transparency offered by various levels and regions within Zhejiang province in implementing a consistent development plan yet with ample region-specific flexibility were important for its economic success and overall accommodating investment environment.

Zhuji 13-5	
Top 5 desirable objectives	
GDP growth rate	7.5–8%
GDP per capita (CNY)	13,500–13,800
Service industry share of GDP (%)	46
Urban resident average disposable income (CNY)	73,000
No. of beds per thousand senior	45
Top 5 must reach objectives	
Arable land stock (10k ha)	77.2
Standing timber volume (10k m^3)	0
Forest coverage (%)	61
Water quality above category III (%)	100
Urban sewer treatment ratio (%)	95

A local 5-year plan needs to both address important local issue and adhere to national and provincial mandate for approval. Thus it can be very difficult to produce a local plan when larger than local social and economic transitions are in motion. Beijing Dongcheng district is one of those local region caught in those transitions. Xicheng and Dongcheng districts are the two most important districts in Beijing, historically with Xicheng mainly tasked for housing the central governance and Dongcheng mainly for housing Beijing city government.

Dongcheng 13-5	
Top 5 desirable objectives	
Green commute ratio (%)	75
Resident disposable income growth (%)	Matching economic growth
Urban registered unemployment (%)	<2
GDP growth rate	6
General fiscal revenue growth rate (%)	5

(continued)

(continued)

Dongcheng 13-5	
Top 5 must reach objectives	
Permanent resident population (10k)	<77.4
Total water consumption (10k m^3)	Matching city requirement
Total energy consumption (10k coal tonnage)	Matching city requirement
Total energy consumption per unit GDP	Matching city requirement
Total water consumption reduction per unit GDP	[>15]

Dongcheng's top objectives focused on growth, income and green. What made this plan particularly hard for local bureaucrats to draft and implement were those must reach objectives focusing on reducing district population density and resource consumption, which would negatively impact economic growth generation, without which local fiscal and municipal objectives are difficult to be reached. At national level, Beijing's rising real estate price and deteriorating living environment became synonymous to central bureaucratic expansion, income inequality and big city disease of the past fast growing period. National mandate to reorient the core of Beijing to focus on being a political capital, not a pyramid tip of all things, therefore reducing real estate price and pollution, trickles down to Dongcheng district to severely limit its manufacturing base, to the extent manufacturing hardly exists as an industry in Dongcheng district.

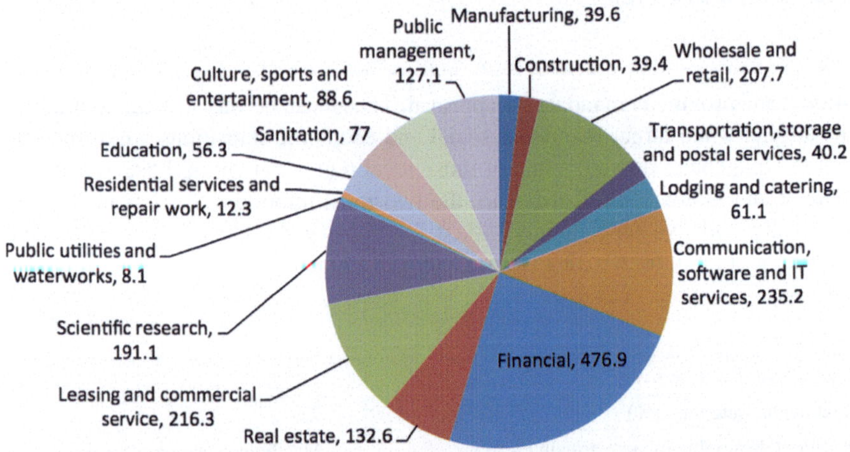

2016 Beijing Dongcheng District GDP by Source (100 million CNY) Dongcheng Bureau of Statistics 东城区统计局

Within Dongcheng's GDP growth contributing sources, education, scientific research, culture/sports/entertainment and communication IT will probably continue to enjoy future growth, while manufacturing, real estate, wholesale/retail segments will expect disincentives as the result of the 13-5 plan.

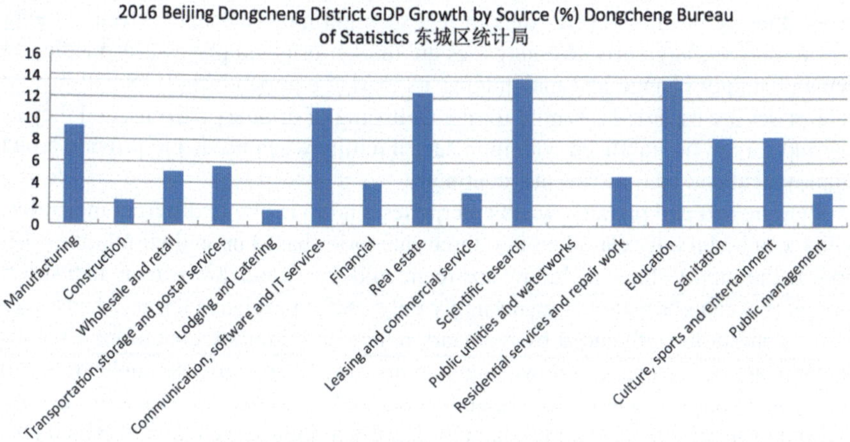

Local plans are the granular level implementation within national developmental plan, and the long-term success of the national economic management system rides on top of those local plan implementation success. Combined studies of local plans and national plans lead to accurate depiction of China's macro economic condition, and individual case studies would shed light on local industrial investment condition and hence helpful for more specific investment strategy formulation.

3.4.4 Corporate Initiatives

Each large economy's corporate world is both complex and unique. China's corporate world is particularly unorthodox from the perspective of the western economists. In contrast to Carl Marx's assertion that "economic foundation shall decide the superstructure", large sections of business can be also heavily influenced if not controlled by its social and political superstructure. In China, that social and political superstructure is governed with the philosophical mixture of Chinese traditional thinking, socialism and capitalism as its guiding principle. The traditional wisdom, the most important of which includes the Confucius thought and the Legalist thought, emphasizes on structural stability and cohesive action for social and economic development. The socialist thought and capitalism thought provide modern extensions crucial for realistic industrial implementation. Past revolution and current reforms might be considered as endless trials and efforts to modernize China's society and economy under those guiding principles.

Traditional Chinese thinking, capitalism and socialist philosophies translate into different management principles based upon different corporate entity types, which we might broadly distinguish based upon ownership, size and industries. Sate-owned enterprises (SOEs) with their perceived inefficiency are accepted as a governmental means for building up operating platforms, upon which private industries can provide products and services. These platforms SOEs are expected to be more capable of weathering business cycles thus in its execution more mandate-driven. Among private players, large private enterprises are market-oriented players, responding to demand supply change and maintaining its market competitiveness. Small private enterprises are regarded essential for the wellbeing of ordinary citizens, and they as a group should be stabilized with monetary liquidity when needed to provide broad employment and income revenue continuity.

State-owned and private-owned enterprises tend to reside in different industries, which can be broadly classified into three categories based upon their relative positions in the supply chain, including upstream, midstream and downstream industries, though this categorization is increasingly only useful in relative terms. Macro economic conditions, influenced by monetary policy and liquidity condition, drive the demand and performance of downstream industries. The downstream industries pull supply and production of midstream industries, and the midstream industries in turn, pull the upstream supply and production. Upstream industries, many of which provide traditional products and services related to raw materials, such as coal, ire ore and aluminum, are often occupied by large SOEs sensitive to policy and regulatory change. The same is true for many traditional downstream client facing service industries, such as airliners and telecoms. Midstream industries, such as electronic components manufacturers, are often occupied by private enterprises. The SOE linkage to market condition change is the SASAC. SASAC acts as a custodian but not a direct manager for state capital, a portfolio of which underwrites SOEs with an obligation to generate appropriate level of capital return for the public. The relative new industries, including e-commerce, smart phone, business logistics and real estate are almost completely occupied by private enterprises.

To describe with most simplified terms, flow events pass through economic structure, and economic structural components respond to those policy and resource flow events, and then generate their responses. Large SOEs in both upstream and downstream industries respond to both policy flow events and market resource flow events, large private enterprises in midstream and new industries more to market resource flow events, and small private enterprises in downstream industries to general health of macro economy and monetary liquidity flow event. So if we break down corporate sectors by ownership types, industries and sizes we could produce better current state analysis and business condition change forecast for designing macro and specific industrial/regional investment strategies.

Since enterprises of different ownership/industry/size operate within the same general macro environment, a high level state analysis of that environment would offer a useful insight. This analysis can be conducted by studying policy initiatives that are often laid out in various levels/ministries of 5-year planning and monetary condition that is managed by PBOC, both of which were discussed earlier. The operating environment analysis can also be conducted by looking into some key macro statistics, especially regarding the energy consumption data.

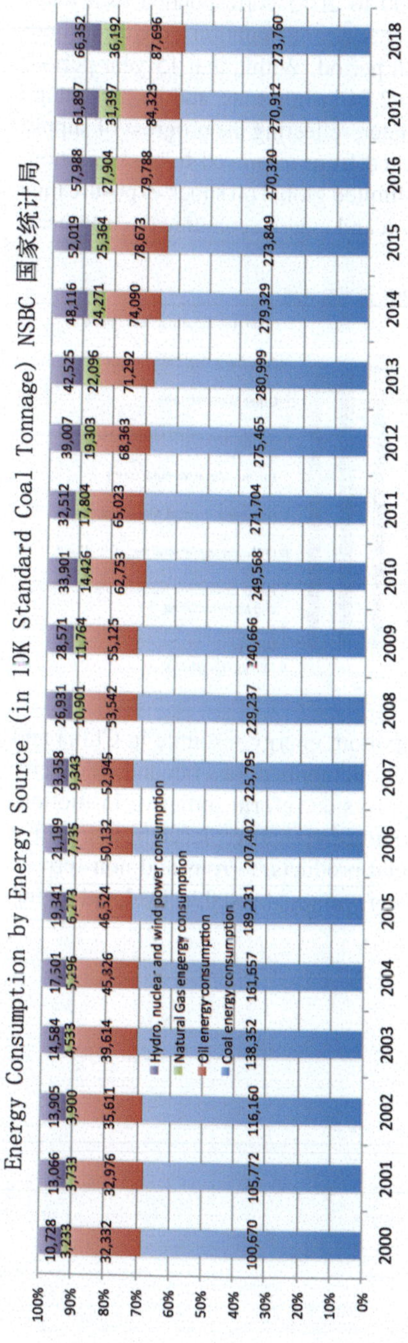
Energy Consumption by Energy Source (in 10K Standard Coal Tonnage) NSBC 国家统计局
Hydro, nuclear and wind power consumption
Natural Gas engergy consumption
Oil energy consumption
Coal energy consumption
100%
90%
80%
70%
60%
50%
40%
30%
20%
10%
0%
2000 10,728 3,233 32,332 100,670
2001 13,066 3,733 32,976 105,772
2002 13,905 3,900 35,611 116,160
2003 14,584 4,533 39,614 138,352
2004 17,501 5,296 45,326 161,657
2005 19,341 6,273 46,524 189,231
2006 21,199 7,735 50,132 207,402
2007 23,358 9,343 52,945 225,795
2008 26,931 10,901 53,542 229,237
2009 28,571 11,764 55,125 240,666
2010 33,901 14,426 62,753 249,568
2011 32,512 17,804 65,023 271,704
2012 39,007 19,303 68,363 275,465
2013 42,525 22,096 71,292 280,999
2014 48,116 24,271 74,090 279,329
2015 52,019 25,364 78,673 273,849
2016 57,988 27,904 79,788 270,320
2017 61,897 31,397 84,323 270,912
2018 66,352 36,192 87,696 273,760

Within the energy consumption data set, the rising total energy consumption expressed in standard coal tonnage from 2000 to 2015 corresponded to a long-running economic growth period and slower energy consumption growth in more recent years to a more moderated GDP growth period. Within that 15-year period, coal's usage had risen from 1.0 billion tons to 2.74 billion tons, and its percentage in total energy consumption rose first and fell later, reflecting the progress of supply side reform to meet green expectation originated from improved living condition. Oil share was consistently around 20%, which limited global oil shock exposure thus providing overall stable energy supply condition and macro economic environment.

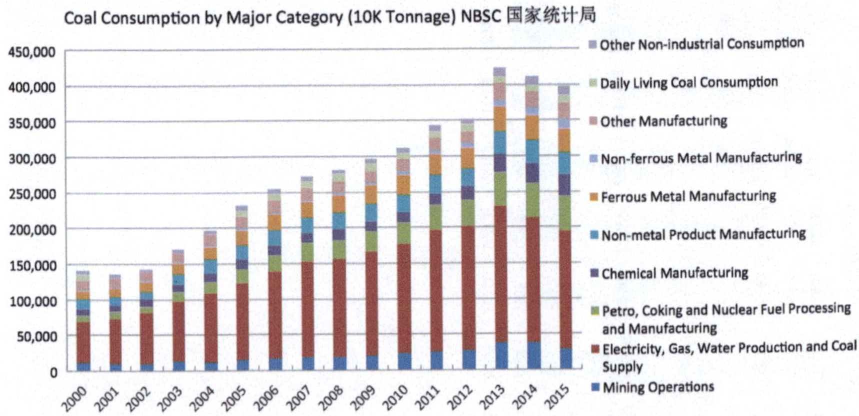

Coal is the most abundant and also the important energy resource in China and has been used extensively in a variety of economic applications beyond electricity generation and fuel manufacturing. With supply side reform initiative in motion, recent coal usage was down in electricity generation and share replaced by alternative energy sources, but its applications in non-metal products, ferrous and non-ferrous metal manufacturing and chemical manufacturing remained at stable level, indicating an overall stable macro condition.

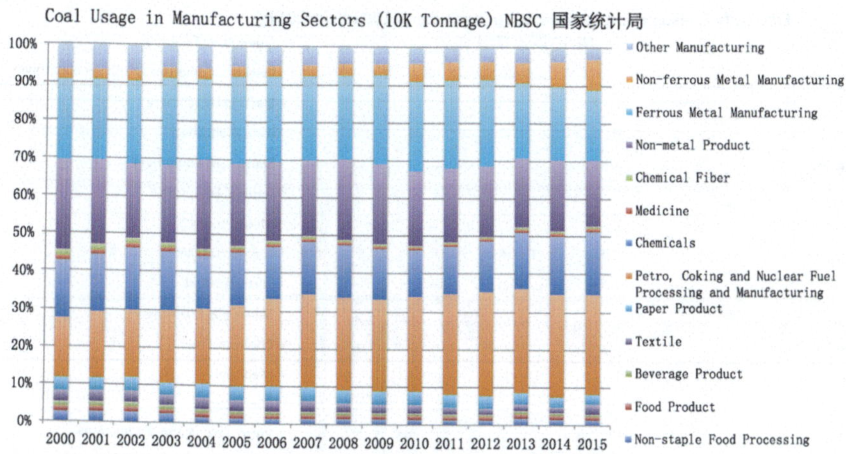

For coal consumption within the important manufacturing segment, the largest share went to energy-related manufacturing. Ferrous metal and non-metal product share decreased, while non-ferrous metal share increased, suggesting manufacturing segment entering a more sophisticated developmental stage.

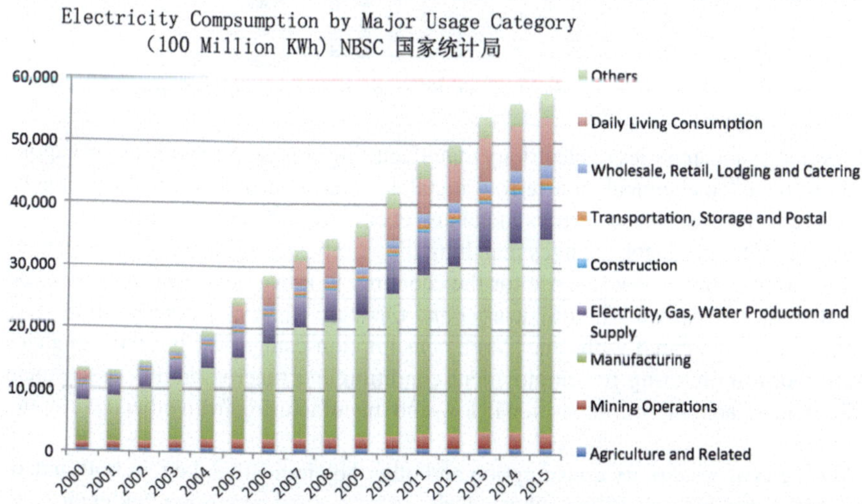

Next to coal consumption data, electricity consumption data is another important piece of information within the energy consumption data set. Electricity consumption data is grouped differently from coal consumption data. Among different categories of electricity consumption, the largest consumption category was manufacturing, following by electricity/gas/water production and daily living. Manufacturing usage growth had slowed, and daily living usage pattern had been stable, pointing to moderated economic growth but stable macro condition.

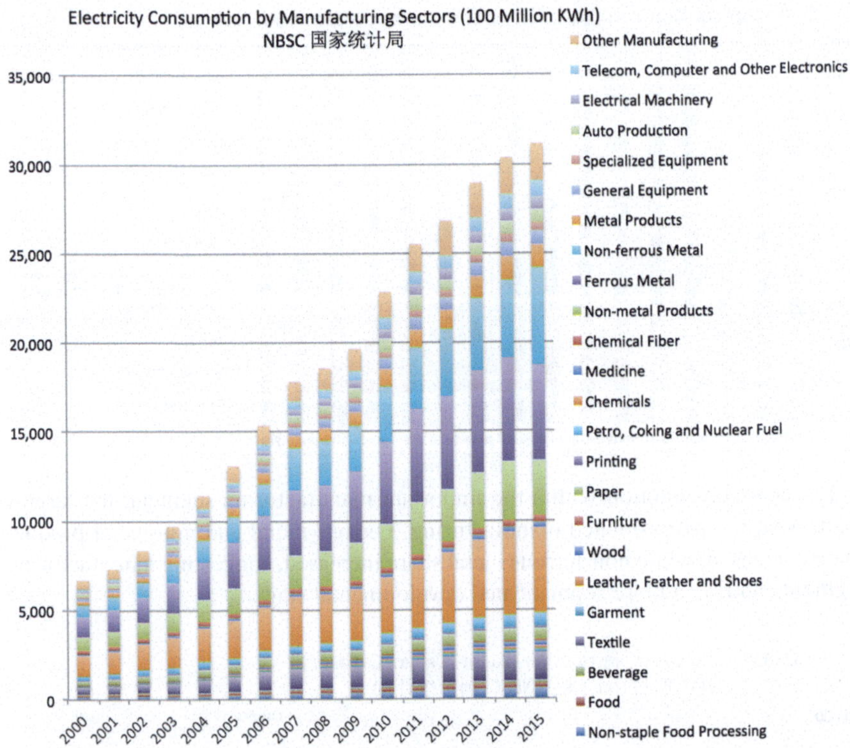

Among subcategories of electricity manufacturing consumption, the largest applications included chemical, non-ferrous metal, ferrous metal and non-metal products. In more recent years, non-ferrous metal and chemicals did better than ferrous metal and non-metal products, changes matching the supply side reform policy initiatives expectation in the broadest sense for the economy to move out of the very low-end manufacturing segment. Textile, leather and furniture electricity consumption were rather small compared with other large consumption categories, but their changes were worth monitoring for employment condition and macro stability assessment when China faces more competition in low-end manufacturing from other developing countries.

Using coal, electricity consumption and other key indicative data, in both macro categories and manufacturing subcategories, with general economic, budgetary and monetary condition analysis being provided, after piecing together policy initiatives, based upon corporate ownership, industry positions and enterprise sizes, we could make reasonable assessment of general corporate condition within different industries and try to predict likely corporate initiatives taken per different flow events for regional and industrial investment analysis.

3.4.5 *Individual Consumer Demand*

Residential consumption formed a third of China GDP, based upon NBSC accounting methodology. Combined with governmental spending, consumption accounted for slightly more than half of China's GDP. The past increase of consumption had been large and steady.

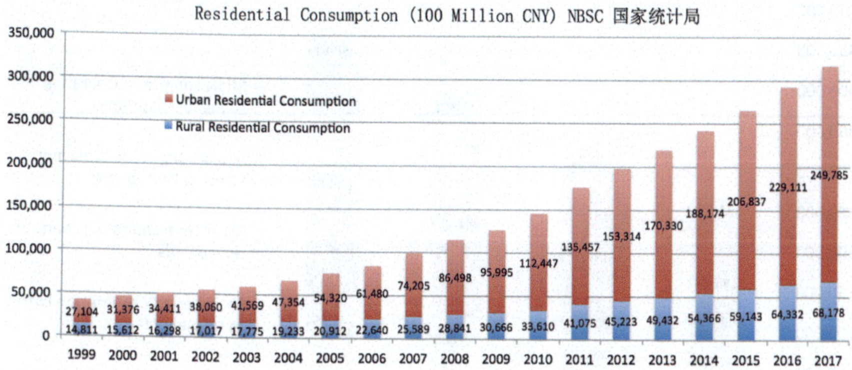

Roughly a third of direct residential consumption went to residential commercial property in 2017. The other large consumption item was vehicle. Total vehicle sale in 2018 was 22.35 million. Out of those, 11.17 million were passenger cars. The high percentage of real estate spending within total residential consumption was caused by a convergence of social desire to have better living space, increased monetary liquidity and a lack of alternative investment venue with enough depth to absorb the excess liquidity. This high real estate share within consumption and its subsequent leverage took a toll on people's spending power on other consumption items. For example, passenger car sale in 2018 was 4% lower versus 2017, with volume drop concentrated in the lower-priced domestic brand segment, where people with lower income were more susceptible to the squeezing effect of rising real estate expenditure, versus foreign brand car segment.

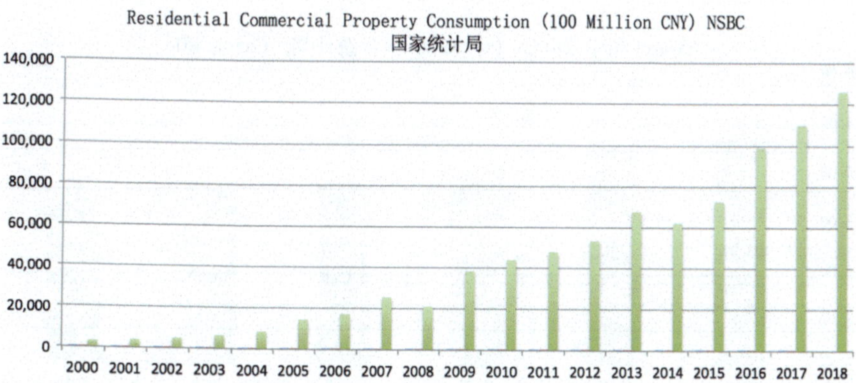

The flow into real estate asset class is financed by both residential savings and loan leverage. Majority of mid and long-term consumption loan issued by banks was used for mortgage. The level of leverage and the consumption expenditure availability both act as constraints on the growth potential of real estate investment class, and growth potential of more general consumption flow event.

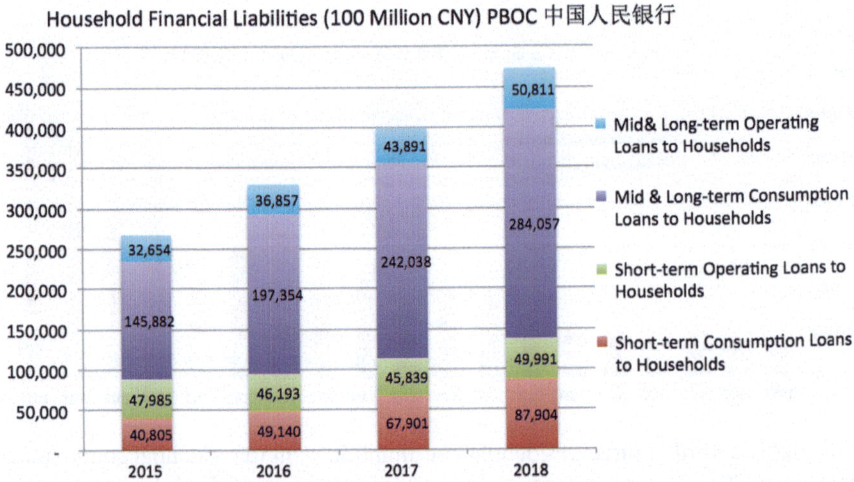

3.4.6 International Trade

International trade was critical for China's integration into global system. Allocation of labor and resources based upon market principle unleashed much increased industrial efficiency. Though export as the percentage of GDP declined, and the net effect of trade (export minus import) is much smaller than that, export retains its criticality as the access window for Chinese industries to the outside world, for technology, and more importantly, for market-based decision making process during resources allocation within various supply chain operations in a society that had its roots in top-down management style.

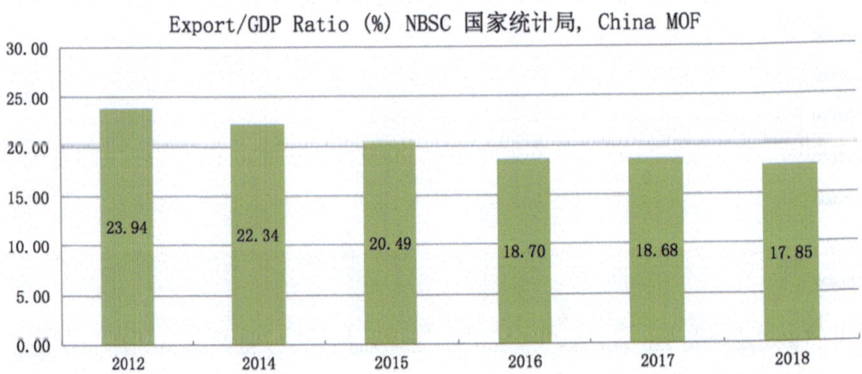

The composition of China's export has been well studied by the business community, academia and policy makers. Large export categories included computer, mobile phone and parts, textile, garments and furniture. The shift towards less energy intensive, more value-added content mixture had been difficult but steady progress was made. Due to China's sheer possible production capacity upon any category entry, its export mix change could bring boom to certain areas and the complete opposite in other areas. Therefore the key in formulating a related and sound investment strategy is to identify where China might or might not gain sufficient progress within a timeframe and make technology and business investment decisions accordingly. For example, knowing China's gradual progress on manufacturing upgrade, large and quickened shoe/toy export decrease might suggest domestic labor and other cost increase gaining speed, and a labor-intensive manufacturing investment decision on China periphery might be worth a look into to receive potential capacity outflow.

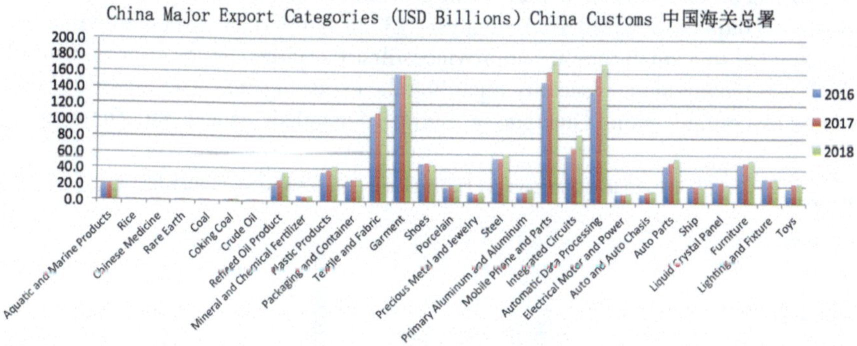

The importing side of China international trade became more important during the period of continuous economic progress both for both industry and consumption purposes. Within the import product categories, the largest were integrated circuit and crude oil, followed by iron ore and concentrate, auto and airplane and their parts, soy and plastic raw material. Iron ore usage is heavily linked to real estate investment flows and consumption flows, and its future demand would be volatile. IC import is dependent upon the future stability of China-US electronic supply chain. Crude oil import growth will be stable to maintain an international oil shock risk limit. To prepare for a long-term investment strategy linked to China import data studies often requires an integrated political and economic analytical approach from China's perspective. For example, knowing China's oil reserve would not grow much, if large crude oil import increase can be observed, building an on-shore refinery facility close to China production capacity by oil exporter countries to lessen China geopolitical concern and bring steady future revenue would probably make sense.

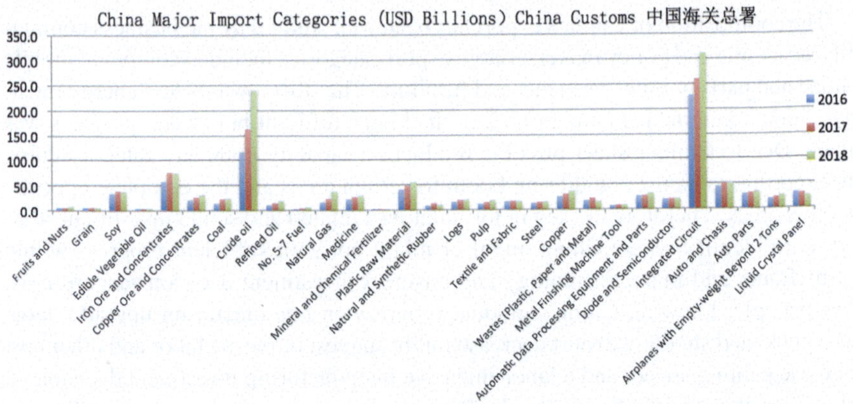

To invest based upon China's economic growth, or integrate into China's industrial growth, all require localized macro analysis. China's import and export activities are concentrated in a small number of provinces/first-tier cities, the most prominent of which was Guangdong, especially regarding the exporting side. The Importing side is more diversified among Guangdong, Beijing, Shanghai, Jiangsu and Zhejiang.

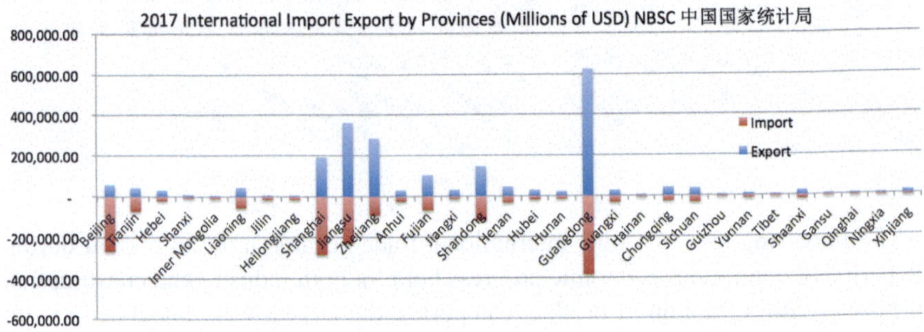

Focusing on international trading activities originated from certain provinces/first tier cities reduces time outlay on China macro analysis, but any conclusion made by latching onto only a few locations for long-term study would be tenuous at best. The process of lessening influence from Guangdong and gaining influence from Yangtze delta and Beijing started in the beginning of 2000 as China entered WTO and that change of fortune was significant as the rest of country started to catch up in the grand economic opening.

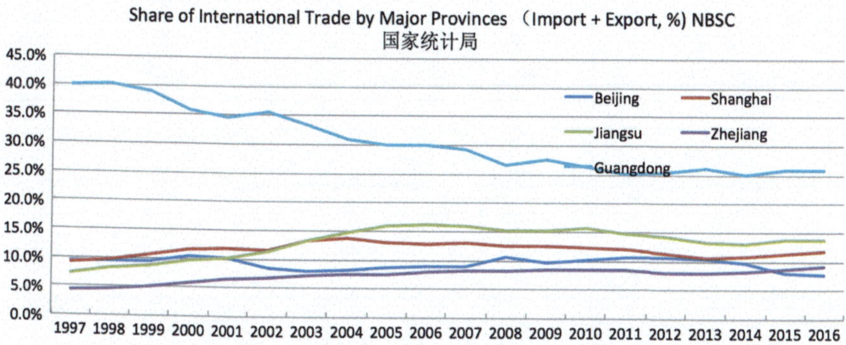

The long-term international trade flow diversification away from Guangdong to more dispersed domestic geography was the result of both improved infrastructure within China and a catch-up in technological hardware and software by other provinces, regional paradigm shifts themselves presenting investment opportunities. For macro assessment and investment strategy formulation based upon China's changing trade flow pattern analysis, practitioners need to look beyond trade data from Guangdong and Yangtze Delta geography, with a time perspective, and remain sensitive to trade product category differences, to generate a multi-dimensional and hence more robust analytical framework.

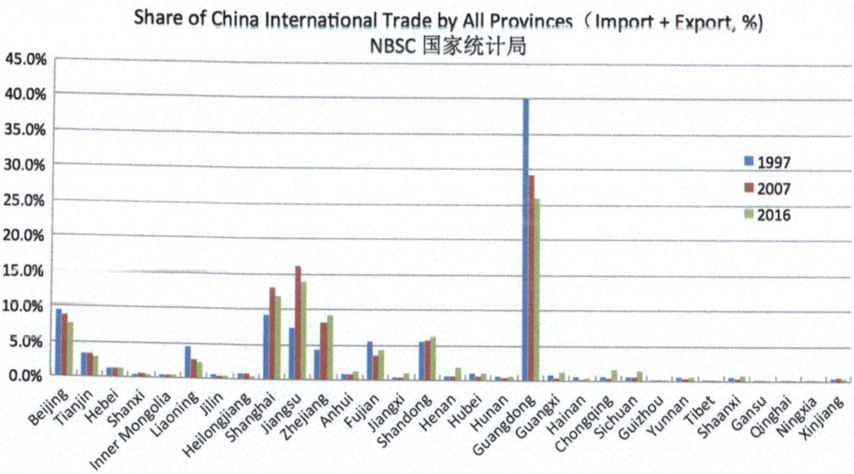

Chapter 4
Structural Reform Agenda

Economic structure and the pattern of resource flows passing through them are not static. After years of freewheeling economic development, massive social and economic stress has been accumulated and needs to be addressed. In response, government has proposed large set of structural reform objectives and implemented many reform proposals. While many of these problems are long-term in nature and cannot be solved with simple quick fixes, progress has been made largely due to the strong determination from the top leadership.

4.1 The Economic and Social Progress

Among many social problems, class immobility and wealth inequality are the two most divisive issues that could have destabilizing effect if not addressed.

4.1.1 Class Immobility and Public Service Improvement

The largest manifestation of class immobility in China is the dichotomy of urban and rural social welfare standard, in particular regarding medical and education services. The number of medical service professions is often two to three times per 10 thousand residents in urban area versus rural area. Taking into consideration that rural residents are more dispersed, the medical service availability deteriorates even further.

X. Zhang, *Mechanical Analysis of China's Macro Economic Structure*,
https://doi.org/10.1007/978-981-15-3840-7_4

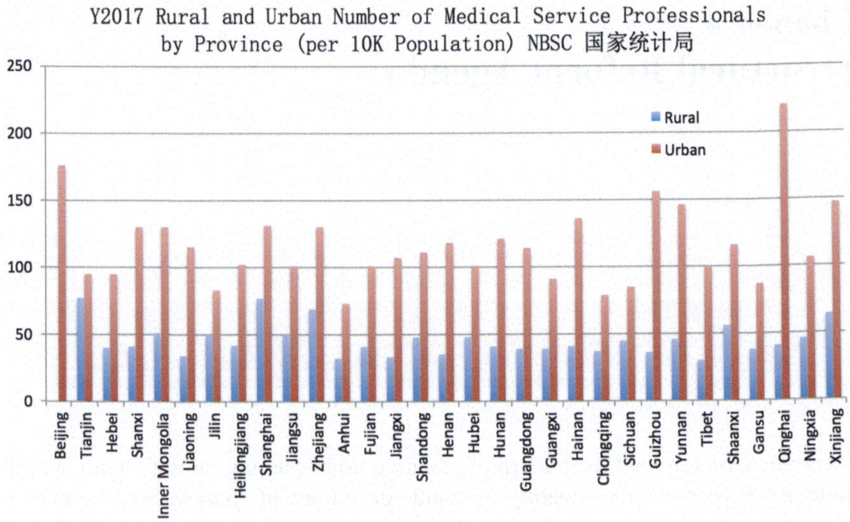

To improve the level of medical services to rural areas, the percentage of fiscal budget allocated to medical services had been increased and in rural area there had been large increase of medical service professionals from 2010 to 2017. But the most audacious reform proposal was the loosening up the urban resident status requirement in 2019 in most cities except the largest ones that are already overcrowded. This was one gigantic step towards finally eliminate the legacy of urban and rural dichotomy so as to allow market force to allocate labor force between urban and rural economic sectors. The trend towards more market-oriented resource allocation is expected to continue to alleviate the stress imposed by class immobility on social and economic growth.

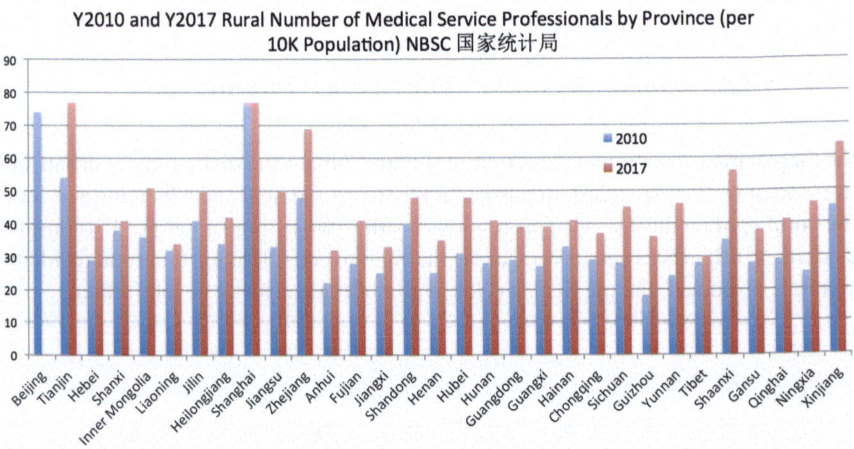

4.1.2 *Real Estate Value Storage and Wealth Inequality*

Real estate is the US equity market-equivalent in China for wealth storage. Though real estate sales data can be influenced by policy initiatives to contain real estate bubble, real estate investment data reflects developer's expectation for future demand. Since 2015 after US Fed started to raise interest and global liquidity started to dry up, China was also in funds tightening mode to drain excess liquidity released during credit crisis. The investment for average apartment became anemic and the investment for the more luxury units had maintained healthy growth, illustrating wider divergence between the general population and the more affluent group during this growth moderation period.

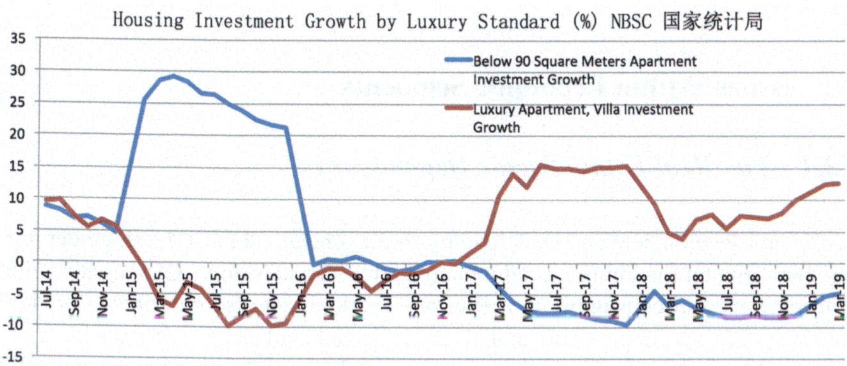

It has become increasingly clear now the global supply chain brought huge economic efficiency improvement without its benefit being widely distributed at either international or domestic level. In US, the beneficiaries tend to be those who have access to technology or capital. In China, the beneficiaries tend to be those that directly participate in the supply chain or the well-connected social group that indirectly participate via providing different essential resources. The beneficiaries with their accumulated wealth then made investment in equities and real estate. Subsequently released monetary liquidity and lowered interest rate cost to deal with the aftermath of financial crisis caused large rise in equities and real estate prices. Rising real estate value brought wealth to those who had means to invest in them in China, leaving behind a large wealth gap.

Particularly hard-hit by the rising real estate price were large number of new entrants into the labor force with comparatively low starting salary. One solution to absorb this better educated labor force into middle class with higher living standard is to improve labor productivity, which means higher industrial sophistication and economic output. This translates into a continuous strong push to advance in various industry sectors in order to support economic growth, class mobility and social stability. We should expect the push to persist with or without a solution on the current international trade negotiation.

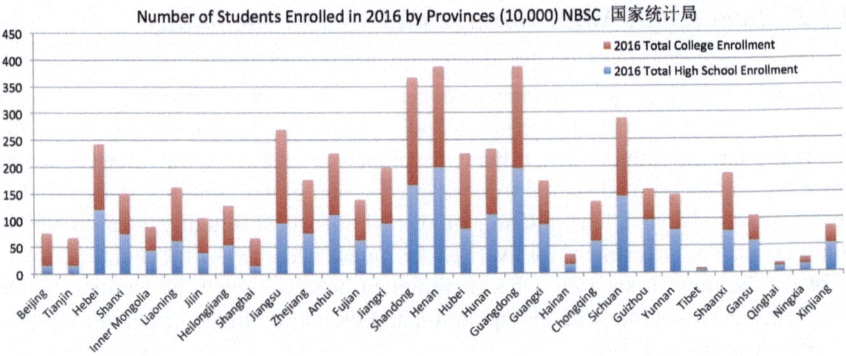

4.2 Issues Within Economic Segments

4.2.1 The Real Estate Sector Dependency

Real estate development and bank lending credit generated in that development process were pivotal for China's rapid modernization. Besides direct GDP contribution in investment and consumption, real estate development also contributes to GDP indirectly, when local government used the collected land usage right transfer fee to fund local projects including highway, subway and other infrastructure projects. But real estate application in economic development had run its course. High real estate price had exacerbated industry exodus, social friction, and risky leverage bubble.

To wean the country off the real estate dependency has proved to be much harder than anticipated. At the stage 4 of industrialization symbolized by steel and concrete material, real estate is considered the last economic force that can pull large economic cylinders. Moving into higher form of Industrialization with advanced economic drivers and higher worker compensation, is a desirable objective, but even after that is achieved, the real estate price in China should still be kept at a rational level. Expensive real estate prices at different global locations are often supported by very specific reasons. With the exception of London being an offshore financial hub, other expensive metros such as Boston, Silicon Valley, Seattle, and to certain extent Munich are innovative centers with monopolistic hold on cutting-edge technologies hence capital and talent attraction, and subsequently high real estate asset appreciation. Without the pricing power from congregating game-changing monopolistic technologies, Germany and Japan are generally very careful with their national real estate value so as to maintain competitive cost edge of advanced manufacturing industries. Therefore, suppressing real estate price should be a long-term developmental objective, if China wants to maintain its role as a manufacturing powerhouse before a true morph into a global innovative center.

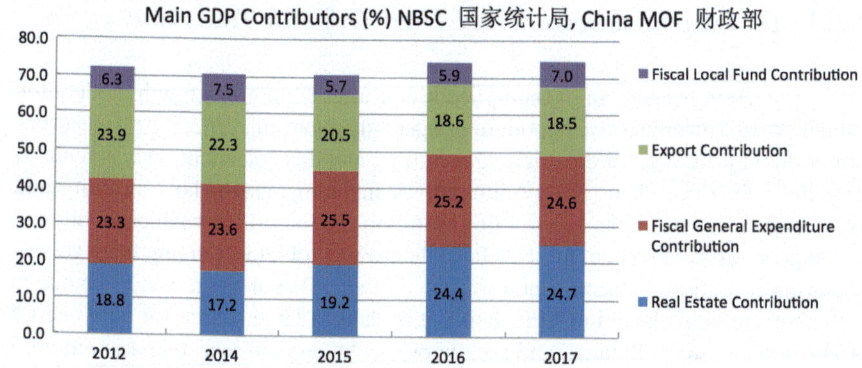

4.2.2 *Platform Corporates and Too Public to Fail*

Platform corporates are often funded with entrust loan and trust loan, both of which are conduit forms of credit that bypass banking limits set per industry or entity. Relatively speaking, more entrust loan originates from Beijing due to top tier SOE presence versus more trust loan originates from Shanghai due to commercial banking activities presence. Platform corporates was pivotal for local government projects funding. Cutting off entrust loan might lead to a surge of trust loan. Since both entrust loan and trust loan are part of shadow banking heavily associated with of local government funding requirement, local government special bond issuance was initiated in 2018 amid a complete crackdown on shadow banking. The burden of regulating platform corporates is therefor transferred from banking regulators to local government with Ministry of Finance as the gatekeeper. The ambiguity of platform true legal status, being governmental or business, remains unsolved. For both its usefulness in providing developmental support to local economy with proven success, but problematic role of direct governmental involvement in broad business arena, persist without an easy solution.

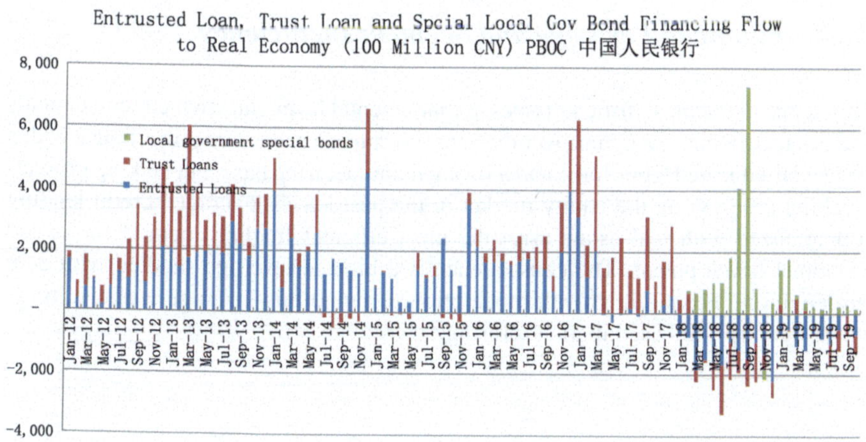

4.2.3 *Oversupplied Sectors and Their Difficult Transition*

Coal production became an oversupplied sector after economic growth moderation amid increased awareness of air pollution especially regarding PM2.5. Its largest consumption purpose was for electricity generation, and this consumption was reduced with the help from clean energy alternatives including gas, solar electricity and hydro electricity. But large amount of gas import, increased solar panel production and huge hydro-related dam projects have their own problems, ranging from geopolitical uncertainty to environmental impact. In the end coal as an energy source is both abundant and cheap in China, hence it remains a large source for both energy production and air pollutants, and continuous technological investment is required to bring down the cost of alternative energy sources and expand their usage scale to reduce coal consumption and its associated air pollution and CO_2 emission. Other oversupplied sectors such as steel and concrete also face difficult transition issues.

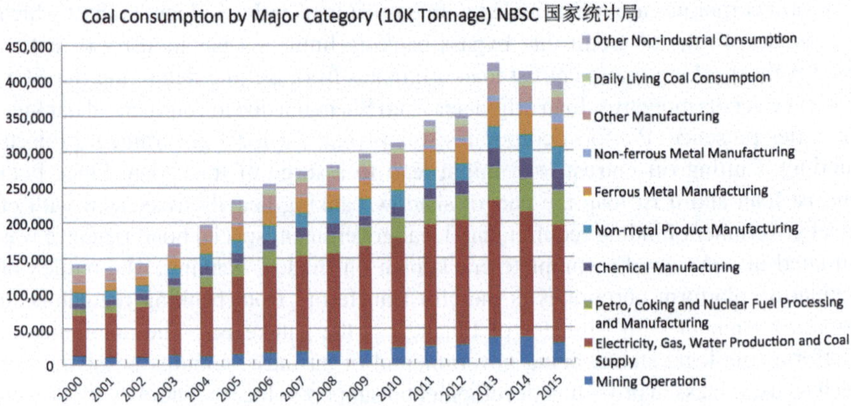

4.2.4 *Financial Leverage and Segment Inefficiency*

This is one of the most difficult issues at fundamental level, intertwined with China's real estate dependency. China over the years became an economic powerhouse with a large well-educated labor force and a strong manufacturing base, but lacking groundbreaking progress on the equity market in the past leaves leveraged credit lending collateralized with real estate asset the most efficient funding method for scaled economic development. The consequence is a bloated leverage saddled with debt burden during economic growth moderation. Unwind this leverage will take time, and assiduous rule-based market reform.

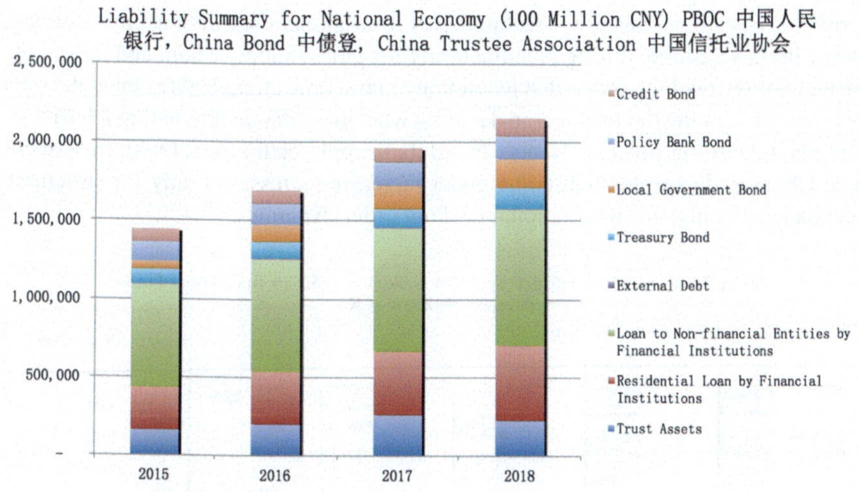

4.2.5 *External Trade Structural Imbalance*

Another persisting issue is the large structural trade imbalance developed during the globalization era. The largest surplus was with the US, concentrating in computer and communication electronics categories. China became the final assembly destination of computers, mobile phones and other electronic products and therefore final surplus origin for large US trade deficit. To achieve this deficit reduction requires an ultimate decoupling of the global supply chain, since it is quite unlikely to find enough volume in other international trade categories to balance out the supply chain surplus amount. The decoupling has enormous global economic ramification if implemented, as US domestically produced iPhone and other consumer electronics products might lose its global pricing competitiveness, while China indigenous innovation capability still can not rival that provided by US research institutions.

Designed by US, global supply chain was created as the most capital efficient international business model, with technology and capital from US, equipment from Japan, Korea Republic, Singapore and China Taiwan, and manufacturing facilities and engineering and other labor from China, pooling together for sophisticated manufacturing at unprecedented level of efficiency. Unwinding that to achieve more balanced global and domestic benefit distribution is only part of the picture. Since WWII, US with its strong but limited size of talent poor and other resources, has gradually let go the total control of global manufacturing arena, and is content with managing global system by using dominating high tech position, supplemented with free capital markets, to allocate roles to different countries to play in global production and trading system. An example was the semiconductor accord with Japan, and the technology and capital flow to Korea Republic to balance out Japan's past semiconductor manufacturing dominance. More recently, when China used its sizable market access to exchange for technologies from global corporations, in combination with fast learning during manufacturing for global supply chain, and moved up on technology pecking order, that technology know-how upgrade threatened the role played by US as the top manager in deciding who does what in international business and manufacturing process. Hence, the global supply chain model with its associated China trade surplus will come under increasing stress, not only for structural imbalance, but also for international pecking order dynamics.

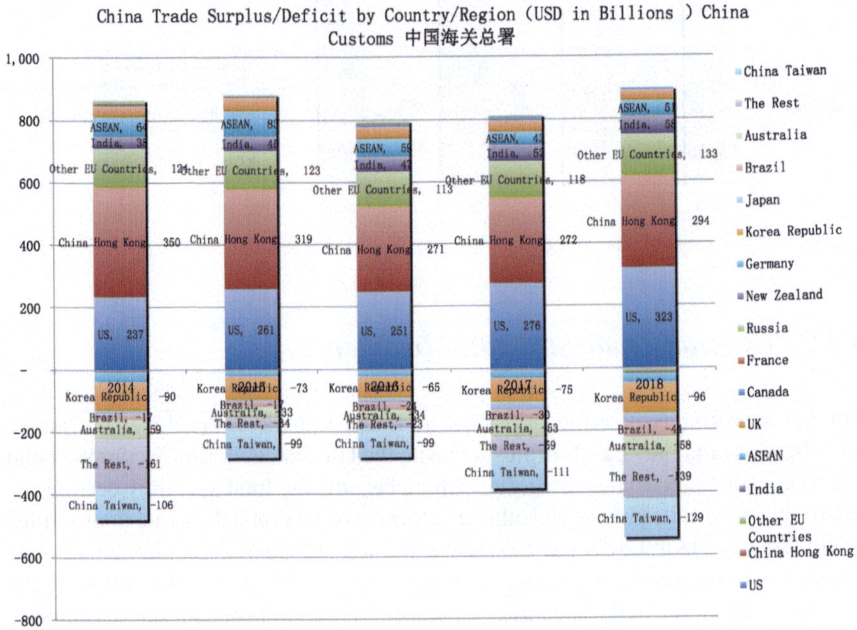

4.3 Issues Within Economic Social Structure

4.3.1 Coal Barons, Internet Moguls and Real Estate Wealth

Coal baron was an extraordinary phenomena during the boom years before the credit crisis crash, typified by the wealthy coal mine owners/operators from Shangxi province rich with coal deposits. Amid rising coal price caused by southern coast energy coal shortage for electricity generation during the export growth period, their fast path to riches from 2004 to 2008 could be illustrated by the quick rising petrol consumption within a very short period, related to increased car consumption. More gentrified tech capital dawned the Internet era crowded with star moguls accumulating extraordinary wealth exemplified by Baidu, Alibaba, and Tencent. Credit easing after the financial crisis also caused an inflated real estate price that further entrenched wealth gap between the very wealthy and the commoners. The expanding wealth gap brought social tension, resulting more bureaucratic control over the wealthy group and that control may strengthen further as a counterbalance to the power of concentrated capital and technology in modern AI era.

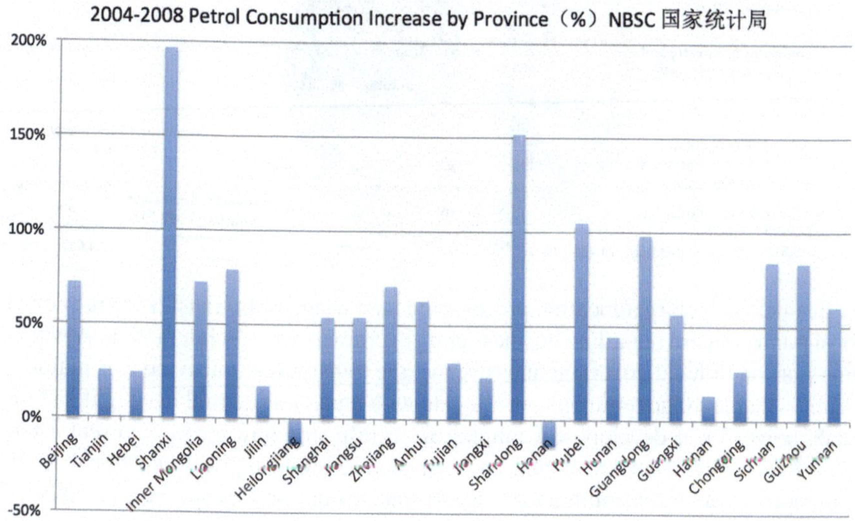

4.3.2 *Bureaucrats and Business Interest Group*

Different levels of Chinese government provide a variety of services to its citizens. They are also directly involved in many local development projects, more so than their western peers. This heavy direct involvement comes with both benefits and concerns. The problem with the direct governmental involvement model is the difficulty in separating bureaucracy function from business function, hence the handling of conflict of interest.

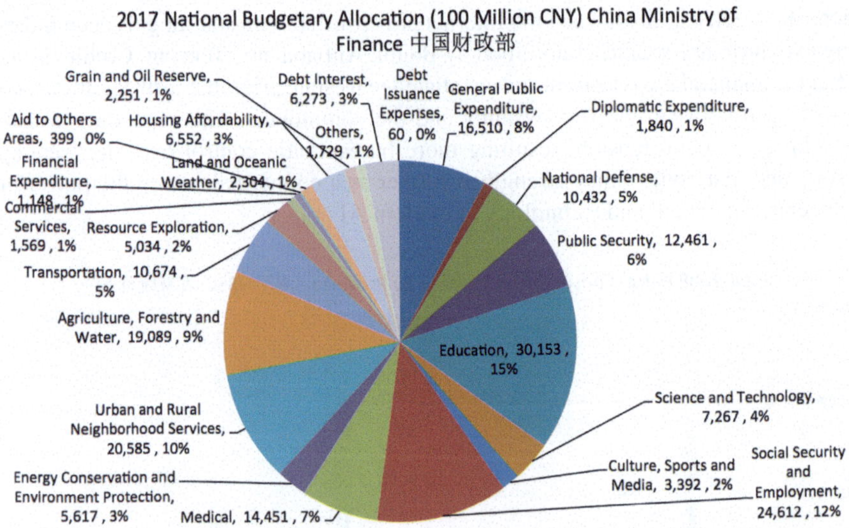

Besides budgetary allocation process, the land usage right transfer fee is another focal point concern regarding business and government interest interaction. A whopping portion of local governmental revenue, the transfer fee is also the vast majority of funds that local government can allocate with much less central oversight and the funds power local development ranging from infrastructure projects to real estate sales. Real estate-related revenue's necessity and its broad application in local development create a thorny combination. Real estate tax has been proposed and expected to replace land usage right transfer fee as a more enduring local governmental income source.

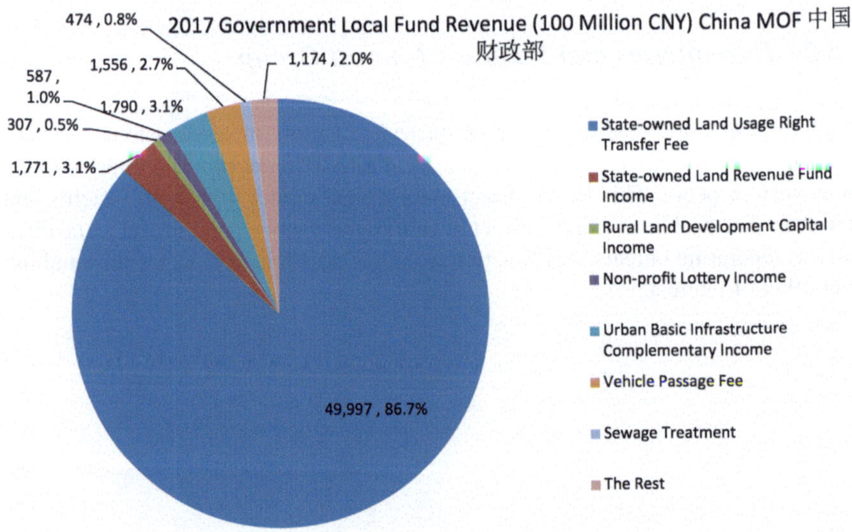

4.3.3 *Class Immobility Without Imperial Exams*

College entrance exam in China is very competitive and remains one of the fairest upward social mobility passages provided to the commoners, but it is still far from the imperial exam in history with more comprehensive and deep mobility impact. What can be used to effectively integrate a wider social spectrum into the ruling group without disrupting the current bureaucrat selection mechanism remains unclear.

4.4 Structural Rebalance Agenda

4.4.1 *Centralized Governance versus Corruption*

How much should be centralized versus how much should be decentralized within governance structure had long been a balancing act in Chinese history. Recent trend was towards more centralization to lessen autonomy especially regarding both regional governance and large SOEs to reduce grey area where corruption might occur with less scrutiny. Different interest groups have different takes on this centralizing trend, but the demand for curbing corruption by the commoners could be hard to satisfy otherwise in the current management structure. Large tax transfer from central to local government can be viewed as exerting central control over revenue and expenditure of the local government. The trade-off is less enthusiasm by the local governance or SOEs to take more proactive approach regarding economic development.

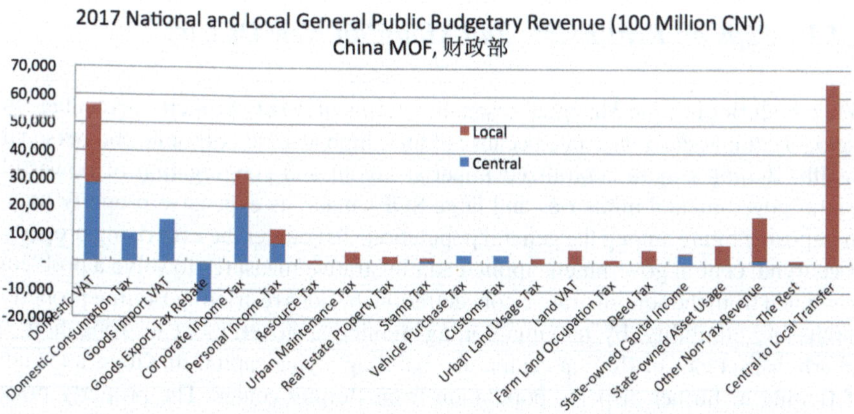

4.4.2 Budget and Wealth Redistribution

Expenditure unsupported by general revenue, when relatively large, shows the degree of a regional economic dependency on fund revenue mostly related to real estate income. Some of those regions, including Sichuan, Yunnan, Shannxi are also in the intense period of urbanization, hence heavy real estate dependency does not automatically translate into economic weakness. The concern is fairness and economic growth sustainability, since whether this largely onetime wealth gain can be well spent and fairly distributed within an administrative region, is heavily dependent upon the experience and foresight of local administration, which has term limits, hence their implementation objectives are not necessarily long-term oriented.

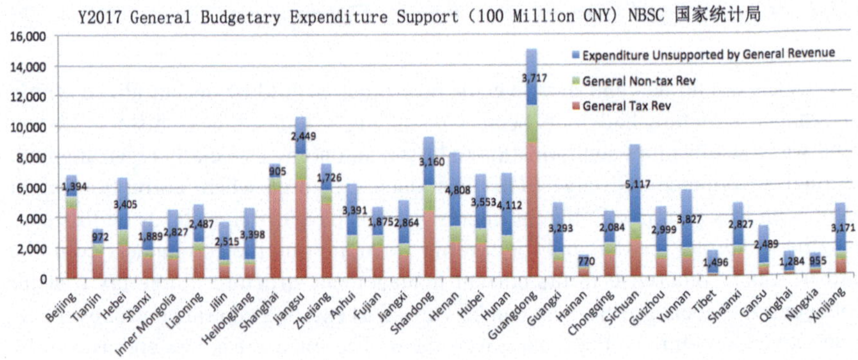

4.4.3 Caps on Real Estate and Xiong'an New District

While both Beijing and Shanghai rose tall in terms of luxury property percentage in regional commercial real estate because of their high level of corporate and personal wealth, Beijing's more centralized imperial layout and congregation of powerful central governmental ministries and large SOEs made its expensive property price an imposing figure among the general population. To counter the ever rising property price trend, central government applied administrative measures to solve a problem originated from the administrative concentration, besides restricting Beijing property purchasing eligibility, by moving Beijing municipal government to Tongzhou, a suburb district east of Beijing center, and building a vice capital in Xiong'an south of Beijing to further disperse population from Beijing center. The property price stabilized since those administrative measures took effect, but the control effort needs to persist to counter the natural tendency of administrative congregation and avoid Beijing's real estate price again becoming a symbol of either unbalanced economic growth or unbalanced wealth distribution.

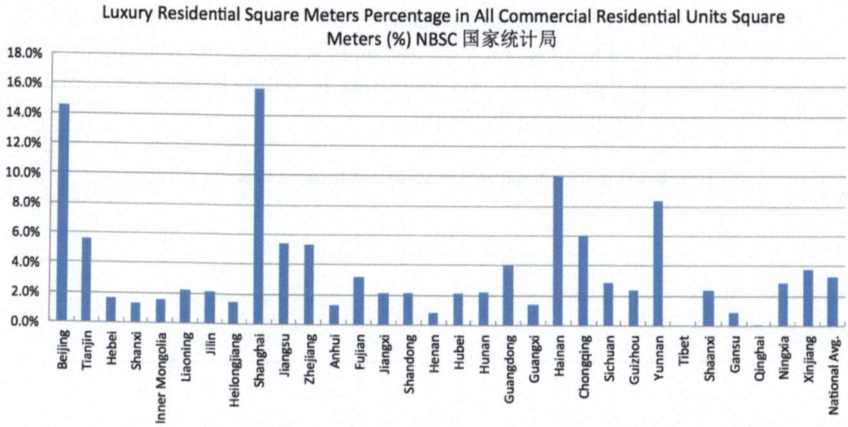

4.4.4 *Environmental Regulation*

There is an increased awareness in China for different environmental issues after the initial fast growth period and subsequently many actions were taken to address those issues. Large effort was made in forest restoration to curb soil erosion and improve the eco system in general. From 2004 to 2011 forest coverage rate improved quite significantly, from 18.2% in 2004 to 21.6% in 2011 at national level, based upon NSBC data.

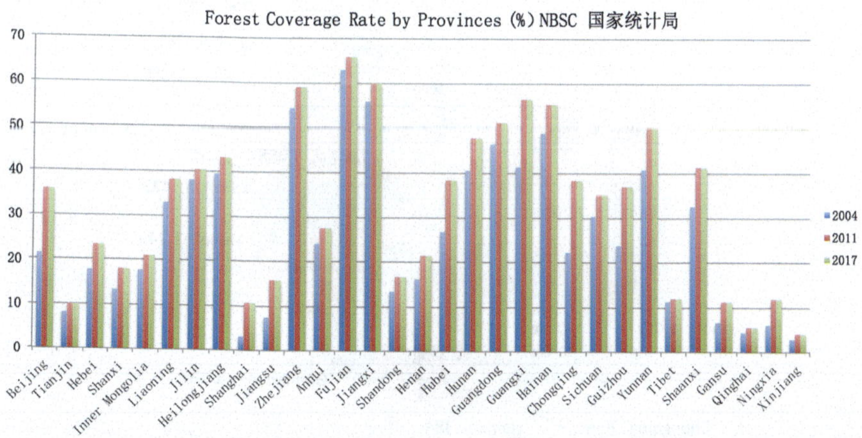

Significant air quality improvement was also achieved. PM2.5 pollution was severe in recent years due to increased coal usage in living and heavy industry sectors. Sulfur Dioxide (SO_2) can be produced during coal and oil burning and its emission reduction can be used as air quality improvement proxy. In SO_2 emission reduction, large improvement could be seen across various regions from 2011 to 2017. Especially helpful to air quality improvement was the reduction coming from areas packed with scaled polluting heavy industries, including Hebei, Henan, Shanxi, Shandong and Inner Mongolia in the North.

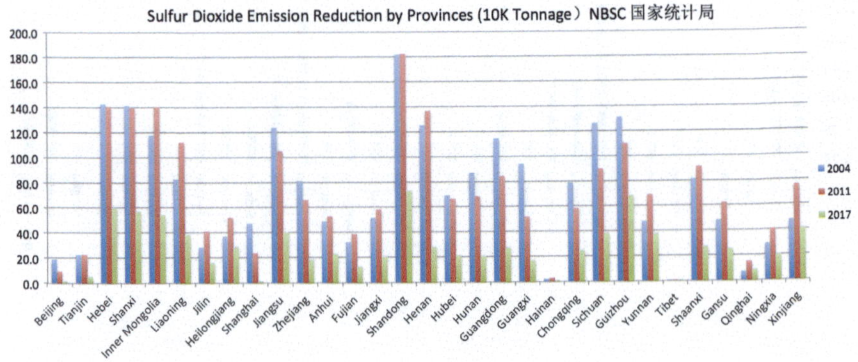

Another large environmental issue is water resource management. Water resources are not evenly distributed in China. This important resource is geographically rich in the south and southwest, and seasonally rich in summer and poor in spring and winter.

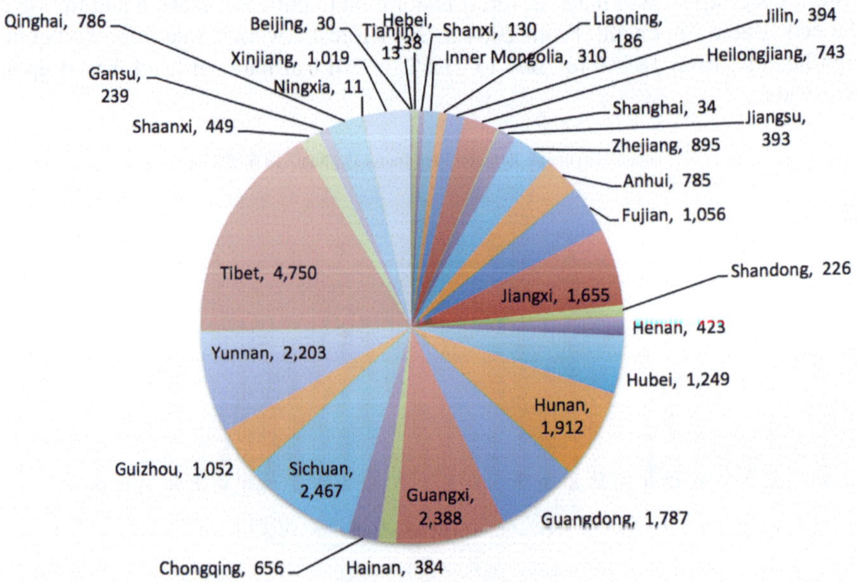

2017 Water Resource Distribution by Provinces (100 Million Cubic Meters) NBSC 国家统计局

The economic constraint imposed by uneven water resource distribution among different provinces can be implied by water resource amount over local GDP ratio.

Some of the most economically dynamic regions, including Beijing, Shanghai, Guangdong, Zhejiang and Jiangsu all have very low water resource/GDP ratios and therefore face resource constraint over their future economic growth.

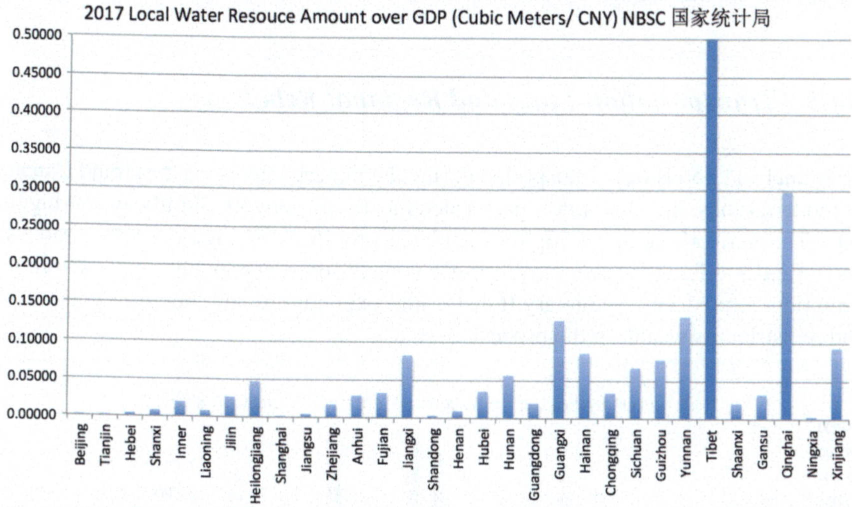

Among those regions, one place with the scarcest water resource available is Beijing, the only mega city in China that is not close to a major river, hence presented with chronic water shortage problem. Ground water was over-pumped causing drinking water quality degradation, land sinking and other issues. Water from south was rerouted in a major engineering effort to supply this city, and since 2014, water shortage problem was somewhat alleviated, with surplus amount pumped back to underground for eco system restoration.

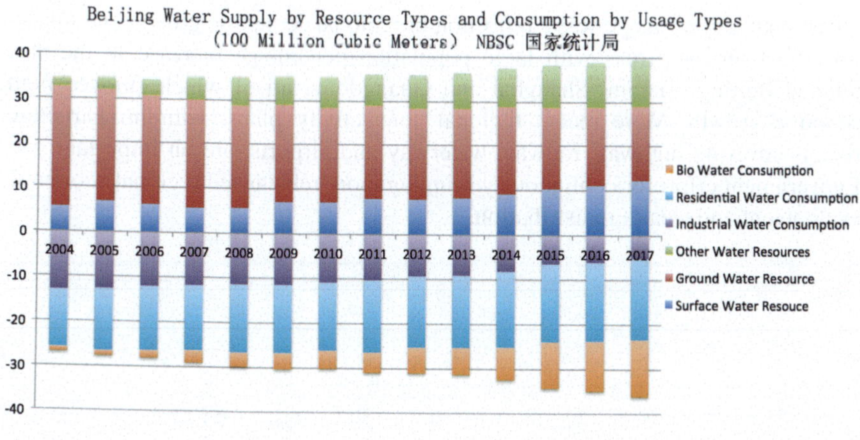

In both SO_2 emission reduction and water resource redistribution management, one common question needs to be answered: how to share the economic growth and environmental cost among different regions, so at geographical, industry, concerned population levels, there is a balanced cost/benefit distribution touch. Finding a feasible solution is more difficult and its ramification more complicated in these days when economic growth moderates and environmental cost rises at the same time.

4.4.5 Transportation Lines and Regional Rebalance

Personnel and goods were transported during the imperial times via the Grand Canal. In modern times, this function is performed mostly by network of railway and highway. The network connects highly populated provinces and remote areas, moves people and goods, and in economic sense, connects different regional supplies to consumptions, transforms budgetary transfer into expenditure and therefore generates and redistributes wealth in the process.

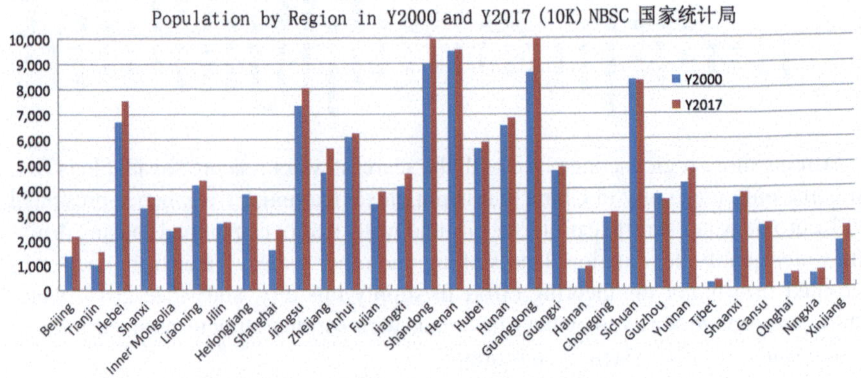

Past population change was a reflection of regional economic growth and migration attractiveness. Areas with large population percentage increase in the past included Beijing, Tianjin, Shanghai and Guangdong, all of which enjoyed high economic growth. More recent regional connectivity plans, with infrastructure projects covering highway, railway, waterway and airports, are an important part of government effort for continuously bringing more rebalanced regional economic development and wealth redistribution.

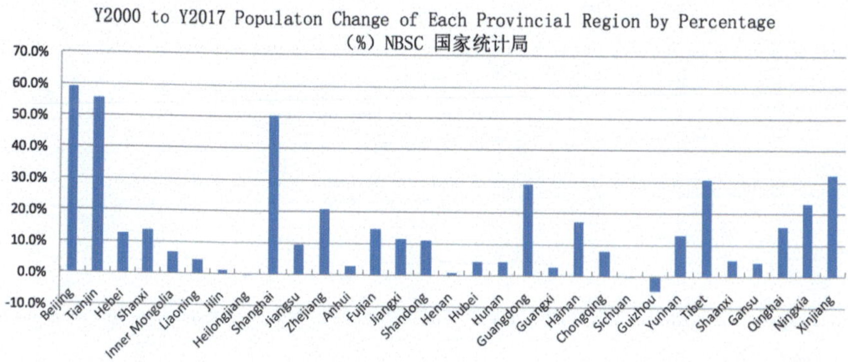

4.4.6 Technological Investment for Trade Balance Mitigation

Trade imbalance with US becomes unsustainable, for a variety of reasons, and largest imbalance category was computer and electronic products. To redress this imbalance, less goods export to US would be desirable, which meant at least a partial unwinding of global supply chain among US, Japan, South Korea, China Taiwan and China Mainland. To keep producing mobile phone and other electronic equipment independently even only for the sizable domestic market requires at least some level of indigenous alternative of US originated technology. This replacement is a working progress, depending upon domestic research capability availability, the intensity and result of international trade conflict resolution and other contributing factors. Therefore large export uncertainty and subsequent technological investment uncertainty need to be assiduously managed.

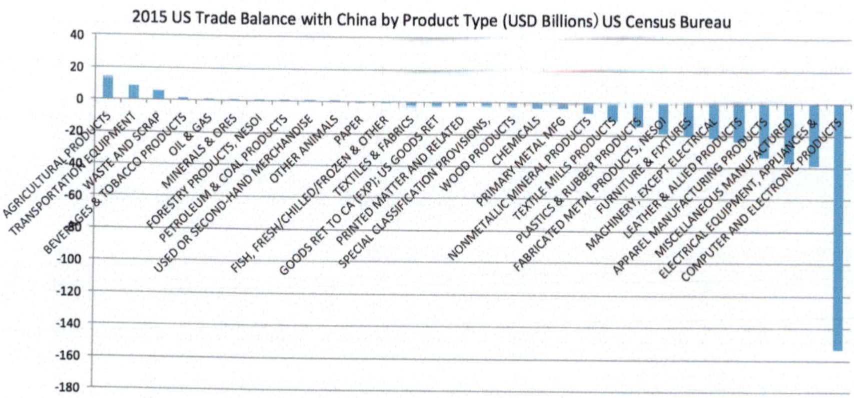

Chapter 5
Investment Flows Dynamics by Investment Entity Types

Correctly assessing general investment flow dynamics within the complexity of Chinese economic structure is fundamental for conducting quality macro assessment and business activities analysis. The general flow dynamics assessment may be grouped by different investment entity types, which includes various levels of government, policy banks, commercial banks, SOEs, private companies, large Internet companies, PE, Trusts, and foreign-owned entities.

5.1 General Investment Condition and the Role of Government

Government initiatives via spending or regulatory actions can from time to time significantly alter the regional economic and industrial structure, therefore change economic assessment and offer investment opportunities at both regional and industrial level for domestic and international corporations and investors. At highest level, Investment condition facilitated by governmental activities should theoretically be in baseline consistency with the NDRC-drafted 5-year plan though the plan itself is not strictly binding. Also, to bestow upon NDRC capabilities in delivering certain results, not only national NDRC and its regional offices are responsible for economic planning, national NDRC is also directly responsible for a small portion of the national budgetary expenditure, the so-called Central Government Expenditure for Capital Construction.

For Chinese economy that is large in scale and complex in structure, its comprehensive national 5-year plan is unsurprisingly packed with general statements and therefore difficult for domestic and international economists to produce quantifiable assessment. On the other hand, local NDRC offices are more focused in plan execution within their respective regions, thus their plan releases offer more clarity in terms of economic developmental target and progress.

X. Zhang, *Mechanical Analysis of China's Macro Economic Structure*,
https://doi.org/10.1007/978-981-15-3840-7_5

Shanghai 11-5	Shanghai 12-5	Shanghai 13-5
Top 5 desirable objectives		
GDP growth 3rd industry % of GDP Center city 3rd industry % of GDP Private industry % of GDP Fiscal revenue	GDP growth Fiscal revenue growth 3rd industry % of GDP Resident consumption % of GDP Private industry % of GDP	GDP growth Fiscal general revenue annual growth Service industry % of GDP Labor productivity (10,000 CNY per person) R&D expenditure % of GDP
Top 5 must reach objectives		
Energy consumption to GDP ratio reduction Social welfare coverage Urban shanty area renovation Social retirement service coverage ratio Social safety index	Affordable housing supply Educational expenditure % of local budget Social retirement service beneficiary Energy consumption reduction per unit of GDP CO_2 emision reduction per unit of GDP	Center city shanty area renovation Permanent resident population Work-related accidental death reduction Energy consumption reduction per unit of GDP Major pollutants emission reduction

Local developmental objective analysis using Shanghai 5-Year plan as an example, would illustrate while GDP growth is still its top priority for 13-5 for Shanghai, labor productivity, R&D expenditure and pollution control are gaining importance. This priority pattern change corroborates national NDRC 13-5 economic pattern change on multiple fronts. To further corroborate national planning change and regional development plan change from a different angle, we can analyze annual budgetary expenditure report published by Shanghai Treasury, and there had been a clear surge of expenditure on education, neighborhood services, social security and technology, therefore aligning developmental emphasis with national NDRC plan on labor productivity and quality of life.

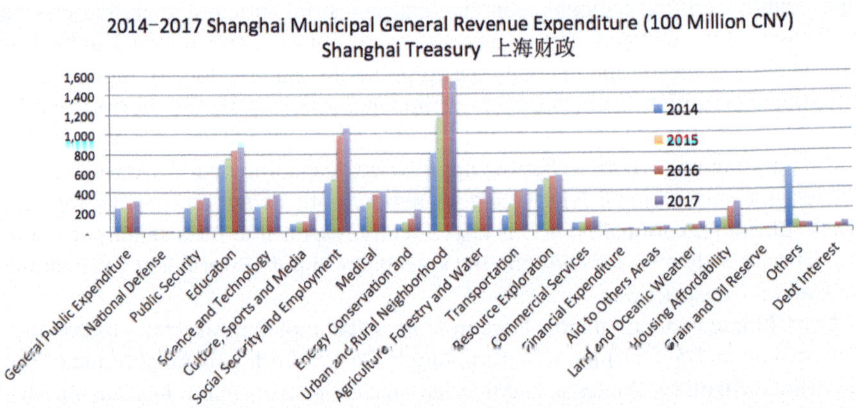

In the trend-setting areas of technology and infrastructure expenditure, which are critical for industrial sectors' competitiveness hence Shanghai regional long-term economic growth, Shanghai has increased spending on product commercialization, highway (though falling in 2017) and special technology projects.

Besides local Treasury report, local SASAC report can also be analyzed to corroborate national and regional 5-year plan priority change. Governmental investment on technology and infrastructure can flow towards SOE and non-SOE entities. Areas with strong SOEs that are more capable of delivering regional plan's execution usually provide quality economic statistics on SASAC reports. With that offered transparency, the execution of some of the most important initiatives brought up in national 5-year plan and itemized by regional 5-year plan can be corroborated via regional SASAC report published by local SASAC offices,

In the case of Shanghai, Shanghai SASAC 2017 report listed the 2nd phase of Everdisplay as one of its main accomplishments, which manufactures display panel product via generation-5.5 technology. Based upon Low Temperature Poly-silicon (LTPS) derived Active-Matrix Organic Light Emitting Diode (AMOLED), this version of display panel product is lighter, thinner and cheaper than older models, though 5.5 generation is not the most up-to-date technology. The LCD and OLED display market in China is dominated by Samsung, LG, FoxConn and BOE, with BOE being the only domestic technology source-based manufacturer. Since SASAC report is primarily a state capital management report and not an industrial report in nature, to make comprehensive understanding of a particular industry development and its impact, it is important to link SASAC point information to the much wider business world information from the likes of IHS Markit, Global Semiconductor Alliance, Semiconductor Industry Association, big four consulting firms and others to create a thorough understanding of those developmental impact. Based upon the current segment analysis, whether Everdisplay's phase-2 factory could create large downstream ecosystem congregation contributing to Shanghai's future economic growth remains to be seen. In terms of promoting advanced local electronics manufacturing business, this Everdisplay catch-up effort was on top of Shanghai AVIC Optoelectronics development, which was listed as one of its past investment recipients during 12-5 period on Shanghai's SASAC own 13-5 development plan, but that technology was based upon TFT-LCD, which could be phased out in avionics segment in the near future.

Also competing in the display segment is BOE from Beijing, a display manufacturer similar to Everdisplay but with much stronger technological capability and production capacity. Beijing SASAC published 2017 earning of BOE at 98.7 billion

CNY after years of volatile revenue and stock performance (its subsequent annual report had a slightly different revenue number). BOE is a public-listed company, in which SASAC is only a minority shareholder (less than 15%), therefore much of its performance and management information is available to the general business news source. For an investor, one way to use SASAC reports as guidance for making business condition assessment is not to be distracted by minority ownership details of SASAC in BOE, rather, the key is to identify the importance of BOE to upstream, downstream industries of the display segment and to Beijing regional economy by its mere citation in SASAC report and expand analysis further using general public business information. SASAC report is concise and only important companies or projects would be included in it. BOE has equipment and material dependency upon Japanese suppliers and downstream exposure to mobile phone manufacturers, thus its future performance could be subjected to potential disruption from current trade dispute. Still, it has strong lead in OLED display segment, if we assume no trade dispute disruption from suppliers to buyers and more accommodative condition from Beijing city government after the current growth austerity, at regional level BOE could generate long-term growth prospect for Beijing and its adjacent area by attracting downstream manufacturers. At industrial level, if we assume no trade dispute disruption, its growth could bolster the supply chain upstream Japanese suppliers, and downstream Xiaomi, which buys display from BOE to make smart phones and is also headquartered in Beijing. One large downstream client in the waiting is Apple, which wants to create a more competitive display supplier situation that has long been dominated by Samsung.

Shanghai's 2017 SASAC report also listed Huahong Grace Semiconductor 2nd phase as one of the local SASAC's main achievements. Semiconductor manufacturing supply chain is a very complicated topic covered extensively by various studies. At this time, the most complex semiconductor technologies are within the front end of the supply chain covering design, equipment and material, which are dominated by US, Japan, Netherlands, South Korea and others. Huahong Grace 2nd phase should be considered a long-term industrial investment versus immediate growth generator for local economy or industry.

The mere mentioning of Shanghai AVIC Optoelectronics in Shanghai SASAC 13-5 plan underscored Shanghai's desire and effort in minimizing the gap on aviation electronic technology versus international players. ARJ-21 regional airplane produced in Shanghai managed to enter commercial services in 2016, with engines supplied from GE and electronics from Rockwell and other global suppliers. Just as in the case of BOE information usage, the key for making solid business condition assessment is, by linking SASAC citation to general public information, sketch out possible future market demand originated within China and ARJ-21 full production as a regional growth contributor and supplier chain expansion contributor in Shanghai, then making macro and investment decision accordingly.

In summary, for a macro or industrial investor, regardless of being domestic or international-based, to properly construct an investment condition view of Chinese regional and industrial economy, it is important to link (1) the national 5-year plan's general agenda; (2) regional 5-year plan specific objectives; (3) regional Treasury budgetary details; (4) regional SASAC specific accomplishment; and finally (5) the broad market information regarding specific industrial segments and specific regions, all 5 pieces together. Corroborating 5 sources of information against each other in combination with self perspective, we may come to a conclusive assessment for the overall investment condition, up which we then conduct further analysis and decide whether to engage in or exit from a regional economy from a macro perspective, or engage in or hedge against a particular industrial development (e.g., participate in upstream opportunities in Shanghai aviation business, downstream opportunities in BOE electronic business, or hedge against heightened competition due to incoming capacity/capability competition).

5.2 Investment by Policy Banks

Since NDRC, which reports to the State Council, in general is not delegated with the responsibility for managing monetary resources required to implement its economic initiatives, therefore investments by policy banks play an important role in the eventual implementation of government economic planning outside the normal domain of budgetary expenditure, especially those that are long-term in nature and less commercially viable or attractive. There are three policy banks in China, China Development Bank, The Export–Import Bank of China and Agricultural Development Bank of China, all under the direct management of the State Council, with each of them playing an important role in its perspective area. CDB is mandated to channel resource flow into infrastructure and urban development projects, EIBC into promoting international trade and cooperation and ADBC into agricultural development.

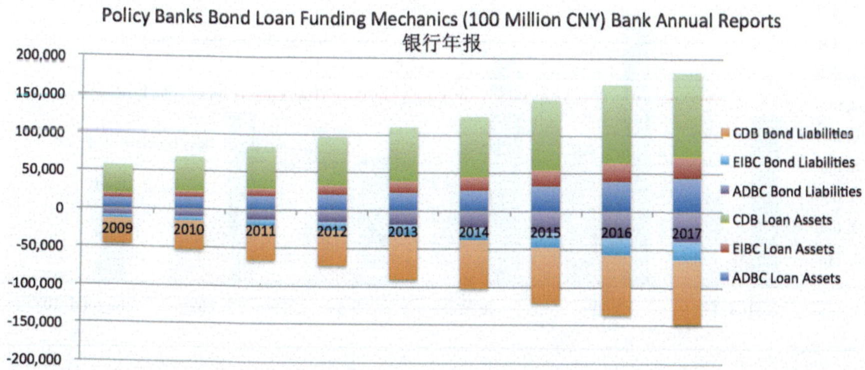

Unlike commercial banks, policy banks do not have extensive retail network to take in client deposit, hence majority of their financing is achieved via borrowing at the more expensive bond market and interbank market. To reduce their financing charge, policy bank bonds are given zero risky capital weight even though they are still subject to tax charges. All policy banks bond issuances are under the supervision of PBOC. PBOC issues annual quotas to three policy banks. These are the upper limits of increases they can have for their outstanding bond amount.

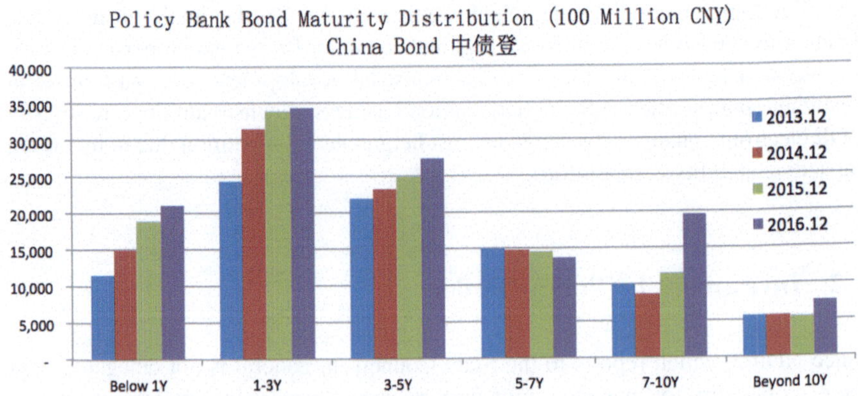

Each of the three policy banks has been given different policy agendas and this has caused their balance sheet financing via bonds to differ in maturity ladder distribution. Both CDB and EIBC have sizable long maturity bond outstanding due to the presence of long-term projects they need to finance in domestic or international infrastructure areas, especially CDB, and EIBC has relatively large short-to-medium maturity outstanding related to trade finance. ADBC on the other hand, has a relatively even distribution of bond amount outstanding across different maturity ladders.

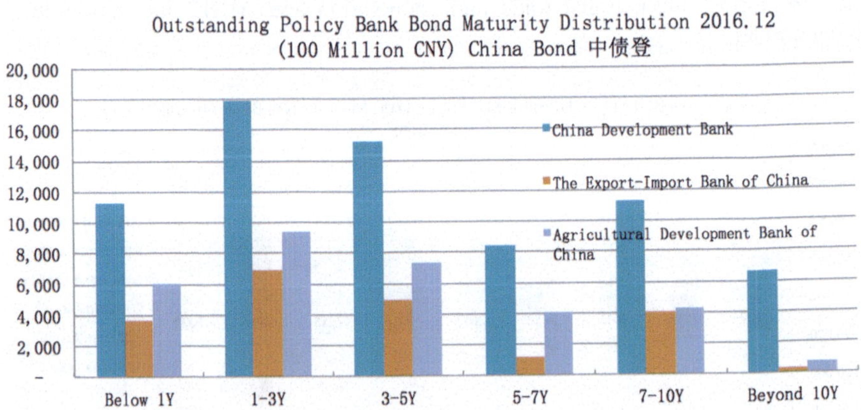

5.2.1 *China Development Bank (CDB)*

Based upon information available on its portal, China Development Bank (CDB) was founded in 1994 as a policy financial institution. It was incorporated as China

Development Bank Corporation in December 2008, and officially designated as a development finance institution in March 2015. As of December 31, 2017, CDB had registered capital at RMB 421.248 billion. Its shareholders included the Ministry of Finance (36.54%), Central Huijin Investment Ltd. (34.68%), Buttonwood Investment Holding Co., Ltd. (27.19%) and the National Council for Social Security Fund (1.59%).

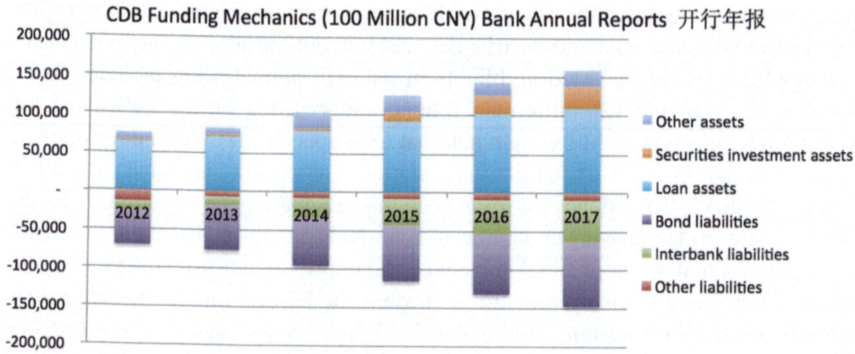

With balance sheet size exceeding 15 trillion CNY by the end of 2017, CDB provides medium to long-term financial resources to fund many long-term economic and social developmental objectives. While interbank money market became more important in recent years, the balance sheet was still financed mostly by bonds. The largest asset class is loan, followed by securities investment. Professional credit rating agencies including Moody's and Standard & Poor's have rated CDB at the same level as China's sovereign rate.

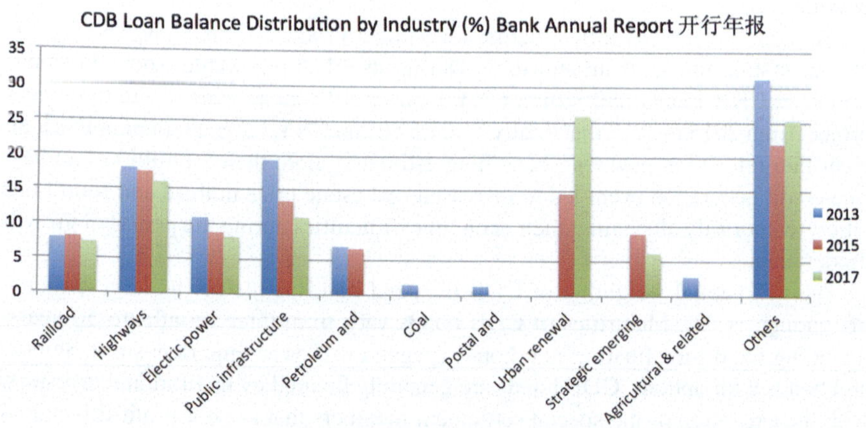

CDB is the world's largest development finance institution. When local government entities and bureaus try to implement their multi-year development plan, especially regarding large long-term infrastructure projects, they would go to CDB to look for funding resources. Whether CDB funding arrangement and its developmental results are satisfying enough in helping local government or bureaus to achieve various national and local developmental goals would be used to benchmark CDB management effectiveness. This was the first institution in China to successfully introduce large-scale urban development project based upon real estate improvement revenue receipt, a credit-generating event that changed the social and economic landscape of the country. CDB also provided support for railroad, highway and other infrastructure projects, while more recently ramped upon urban renewal effort by trying to pull real estate-related industrial demand without introducing large real estate oversupply. Some of its listed highlights in its 2017 annual filing included 147.2 billion CNY loan and 120 billion CNY bond underwriting for the railway sector, with main focus upon eight-by-eight national high-speed railway grid development. Large-scale national and urban rail transportation is a necessity in China. Not only it reduces country's dependency on fossil fuel, thus alleviating air pollution, reducing CO_2 emission and improving economic and national security, it also at the same time addresses regional developmental imbalance and improves industrial integration efficiency. CDB's large railway investment made it the biggest railway lender among domestic financial institutions. Within that 2017 financial package, 13.5 billion CNY loan was provided for major rehabilitation of railway transportation equipment of China Railway, 103.1 billion CNY loan was issued for urban rail transit system. In other infrastructure areas, 96.7 billion CNY loan was issued to fund water resource projects. 78.8 billion CNY loan was issued to clean energy sector, accounting for 40% of total China clean energy investment in 2017. Many of these projects are long-term projects without possessing attractive risk return profile for private investment, so CDB walks a fine line between sufficiently funding country's crucial infrastructure development and making sure appropriate return can be generated on top of safe principal payment, to ensure CDB as a long-term viable development funding provider.

An area where CDB infrastructure investment produces immediate and significant economic impact is urbanization. During its urban renewable (social housing) initiative, CDB issued 880 billion CNY loan in 2017 alone, part of the three-year project from 2015 to 2017 that totally 3,407.5 billion CNY. Large amount of this loan went into relocation payment, benefiting estimated more than 20 million families. The credit generation event led to increased real estate price in third and fourth tier cities, temporarily alleviating their economic difficulties during the period of growth moderation.

The risk capital weighting of CDB financial bonds, which is its largest source of funding, is 0%. Maturities of CDB bonds vary from three months to 50 years, including fixed rate, floating rate bonds (pegged to 1-year time deposit or Shibor) and bonds with options. CDB bonds are generally favored by institutional investors, with the exception of the special settlement members that are not profit-driven and prefer treasury bonds for their tax-exempt status and liquidity comparable to CDB bonds. Besides their low risk while making relative higher interest payment than treasury, CDB bonds availability in large quantities in long maturity between 7 and 10 years also makes CDB bonds very attractive for insurance companies.

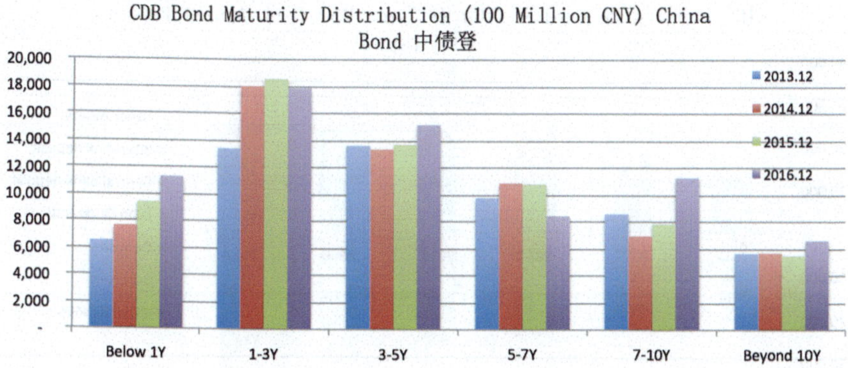

As a critical part within China economic institution, CDB provides resources in scale to both policy and commercial areas, and this has proved challenging when public due diligence concern has to be addressed. Large anti-corruption effort was eventually initiated to introduce more stringent oversight. Nevertheless, CDB is expected to continuously play a critical role in China's economic development hence its business and investment data analysis are critical for China's long term regional and industrial economic assessment.

5.2.2 *The Export–Import Bank of China (EIBC)*

Founded in 1994, the Export–Import Bank of China is a state bank solely owned by the government. Its international credit rating is the same as China's sovereign rating. The Bank has established correspondent banking relationship with more than 1,000 banks. More focused than CDB, EIBC's main mandate is to facilitate the export and import of Chinese mechanical and electronic products, complete sets of equipment and new and high-tech products, assist Chinese companies with comparative advantages in their offshore project contracting and outbound investment, and promote international economic cooperation and trade. Since EIBC business activities are directly related to the current state and the future direction of China's international trade pattern, and related to the State Council assessment of China international trade condition and consequently its proposed policy agenda, therefore understanding where and how EIBC sets its policy and resource allocation priorities is important for conducting China's macro and industrial analysis, especially regarding the international trade-related industries and regions.

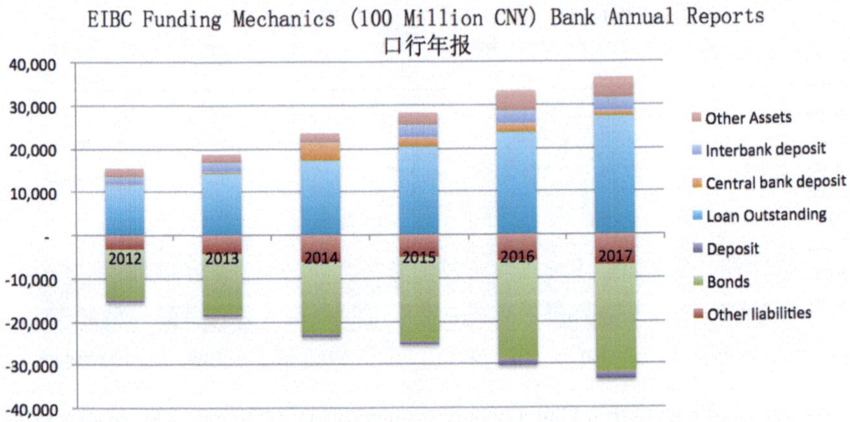

In terms of its funding mechanics, EIBC mostly uses bond market to finance its balance sheet, more so versus CDB that also has an active usage of interbank money market. Its largest asset is loan, more so versus CDB that also has a sizable securities investment portfolio. Stated on its 2017 annual report, "the bank's main mandate is to facilitate national development strategies, and build a policy bank which has clear-cut market positioning, well-defined business portfolio, unique functions, sufficient capital, good governance, strict internal control, safe operation, high quality service and sustainable development capability. Its financial support goes to foreign trade, cross-border investment, the Belt and Road Initiative, international industrial capacity and equipment manufacturing cooperation, science and technology, cultural industry, "going global" endeavors of small and medium enterprises, and the building of an open economy." EIBC's main business lines include various types of loan underwriting, entrusted loan underwriting, trade finance, deposit taking, bill acceptance/discount, guarantee, insurance, advisory services, consulting, foreign exchange, banking activities, interbank lending and borrowing, syndication and securitization, when they are international trade-related.

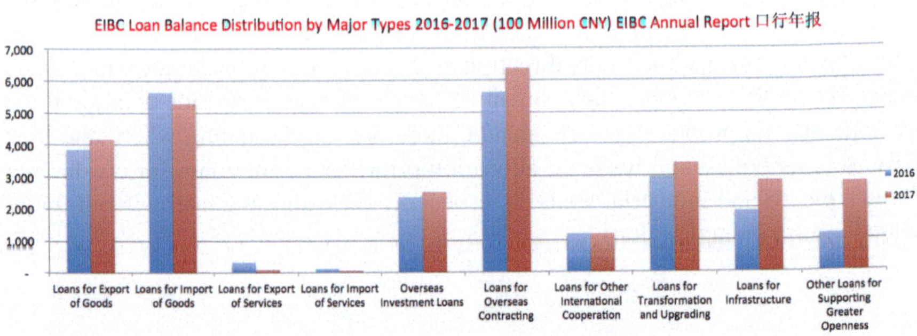

EIBC's largest asset class is loan. Foreign trade loans, which include export trade loans and import trade loans, are provided to support trade of merchandise, labor and technology between China and foreign countries or regions. Overseas investment loans are provided to Chinese funded companies (including share-holding companies) that are registered overseas to support their overseas investment. International cooperation loans are provided to clients to support their cooperation with governments of foreign countries or regions, financial institutions and companies with sovereign guarantee. Loans are also provided to Chinese companies for conducting overseas contracting projects. In recent years, while international trade growth has slowed, which has contributed to anemic performance in goods and service-related loan underwriting, EIBC has increased its effort in supporting China's trade growth, especially in overseas contracting and international infrastructure areas. Some of the listed achievement in its 2017 annual filing, included international infrastructure projects such as Budapest-Belgrade railway project to boost regional infrastructure development and connectivity, and equipment manufacturing projects such as the 38,000dwt stainless steel chemical and oil product tanker capable of providing flexible and efficient transport service with a cargo capacity of 46,000 m^3 and 43 duplex stainless steel cargo tanks. Bank's increased effort in infrastructure area has led to larger bond issuance in 7–10 year long maturity ladder.

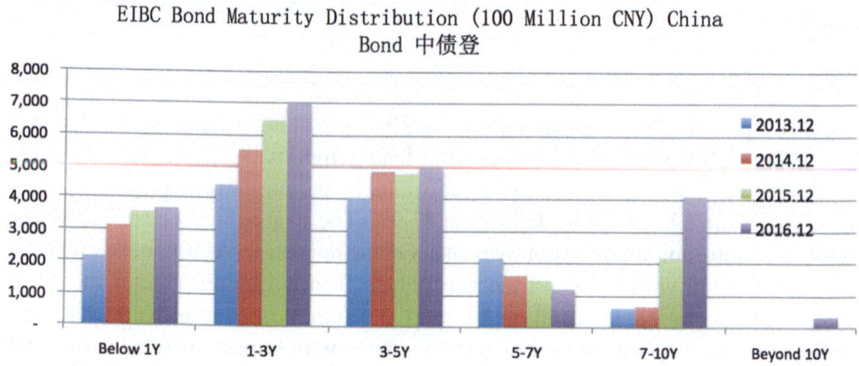

In its 2017 filing, the bank's balance sheet size stood at 3.638 trillion CNY, 75.6% of which were outstanding loans. 74.0% of the financing was achieved via bond issuance. Among the loans being made in 2017 filing, 963.8 billion CNY were foreign trade loans, majority of which were for import of goods; 252.1 billion for overseas investment; 756.7 billion CNY for international cooperation loans, most of which were for overseas contracting; 904.1 billion CNY for supporting greater openness, most of which were loans for transformation upgrading and loans for infrastructure.

Regarding bonds issued by EIBC, the investor base for EIBC bond is similar to the base for CDB bond. EIBC bond offers slightly higher yield versus CDB bond to compensate its slightly lower liquidity. The investor base that prefers buying CDB bond rather than buying Treasury bond also prefers buying EIBC bond rather than buying CDB bond for the same reasons. For those institutions that prefer Treasury bond, such as special settlement members, EIBC bond slightly higher yield is not enough to compensate for treasury tax-exempt advantage.

5.2.3 Agricultural Development Bank of China (ADBC)

Similar to the Export–Import Bank of China, Agricultural Development Bank of China is a state bank solely owned by the government, therefore it enjoys the same rating as CDB and EIBC, and its international credit ratings are the same as China's sovereign ratings. ADBC's main focus is to raise funds to support the agricultural sector within the Chinese economy.

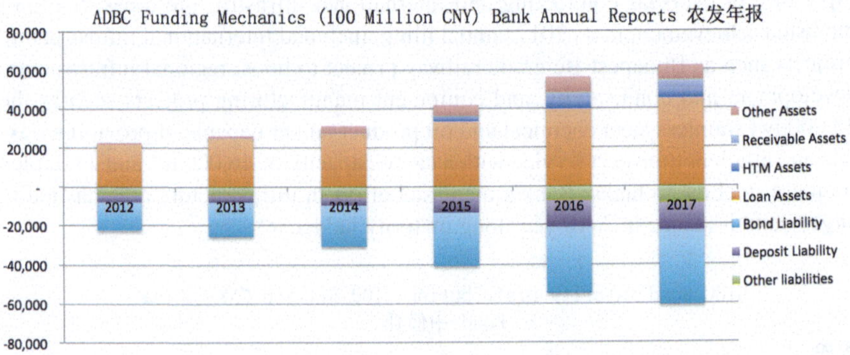

Based upon its 2017 annual report, its 2017 year-end balance sheet size was 6.22 trillion CNY, with 72.4% assets from loan activities, 8.4% assets from HTM investment and 6.9% from Accounts Receivable. Its liability was mostly financed by bond issuance at 62.7% and by deposits at 23.9%. The sizable presence of deposits at ADBC is unique among three policy banks. On the bond side, ADBC bonds investor base is also unique with higher presence by players from agricultural sector, including village commercial banks, rural credit coop and rural commercial banks. Notably ADBC in recent years increased its bond issuance with longer maturity to strength financing for long-term agricultural project.

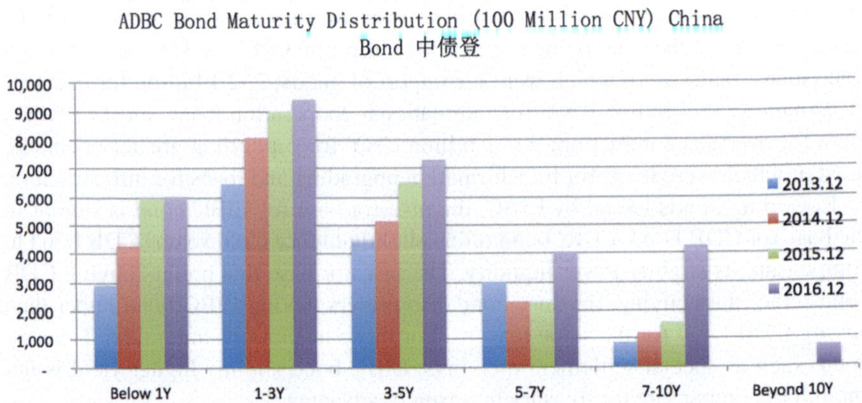

ADBC business overview stated one of its main functions as providing loans for purchase, stockpiling, regulation, and distribution of key agricultural products such as grain, cotton, edible oil, sugar, pork, and chemical fertilizer. To fulfill that policy bank mandate, ADBC in its 2016 annual filing elaborated on commodity purchase loan program that provided price support and improved economic and farmer income security. Loans amounting to RMB454.7 billion were granted for the purchase and stockpiling of grain, cotton, and edible oil during the year, supporting the purchase and stockpiling of 427.42 billion catties of grain and edible oil and 45.08 million piculs of cotton. ADBC also provided active assistance for the "destocking" work, and supported the sales of 202.63 billion catties of policy-backed grains and 76.12 million piculs of cotton in stock.

ADBC business overview's other stated main functions included providing loans in support of the construction of agricultural and rural infrastructure projects, water conservancy projects and circulation systems; providing loans for projects in support of integrated agricultural development, means of production and agricultural science and technology; providing loans for projects in support of renovation of shack settlements and construction of concentrated housing for farmers; providing loans in support of poverty alleviation through relocation, infrastructure in poor areas, development of special industries and special poverty alleviation projects; providing loans in support of town construction, land purchase and stockpiling in counties; providing loans in support of small agricultural enterprises and leading industrial enterprises.

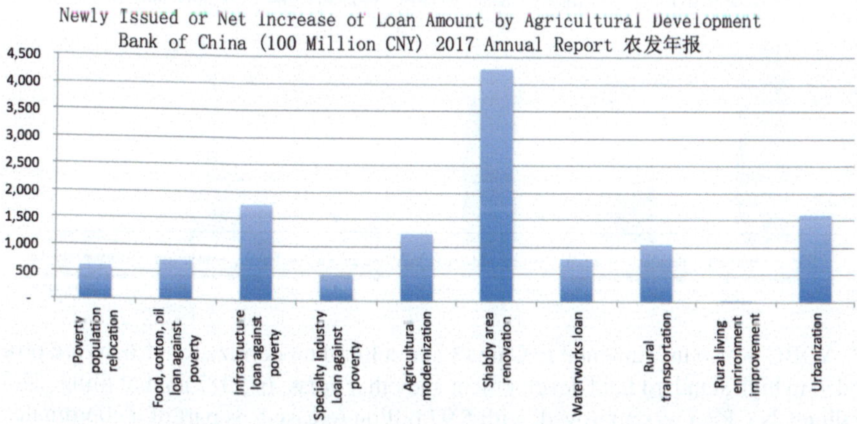

Newly issued or net increase loan data from annual filings detailed further on how ADBC allocates its resources to implement its developmental agenda. Largest amount would go to shabby area renovation. Similar to CDB's urban renewal initiative, shabby area renovation is a credit-generating event that pulls demand from real estate-related supply chain with macro economic stimulus effect without producing large real estate oversupply. Other large resource allocations would go to urbanization, poverty alleviation and agricultural infrastructure building, important for sustainable and balanced growth initiative.

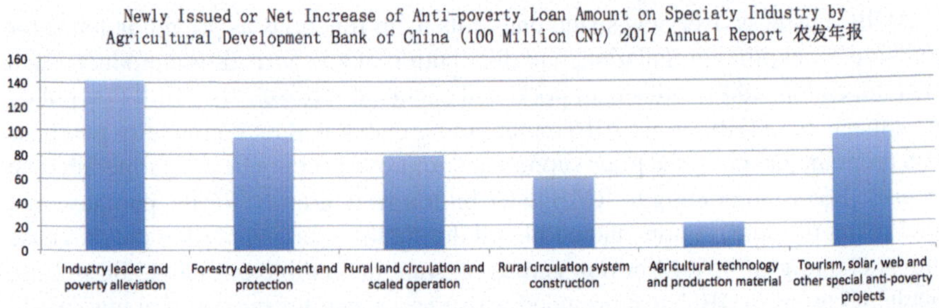

One of the critical objectives of balanced social and economic growth is to shrink the wealth gap between the urban and rural area. ADBC plays an important role in this area, by issuing loan specifically targeted for alleviating rural poverty, while trying to create agricultural industry leader, protect forestry and improve production, etc. One of its listed investment effort on 2017 annual filing was loan support for cane sugar industry in Dehong Autonomous Prefecture in province of Yunnan. A relatively impoverished remote and mountainous region with many minority residents and a less educated workforce, the area is rich with water resource. Cumulatively 9.9 billion CNY loan was provided to Dehong's cane sugar industry to improve industry infrastructure condition, production and to facilitate sugar purchase payment.

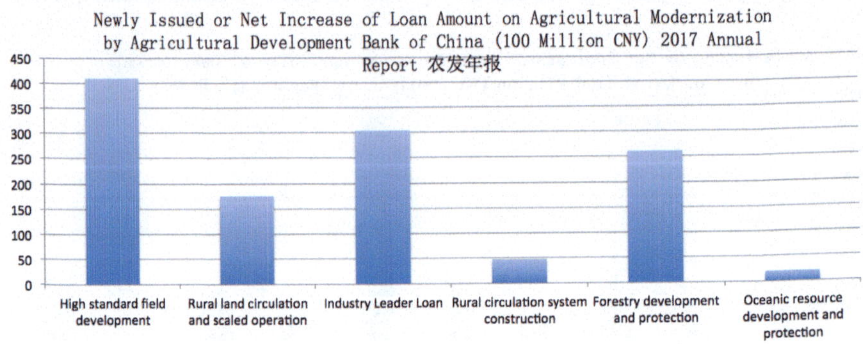

ADBC is also instrumental in China's agricultural modernization. Loans are provided in high standard field development and other areas. In 2017 annual filing, 24.2 billion CNY loan was approved, with 5.97 billion released, as part of a coordinated and comprehensive plan to build high standard land across various counties in Jiangxi province. Total estimated loan requirement for the project would be 34.8 billion CNY. Jiangxi is one of the most important agricultural bases in China. High standard field will improve farmer's income level, reduce poverty, and increase China's economic security.

5.3 Investment by Commercial Banks

Analysis in earlier chapter on aggregated social financing illustrated loan, trust loan and entrusted loan as the most important sources of financing for the macro economy and banks as the most important financial intermediaries in China. PBOC releases data on sources and uses of funds by depository institutions, which include central bank, policy banks, commercial banks, and some other financial entities. The amount of funds sourced by depository institutions was by the end of 2018 at 196.233 trillion CNY.

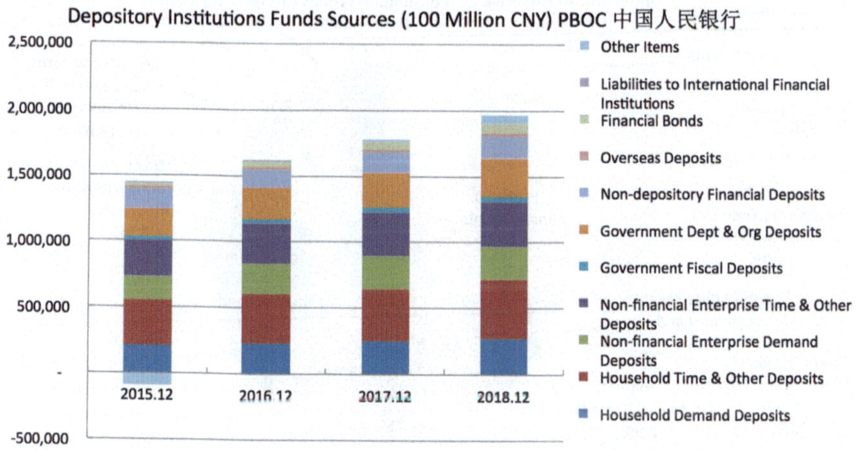

Within that close to 200 trillion CNY of funding liabilities, most of them, roughly around 80%, were sourced from different types of deposits. The cost of deposit thus forms the funding cost baseline of China macro's aggregated social finance, with layers of spreads being the channel cost, risk premium cost and regulatory cost added on top of that baseline cost to fund different activities throughout the general economy.

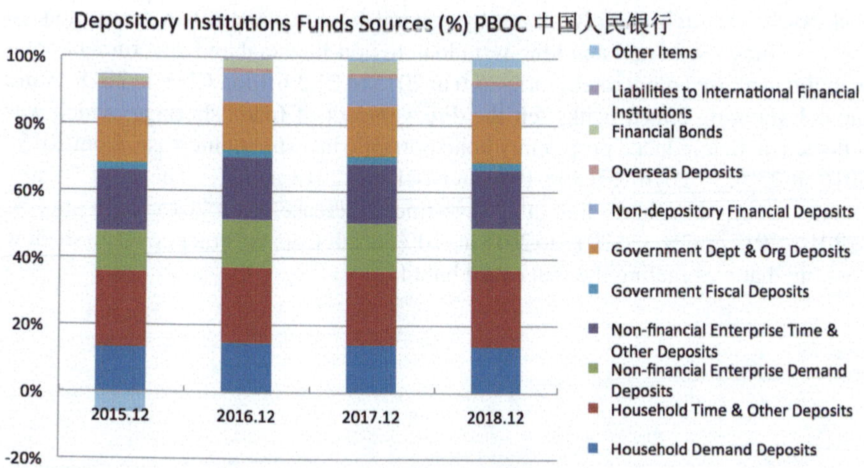

Funds sourced by depository institutions are put into different usages. From 2015 to 2018 year-end average, 3.7% went to short-term household consumption loan, much of that related to credit card usage; 13.0% went to mid to long-term household consumption loan, majority of that related to household real estate loan; 17.2% went to portfolio investment, much of that related to bank bond investment; 16.8 and 25.8% went to short-term, mid to long-term non-financial and government entity loans; 11.4% went to share and other investment, much of that related to shadow banking in the form of entrusted trust and trust loan.

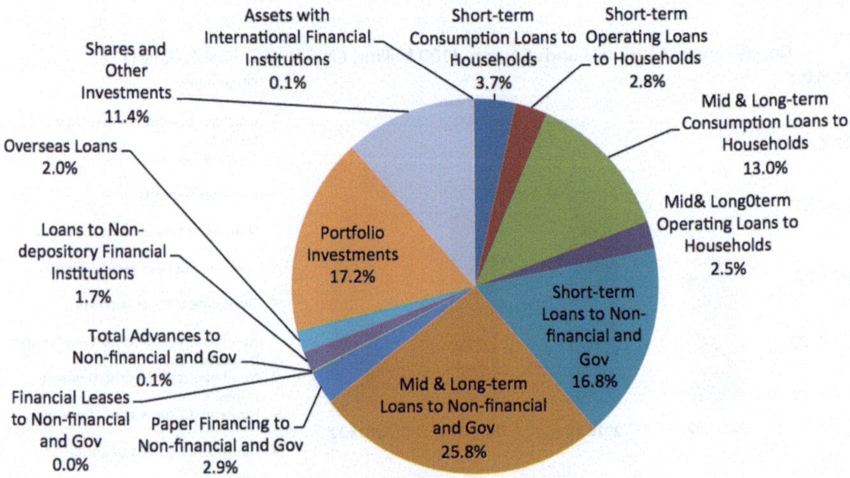

Depository Institutions 2015-2018 Average Fund Uses (Year End, 100 Million CNY) PBOC 中国人民银行

From 2015 to 2018, depository institutions saw their largest major fund use increase in short-term household consumption loan in terms of percentage increase. The most economically significant fund use increase was in mid and long-term household consumption loan, from 14.6 to 28.4 trillion CNY, when resident appetite for real estate was high, mainly driven by general liquidity and urban renovation. In contrast, fund use in mid and long-term loan to non-financial and government organization increased moderately form 35.6 in 2015 to 51.3 trillion CNY in 2018. Amid the deleveraging effort, banks felt the direct impact of funds shortage, which was reflected in their reduced proprietary bond portfolio investment increase, from 2015–2016 at 23%, to 2016–2017 at 19% and 2017 to 2018 at 12%. The most volatile change occurred to shares and other investment increase, from 2015–2016 at 65%, to 2016–2017 at -2% and 2017 to 2018 at -10%, result from the crackdown on shadow banking that was fueling the real estate bubble.

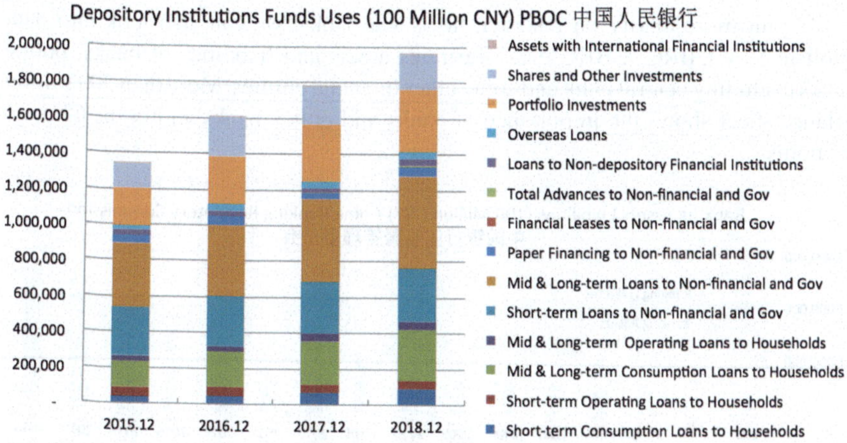

Breakout points of the depository institutions funds use month-to-month change are closely associated with macro economic condition change and subsequently taken macro and monetary policy actions. The expected strengthening of US fed fund rate, in the beginning of 2017, triggered USD appreciation expectation versus CNY. Paper Financing dropped due to crackdown linked to phony trade financing for capital outflow purpose and other well-publicized paper financing fraudulent events. The continuous increase of mid and long-term household consumption loan issuance since mid 2015 was related to liquidity storage function of real estate after the equity bubble in 2015 and continuous eased liquidity condition and leverage transfer from nonresidential to residential sector. To prepare for the expected increases of fed fund rate, since early 2017 liquidity was tightened and this had contributed difficulty in entrusted and trust loan area, which was further compounded by deleveraging effort in the trust loan segment by the regulators. Bond portfolio often decreases in the beginning of each year, mirroring the increases of loan issuance during that time, reflecting proprietary bond portfolio as a liquidity storage place before annual credit quote is available for new loan issuance when new year starts.

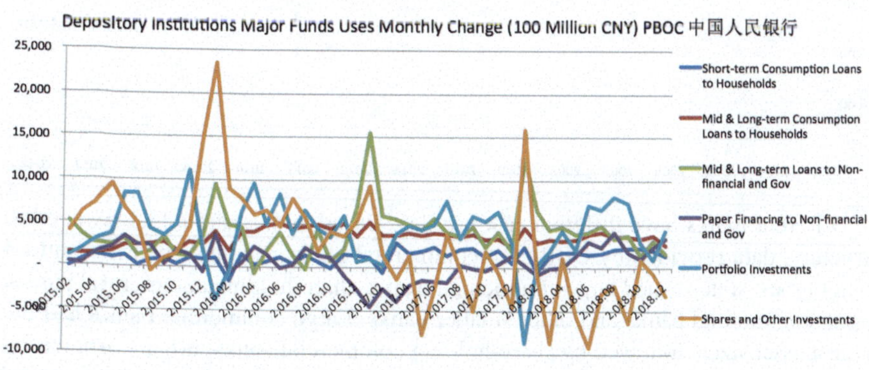

To gain more clarity on resource flows via banks, we can also look into data published by CBRC. CBRC data illustrates assets and liabilities of banks, policy banks excluding central bank and some other financial entities. More than 200 trillion balance sheet shows the importance of banks and policy banks within the Chinese economy.

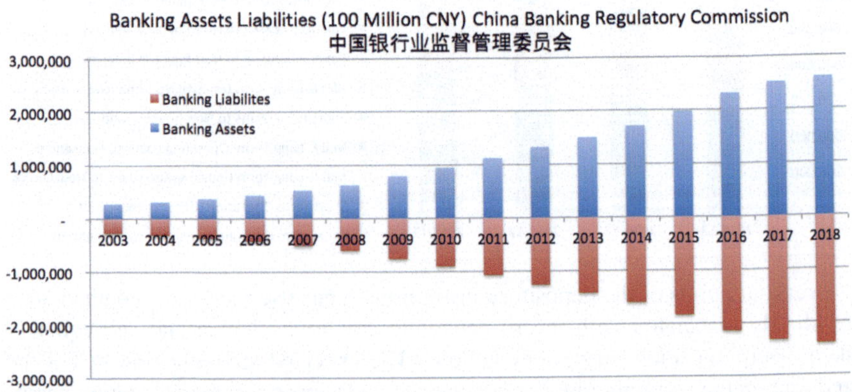

One health indicator of China's banking industry and the broader economy is banking industry's leverage ratio. A simplified calculation of leverage ratio, using assets/(assets − liabilities), shows a long trend towards leverage reduction in the banking industry, which is contrary to the general increase of leverage for the wider economy.

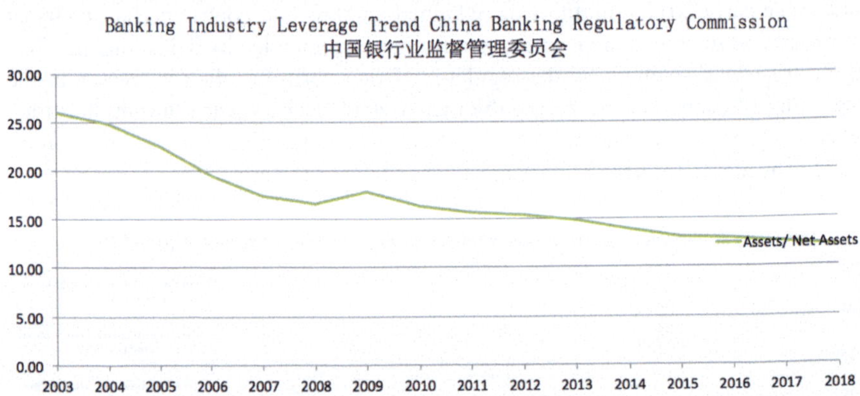

Different banks have different risk profiles. Based upon shareholder ownership structure, data provided by CBRC on commercial banks can be categorized into 4 major types: state-owned large commercial banks, share-holding commercial banks, urban commercial banks and other smaller banks. Large commercial banks had the largest asset sizes, followed by share-holding commercial banks, urban commercial banks, and other smaller banks. 3 policy banks combined based upon their annual filing had around 24 trillion CNY worth of assets in 2017.

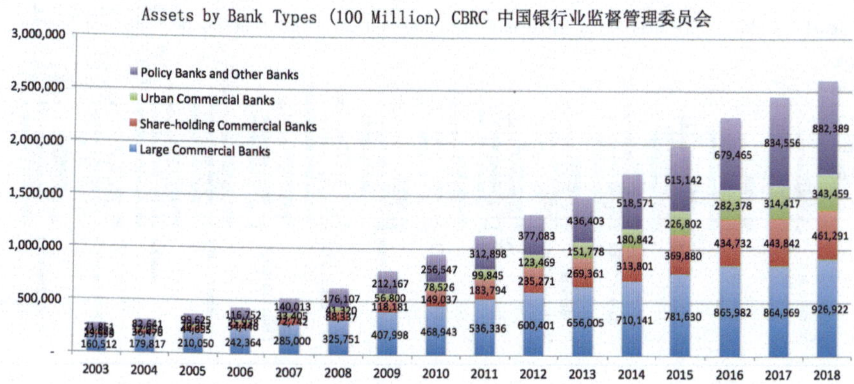

Within 5 large state-owned commercial banks, In terms of asset sizes, ICBC led the pack, followed by CCB, ABC and BOC. State-owned commercial banks are generally much larger than share-holding commercial banks and share-holding commercial banks are generally much larger than urban commercial banks.

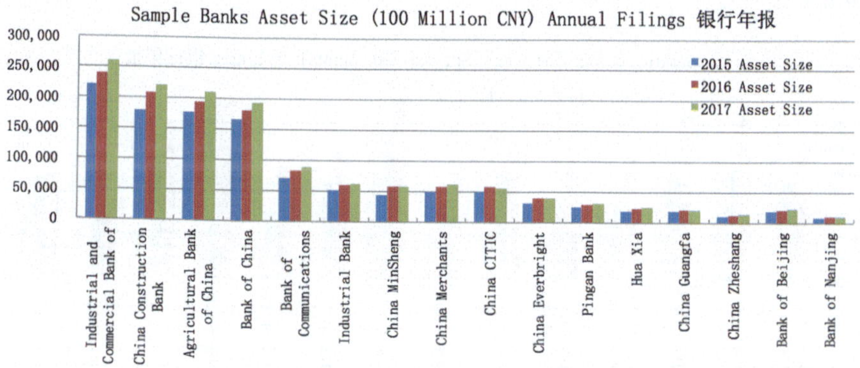

The size of a bank's balance sheet remains a good indicator of its marketing penetration capability for lowering cost of funding via attracting deposits from a wider client base. That funding cost translates into bank-channeled resource flow cost within Chinese macro economic structure. Among the sampled banks, largest banks including ICBC, CCB, ABC and BOC had the lowest cost of funds, less than 2% from 2015 to 2017. Funding cost for most of share-holding banks, with the exception of China Merchants, would be 0.5% higher. The lower cost of funds is typically caused by relative higher portion of funds coming from cash deposit, while the higher cost of funds is usually caused by higher portion of funds coming from term deposit, interbank borrowing and wealth management products.

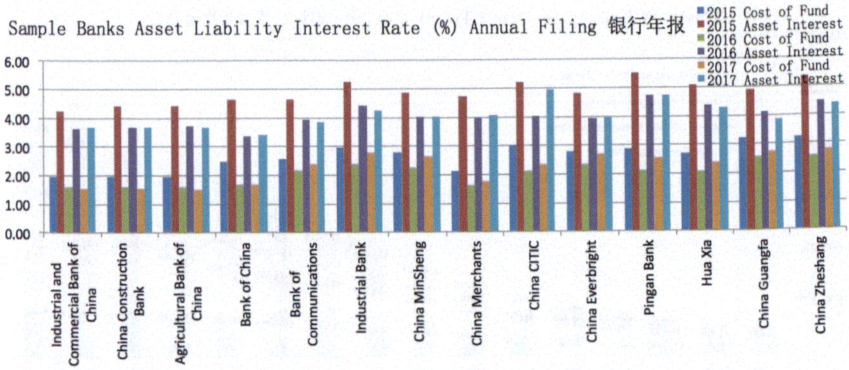

Lower cost of funds often translates into higher interest rate spread. Alternatively, to generate the same level of interest rate spread, a bank with higher cost of funding might pursue riskier assets. Hence when liquidity is drained the more market-driven share-holding banks and urban commercial banks ironically may have higher risk exposure and are more likely to become sources of instabilities within the economic structure.

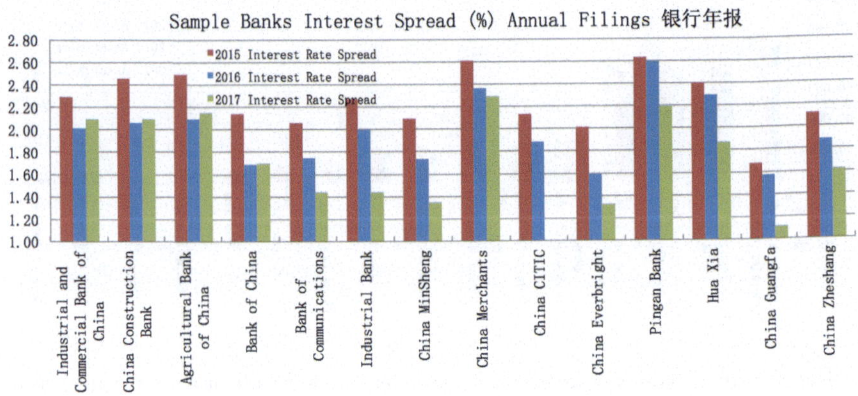

Over the recent years, all financial institutions participated in Chinese economic growth with their asset sizes increased substantially and share-holding commercial banks and urban commercial banks grew even relatively faster than their large commercial bank peers. Large national banks share of the total banking balance sheet dropped from 52.6% in 2009 to 36.7% by the end of 2018. Share-holding commercial banks and urban commercial banks increased their share from 14.2 and 6.5% in 2009, to 17.5 and 12.8% by the end of 2018, respectively. But large commercial banks retained their dominant positions in terms of extensive reach of their resource flows within the economic structure, hence the most feasible target in macro liquidity and monetary policy management by PBOC and other regulatory bodies.

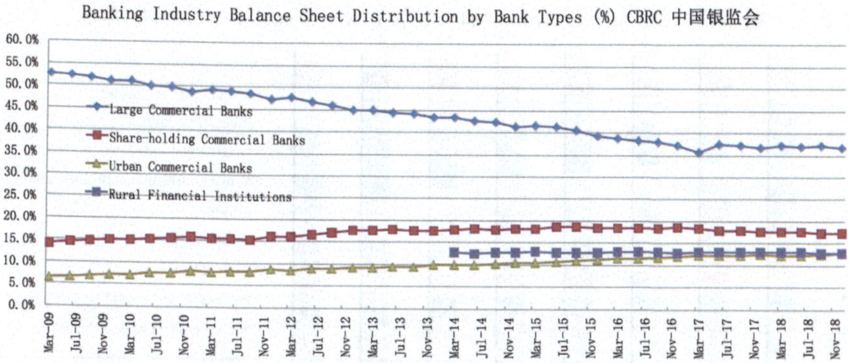

The loan data from ICBC, which is the largest bank within CBRC large commercial bank category, sheds light on significant and volatile economic change occurring in China over the recent years. A list of quantitative easing measures from US Fed, culminated in the announcement of QE3 in September of 2012 and QE4 in December of 2012 to deal with the 2008 financial credit crisis, accompanied by synchronized easing measures from PBOC to stabilize domestic economy and exchange rate, finally started to have irreversible impact on Chinese economy. Within the ICBC combined personal loan and corporate loan portfolio, the share of residential mortgage loan started to increase drastically in 2013, from a paltry 0.14% year-over-year change in 2012 to 2.5% increase in 2013. The increase continued during 2014 at 2.2%, 2015 at 3.0%, 2016 at 5.1% and 2017 at 2.4%. 2013 proved to be a turning point, during which US had finished repairing its balance sheet damaged by the credit crisis.

During the 2013 to 2017 period, share of ICBC loan allocated to manufacturing segment within its combined personal and corporate loan portfolio was significantly reduced. Since the financial crisis, China export segment growth stalled, reducing export-related manufacturing financing demand. Simultaneously, domestic and international monetary easing measures made investment in real estate more profitable, further shifting financial resources away from low margin manufacturing sector. The share of manufacturing segment loan within total ICBC personal and corporate loan started to shrink in 2013, from 2012 year-over-year increase at 1.53% to 2013 decrease at −0.6%. The year-over-year decrease continued at −0.77% in 2014, further accelerated in 2015 at −1.3%, 2016 at −1.6% and 2017 at −1.4%. One important reason for accelerated manufacturing segment loan share decrease from 2015 to 2017 was US economy entering stronger growth period pushing up the US dollar index, and the USD CNY exchange rate largely remained the same during that period, and this exchange rate up movement proved detrimental to low margin China manufacturing segment, especially within the export sub-segment.

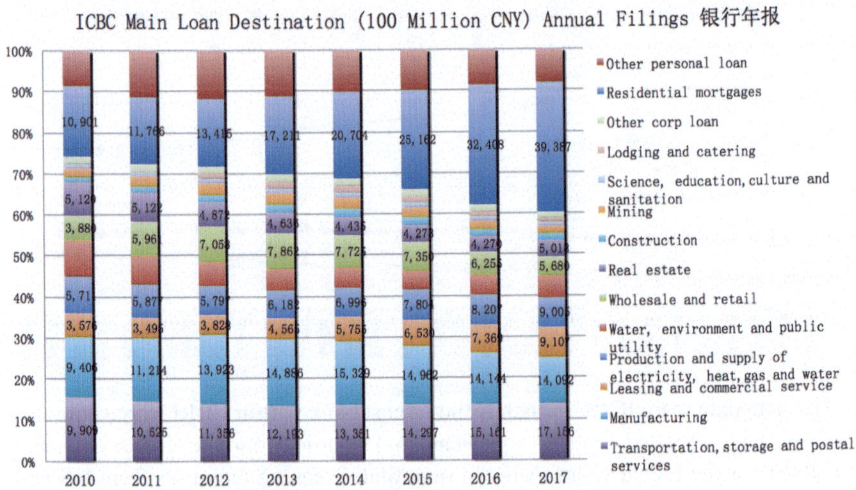

The ICBC loan distribution data from 2010 to 2015 within the manufacturing segment further sheds light into China's macro structural change. During the 2010 to 2015 period, for sub-segment share change within ICBC manufacturing segment loan, largest percentage reduction came from petroleum processing coking at −4%, iron and steel at −2%, and the largest increase came from chemical industry at 2%. This allocation change within manufacturing loan portfolio suggested an economic model shift away from energy and raw material intensive pattern to a more advanced growing pattern.

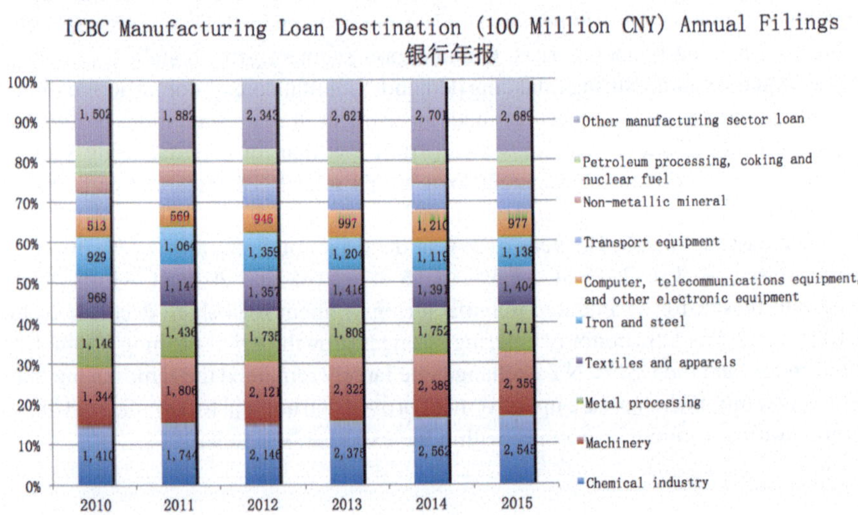

Slightly smaller in terms of its balance sheet size but mostly regarded as a competitive peer vis-a-vis ICBC, China Construction Bank (CCB) also saw its residential mortgage loan share increase and manufacturing loan share decrease within its combined loan portfolio. The residential mortgage loan share YoY increase picked up speed from 0.4% in 2012, to 2.0, 2.2, 3.9, 5.1 and 1.1% during 2013, 2014, 2015, 2016 and 2017 respectively, while the manufacturing loan share YOY change reversed from 0.3% increase in 2012 to decrease by −1.4, −1.7, −1.9, −1.6 and −1.4% in 2013, 2014, 2015, 2016 and 2017 respectively.

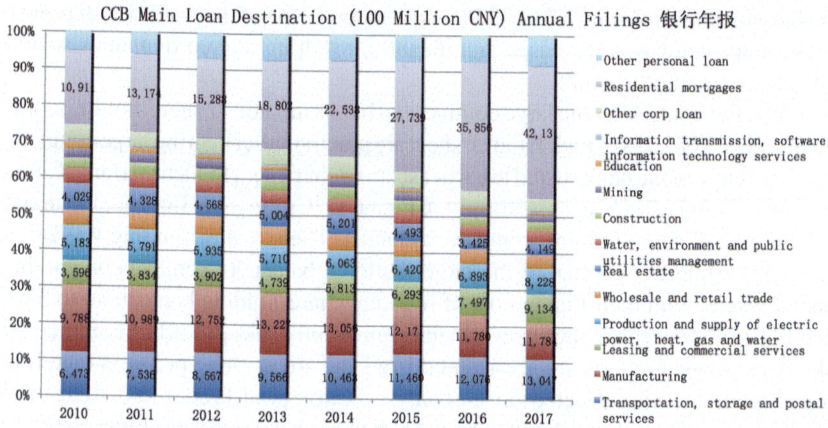

As another large bank within the top echelon, Agricultural Bank of China (ABC) also saw residential mortgage loan share increase and manufacturing loan share decrease within its combined personal and corporate loan portfolio. The residential mortgage loan share YoY increase picked up speed from 0.7% in 2012, to 0.8, 1.6, 3.2, 5.6 and 1.5% during 2013, 2014, 2015, 2016 and 2017 respectively, while the manufacturing loan share YOY change reversed from 0.3% increase in 2012 to decrease by −1.4, −1.7, −1.9, −1.6 and −1.4% in 2013, 2014, 2015, 2016 and 2017 respectively.

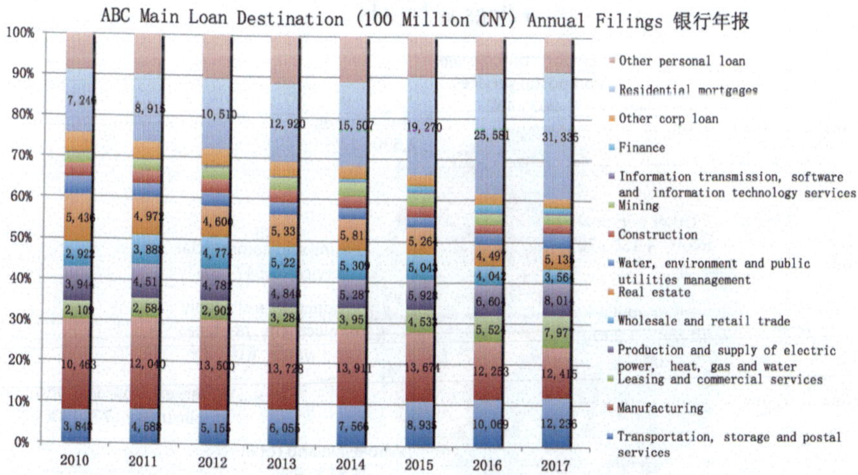

If we combine ICBC, CCB and ABC loan portfolio together, excluding overseas business or bill discount amount, the manufacturing loan amount of the three largest banks was at 2.97 trillion CNY, residential mortgage loan amount was at 2.91 trillion, out of total loan amount at 16.4 trillion in 2010. In 2017, the manufacturing loan amount stood at 3.83 trillion CNY, and residential mortgage loan amount stood at 11.3 trillion, out of total 34.3 trillion personal and corporate loans. Three banks' manufacturing loan share decreased from 18.1 to 11.2%, while their residential mortgage loan share increased from 17.7 to 32.9%. The macro dependency and risk exposure to real estate sector was increased significantly, resulting altered dynamics within the macro economic structure.

The next tier banks after the large commercial banks include 12 share-holding commercial banks. The sizes of their balance sheet are much smaller than the large commercial banks. Some of the banks listed in earlier section/chart, e.g., Industrial Bank, China Merchants, China Minsheng, Everbright, China CITIC, Pingan, Hua Xia, Guangfa, Zheshang are all share-holding commercial banks. Their cost of funding was often 0.5% to 1.0% higher than that of the larger national banks. To achieve comparable financial results with their higher cost of funding, share-holding banks tend to have higher risk preference than the state-owned commercial banks and urban commercial banks. Their annual reports are less standardized and are working progress therefore only a couple of them are selected into the analysis sample pool. In addition to Industrial Bank, Huaxia and Minsheng that are share-holding banks, Bank of Beijing is selected into 2nd tier bank analysis pool for being a leading urban Commercial bank. Four banks' weighted average loan exposure to real estate was average at 20% in 2016 and 2017, and their weighted loan exposure to manufacturing was average at 12% in 2016 and 2017. Compared to three large commercial banks studied earlier, their residential mortgage exposure was lower, but other personal loan exposure was far higher at 20%.

China Merchant, Industrial Bank, Hua Xia, Minsheng and Bank of Beijing 2016–2017 Average Loan Allocation by Industry (100 Million CNY) Annual Filings 银行年报

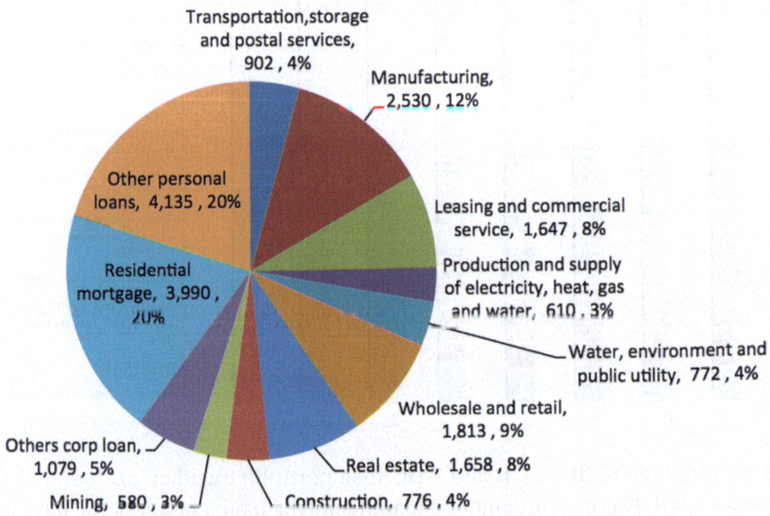

The difference regarding residential mortgage loan share within loan portfolio between larger and smaller banks, came from smaller banks' active pursuing of consumer business in credit card and micro lending areas where share-holding, urban and rural commercial banks are in general far nimbler players versus larger banks. Based upon CBRC data for the period between 2015 and 2018, in small and micro loan segment, urban and rural commercial banks had increased their level of activities, while large commercial and share-holding commercial banks level of activities largely remained the same.

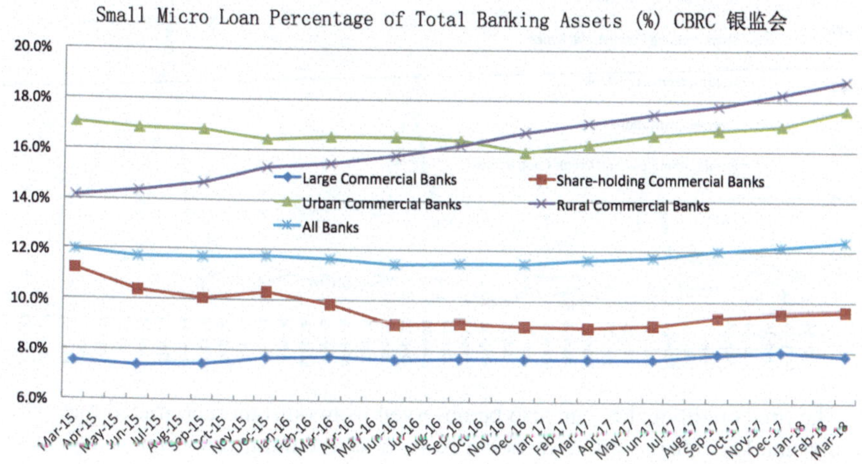

Smaller banks' active pursuing in consumer business and micro lending provides crucial resource flows into economic structural segments outside the more orderly governmental entities, large corporates and mortgage lending world. While befitting the macro policy push from the government for helping employment and social stability, these flows also come with higher lending risks. Smaller banks, especially rural commercial banks, have much high percentage of non-performing loans.

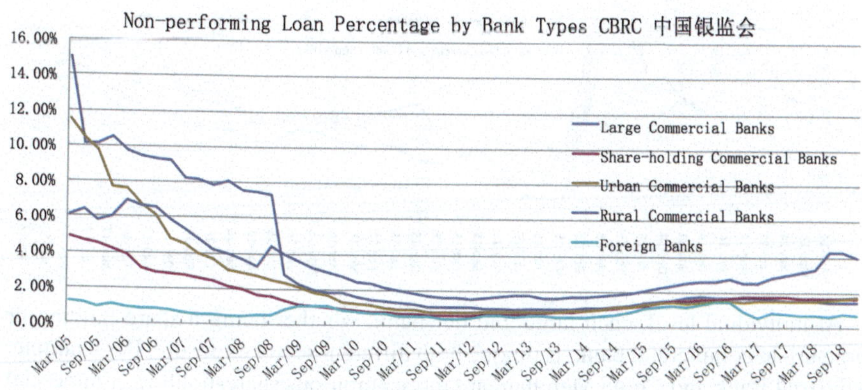

This observed pattern of resource flows by various bank types through different economic structural components led to tiered credit quality, which can be quantified from outright repo trading activities in the money market. Urban commercial and rural commercial banks are more active in pursuing risky assets while having persistent funds shortage, hence they have higher trading presence in the more expensive outright repo market.

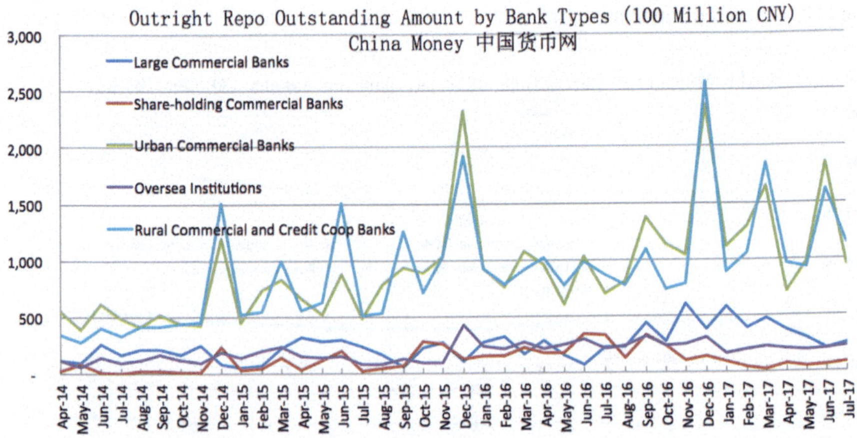

The tired credit quality can also be observed from outright repo traded rate. The capital markets charge different-tiered banks risk premium based upon their perceived level of credit quality, requesting the large commercial banks borrowing at the lowest cost, followed by share-holding commercial banks, urban commercial banks. Rural commercial banks and oversea institutions pay the highest credit premium for their overall lower credit standing.

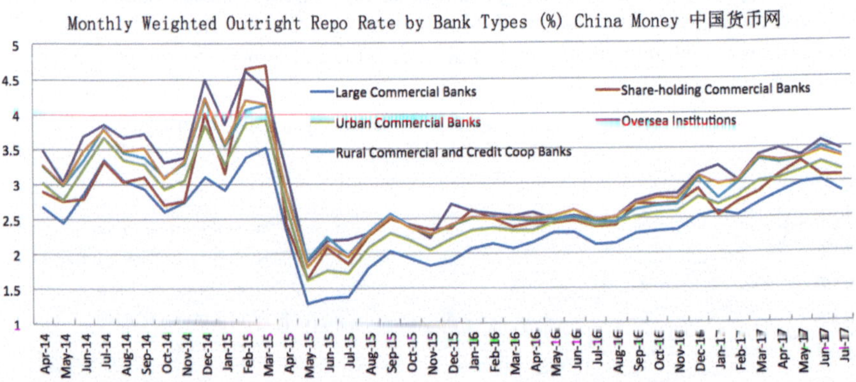

At individual level, each large 2nd tier bank, whether being a share-holding or large urban commercial bank, is unique with different sector exposure. For example, Industrial Bank and China Merchant are more ambitious share-holding commercial banks with larger residential mortgage portfolio.

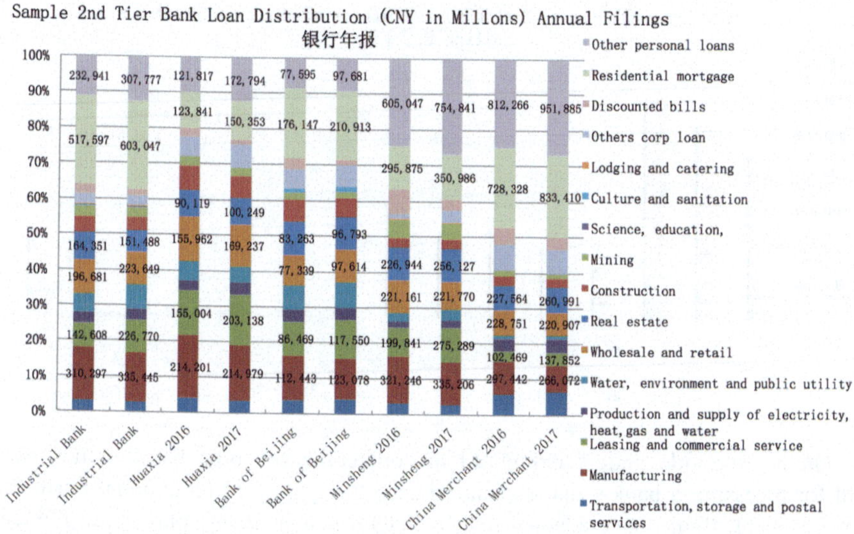

Investing at regional or regional industry level requires detailed local understanding, and knowledge of local urban and rural commercial banks is one critical piece of that local understanding puzzle. Urban commercial banks usually originated from a series of merger of local credit institutions within a metro area during the start of economic reform. As a result they often obtained local government support and in return provided feedback support to regional economy. Similar to urban commercial banks, rural commercial banks were the result of mergers of regional rural credit institutions and they lack extensive retail network but have access to local projects. To compensate for their lack of extensive branch coverage in attracting deposit, both urban commercial banks and rural commercial banks make extensive usage of interbank money market to fund their balance sheet expansion, but still maintain a heavy reliance on cash deposit especially from their retail customers.

On the liability side, deposit is the main source of urban commercial banks funding and its size is a good measure of both a bank's competitiveness and the level of local economic development. The mixture of a bank's deposit type is just as important. Cash deposit pays much lower interest for both retail customer and institutional clients, at less than 1%, while the term deposit's return is often at more than 3%, depending on the deposit maturity. Higher percentage of deposits coming from cash may reflect the general strength of local wealth, in this case Bank of Beijing, or possibly just the opposite, the potential room for improvement on termed investment services, in this case Huishang, an urban commercial bank located in Anhui province. The following figure illustrates the size and composition of 5 sampled urban commercial banks' reported deposit from 2015 to 2017.

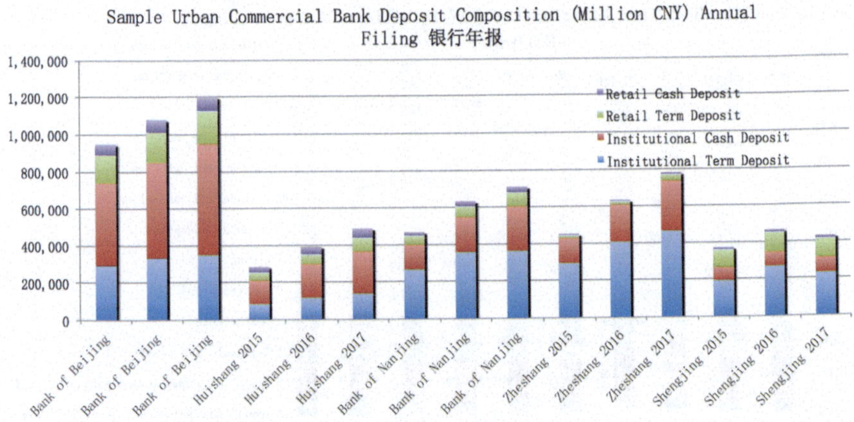

On the asset side, understanding of loan collateralization type distribution is useful for assessing a bank's risk exposure hence the quality of its regional business environment. Banks have adapted their collateral management approach to reduce risk exposure in their respective business environment. The most stringent form of lending collateralization is collateralized loan, followed by pledge loan and bridge loan, while the least stringent form is the credit loan. Bank of Beijing's relative low percentage of collateralized loan and higher percentage of credit loan might point to the overall better economic structure quality in Beijing. Banks situated in less prosperous area, such as Huishang and Shengjing (a urban commercial bank located in northeastern Liaoning province), on the opposite, had much higher percentage of pledge loan and collateralized loan. Not an urban commercial bank, Zheshang as a regional share-holding commercial bank, had higher collateralized loan percentage, revealing a loan quality problem originated from the stagnation of the regional export industry.

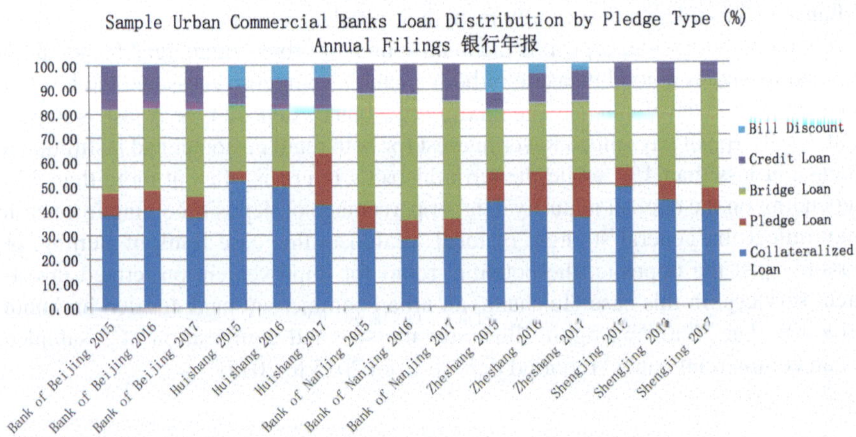

Another way for assessing regional economic vitality using 2nd tier bank data is to compare regional commercial bank's interest income percentage within its total revenue. Bank of Beijing and Zheshang are in more developed regions and have lower interest income percentage therefore more diversified income sources, while Huishang and Shengjing are in relatively less developed areas and have much higher dependency on interest income, and their dependency had increased from 2015 to 2017, indicating possibly a less favorable investment environment versus Beijing or Zhejiang.

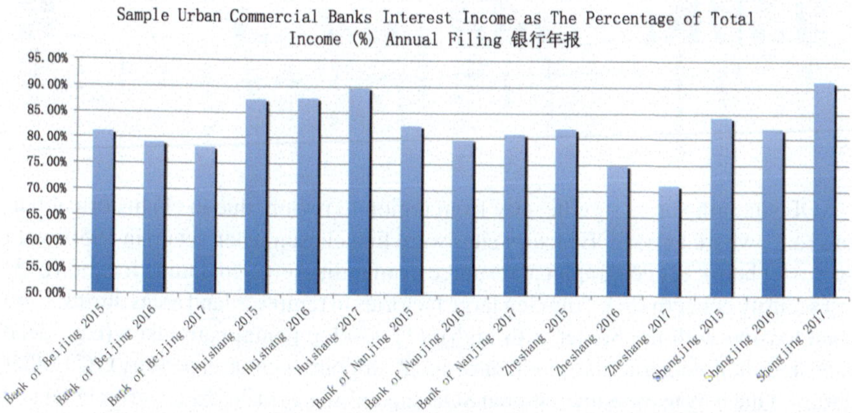

In a nutshell, large commercial banks, share-holding commercial banks, urban and rural commercial banks, are the most important financial intermediaries in China to channel quantity resources into different regional and industrial segments within China's macro economic structure. The deciphering of their different sizes of resource flows into different recipient destinations, their funding base, funding cost level, loan collateralizing type distribution, helps us to understand the state and possible future direction of macro, local economy and local industries to build up more informed macro analysis and formulate more informed investment strategies.

5.4 Investment by SOEs

Based upon reports published by Ministry of Finance on state-owned enterprises including both the central and local level SOEs, the statistics at sector level were quite indicative of the economic reforms that were taking place. Coal industry underperformed for overcapacity reduction, especially in the steam coal segment where coal was being used for electricity generation. Transportation outperformed for various infrastructure-building initiatives implementation, including high-speed train, urban subway projects, and the auto industry. Other areas that have outperformed included machinery, investment services, education, and research-generated revenue, are all results from the larger reengineering effort to transform the economy into a more self-sustaining growth model that is less dependent upon old-styled industrialization and export.

State-owned Enterprises Profit by Sector (100 Million CNY) China Ministry of Finance
中国财政部

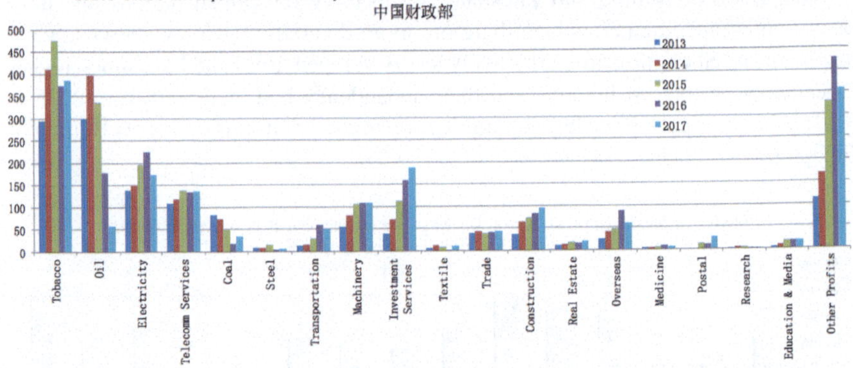

SOE strength varies significantly from region to region, due to (1) historical reasons (e.g., where large SOE factory sites were first chosen when set up in 1950s with the Soviet help); (2) geographical resource availability (e.g., coal mine location); (3) past security concerns (e.g., moving large factories to remote inland areas during 1960 when tension with the Soviet with high); (4) developmental path taken (e.g., deep water terminal construction to enhance local shipping center capability); (5) other reasons. One way to measure regional SOE capabilities in utilizing governmental and commercial investment flows is via past SOE tax revenue generated, which partially corresponded to their strength. In 2017, excluding state-owned financial institutions, central-owned SOEs paid tax revenue at 3.0813 trillion CNY, versus local-owned SOEs paid tax revenue at 1.1533 trillion CNY. The strongest economic provinces often deliver largest SOEs tax revenue. A caveat is that the numbers shown in the pie chart are not exact reflection of regional SOEs strength, since it only includes tax revenues reported by regional SOEs. This creates a statistical bias against Beijing, which is the home to many central-owned SOEs and state-owned financial institutions.

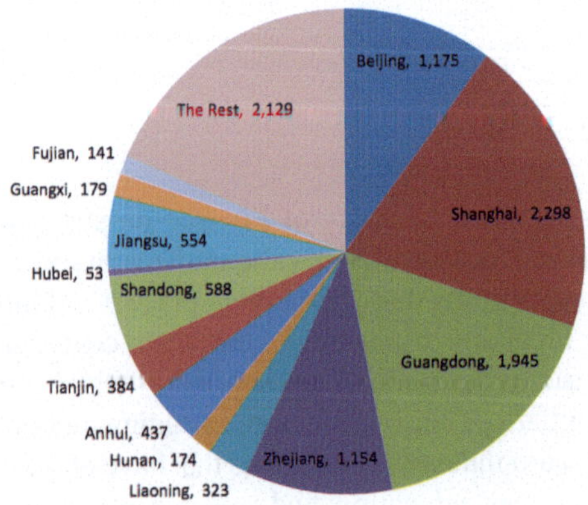

2017 State-owned Enterprises Corporate Tax Payment by Province
(100 Million CNY) SASAC 国资委

Where are the destinations of SOEs investments is dependent upon the national priority for economic platform development and also upon commercial viability. To fight against corruption and prevent the loss of state assets during investment flow implementation, SOEs management line is centralized and strictly hierarchical to produce clear managerial lines of responsibilities, and that makes SOEs risk-averse and possibly slow movers. But when acting as platform providers much as western utility companies or mature tech monopolies, upon which private industry players and citizens can carry out their diverse and creative activities, SOEs though not being the most efficient type, are well-resourced, well-informed and well-organized to process investment flows with their national matrix reporting lines and top down management structure. To reduce export trade dependency and distribute more economic benefits domestically with internal development, investment is expected to flow into 5G network infrastructure, transportation, natural gas and other alternative energy sources, urbanization, much along the lines of national 5-year plan. More specific industry examples will be discussed in Chap. 6.

5.5 Other Not State-Owned Companies

Large non-SOEs dominate in the areas of E-commerce, business logistics, mobile phones, home appliances, and real estate. Some of the large non-SOEs, such as Haier or Gree in home appliance sectors, were theoretically controlled by local SASAC in the past but government involvement at operational level remains rather limited and they act much like private companies. Since large non-SOEs are market-driven, their investment flows are largely directed based upon where their end demand is and where the end demand will come from in the future. PBOC started to ask banks to generate more lending activities since 2018 with more clarified state ownership definition to provide better financial support to non-SOEs.

The state of non-SOEs investments can be used as barometers for measuring macro or sectorial economic trend and conditions since they are sensitive to market condition change, in terms of supply, demand, financial liquidity, trade conflict, currency rate and policy changes. Their investment decisions and results can be gathered from their executive statements, annual filings and industrial consulting reports.

5.6 Investment by BAT and the Like

Particular importance should be assigned to investment data from BAT and the like. Dominating in the innovation arena, Baidu, Alibaba, Tencent, and Xiaomi act as FOF to either buy entrepreneurial projects or fund competing projects when market condition is right. The data in this area is sketchy and often only available from industrial consulting report.

5.7 PE and High-Net-Worth

The personal income tax/ regional budgetary expenditure ratio showed Beijing and Shanghai not only led the regional personal wealth pack, both of them actually extended their lead in personal wealth during the 10-year period from 2006 to 2016. Other leading regions, including Zhejiang, Jiangsu and Guangdong, still maintained their lead but witnessed their personal wealth generation capacity relatively losing ground, due to the economic moderation in more recent years. High-net-worth population from those wealthy regions and other areas invest their wealth into different asset classes such as real estate, equities, and bonds. Real estate is an important asset class in China, more so versus equities that only play a minor role in China's aggregated social financing activities. Luxury real estate square meters percentage within residential commercial property square meters, when higher than average for a region, could indicate where high net worth individuals might prefer to physically reside or park capital for asset appreciation hence they direct invest flows into real estate class towards those particular regions. Data indicated those areas included Hainan, a Chinese Florida-equivalent region popular for retirees and resort goers, in addition to Beijing, Shanghai, Yunnan and Chongqing.

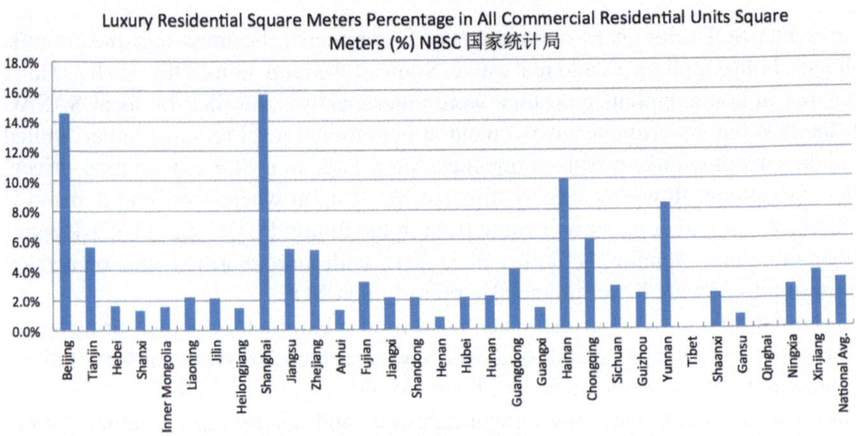

Though high-net-worth real estate investment flow may have geographical preference, in absolute quantities, approximated by regional luxury property purchase flow, it may still largely follow wealth generation geographical distribution pattern. The largest luxury real estate investment destination was Shanghai, followed by Guangdong, Jiangsu, Zhejiang and Beijing, a list of regions with highest personal wealth generation based upon income tax/ regional budgetary expenditure ratio. The surprise was the lowered rank of Beijing, which could be partially explained by Beijing's dense city core making it difficult for developers to build large units that residents would actually want to purchase. 2.9 trillion CNY flew into luxury real estate units from 2011 to 2016, making an average annual flow close to 0.48 trillion CNY.

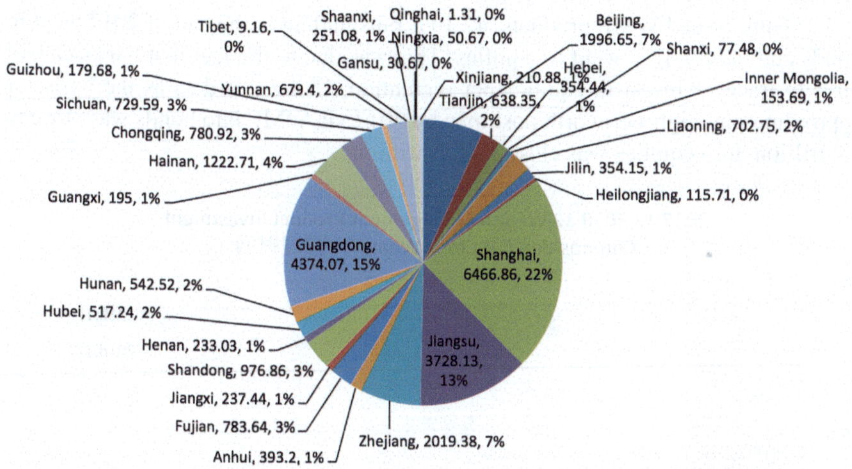

2011–2016 Luxury Property Purchases by Province (100 Million CNY) NBSC 国家统计局

Besides real estate, high-net-worth individuals also purchase fixed income assets from banks for yield and safety. Since they cannot directly buy interbank bonds (vs. saving bonds) that form the majority of China's bond market, they would purchase wealth management products (WMP), a termed investment instrument issued by banks, either with fixed or floating rate of return. WMP's term is often short, so investors need to reinvest received proceeds once existing investment matures. WMP outstanding at the end of 2017 for the high-net-worth individuals stood at 2.91 trillion CNY. From 2013 to 2017 year end, outstanding WMP increased by 4.8 trillion CNY per year average, taking into account that high-net-worth individuals holding about 10% of WMP, annual net flow into WMP investment by the high-net-worth might be approximately at 0.48 trillion CNY.

Wealth Management Product Outstanding by Investor Type (CNY in Trillion) ChinaWealth 中国理财网

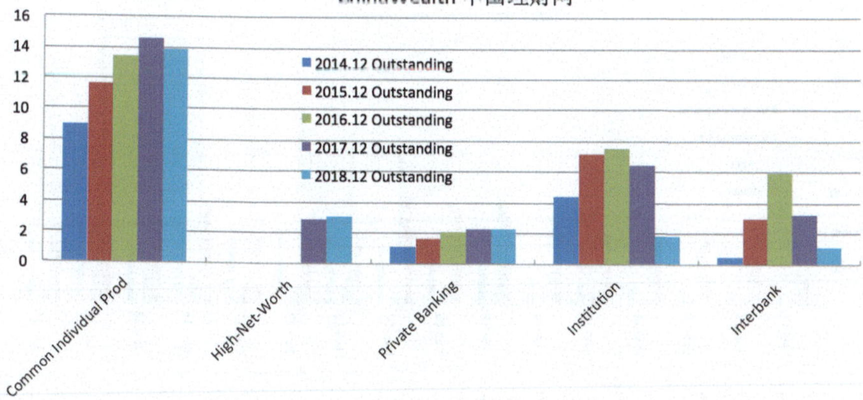

For bank-issued WMP products, 42.19% outstanding at the end of 2017 went to bonds and only 9.47% went to equities. This was due to the fact that banks cannot directly trade or invest in equities per regulation. Using this data as the basis for approximation, high-net-worth positions by 2017 via WMP into bonds was close to 1.2 trillion, into equities was close to 0.28 trillion.

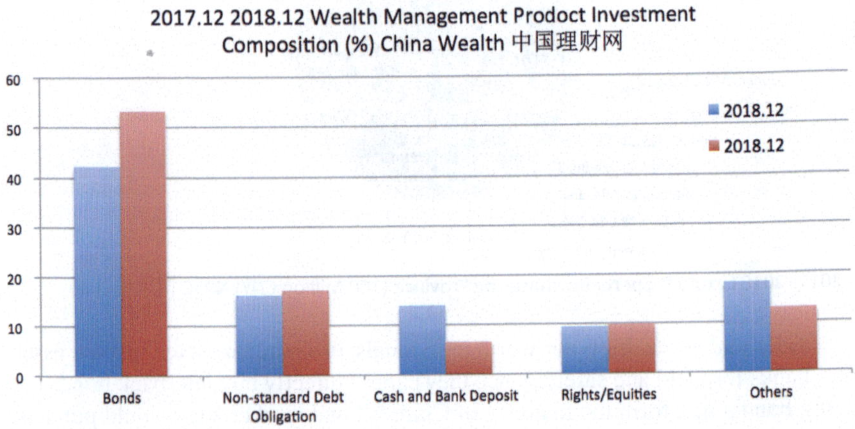

High-net-worth investment flows into equities can take indirect paths, such as WMPs, or direct paths, such as equity trading and private equities. Private equities allocate most of their assets into equities. From the end of 2015 to the end of 2018, outstanding equities amount increased from close to 2 trillion to close to 8 trillion CNY, a 2 trillion CNY increase per year. Though how much of that increase belonged to high-net-worth individuals is unclear.

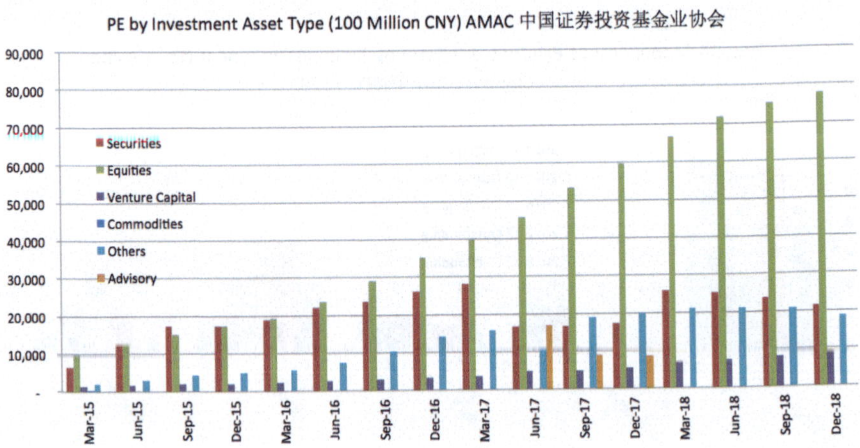

5.8 Investment by Trusts

Regulatory agencies and their policy directives can have significant impact on the size and direction of trust investment flow. Based upon market segmentation befitting China's regulatory framework, trust investment can be classified into 8 types: bonds, equities, mutual funds, real estate, basic industries, financial institutions, commercial corporates, and others. Bonds and equities are regulated by CBRC and CSRC. Mutual funds, due to their composite assets mixture, are overseen by PBOC, CSRC, multiple exchanges, and others regulatory bodies. Others 4 defined categories fall under the jurisdiction of NDRC for development planning directives, CBRC for bank lending industry limits directives, local government, and other agencies. The largest trust investment flows went into commercial corporates, financial institutions, basic industries, and real estate categories, supporting companies' collateralized financing, interbank capital arbitrage, local governmental development projects, and real estate projects, respectively.

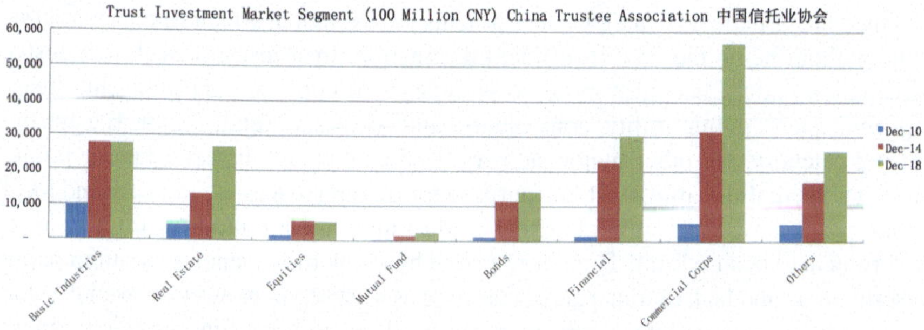

In addition to regulatory-conforming market segmentation, destined industry-conforming market segmentation can also be used to delineate where trust resource flows are being consumed. Real estate trust had been profitable but its risks include large inventory, high leverage, real estate and trust funding arbitrage policy violation, and real estate bubble. Leasing trust made more efficient usage of existing capital base and therefore was generally encouraged. Retail trust had been on the rise, a lot of which was associated with outlets and other related projects. Commercial corporates trusts often provided liquidity lending support for companies.

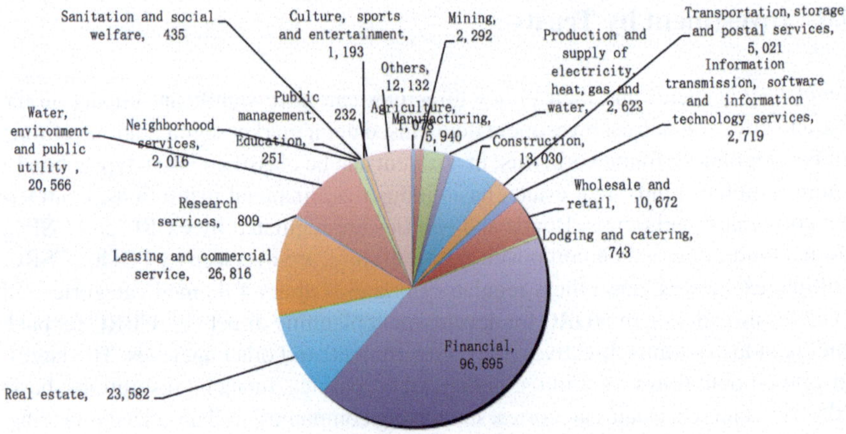

2017.12 Trust Funds Major Industry Usage (100 Million CNY)
China Trustee Association 中国信托业协会

Once the "Financial" category investments are excluded, which often act as conduits without being the final investment destination, trust investment flow industry distribution pattern becomes more observable, with large amount going into leasing, real estate, public utility, construction and wholesale retail sector. Except the leasing category, the other major industry destinations are all real estate or public project related, illustrating trust true purpose for funding real estate industry and local public projects without hitting banking credit limit, banking industry limit or local government exposure limit. Though censured by regulatory agencies for often being unscrupulous and lack of transparency, as long as trust segment exists, especially due to the persisting real estate dependency and local government funding requirement, its large investment flow amount could influence macro and local economic condition and monitoring that amount would be useful for making macro growth forecast and investment decision.

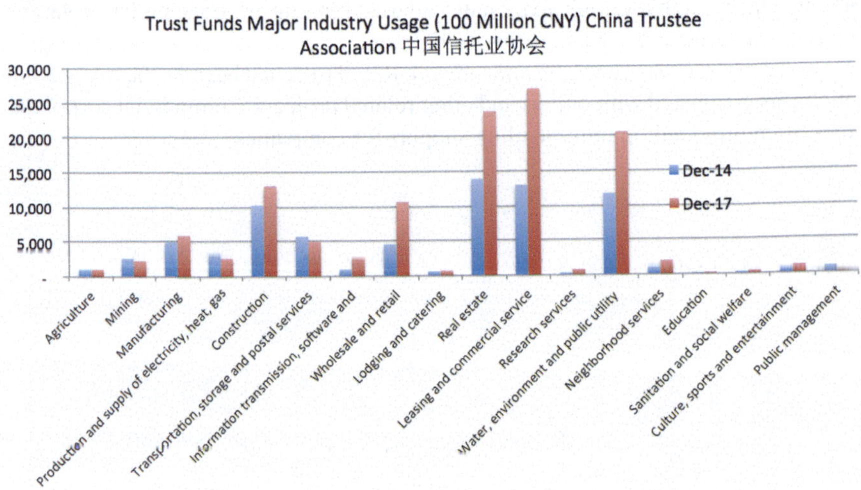

Some less common investment destinations for trusts, including those in Research, Social Welfare are seeing higher growth rate, a reflection of country's changing developmental direction under the new leadership.

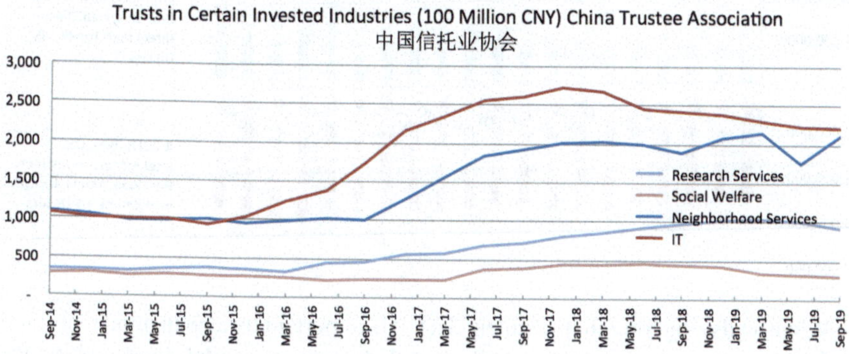

5.9 Foreign Entities

Foreign investments had been instrumental for China's entry into modern industrial age. It was investment from China Hong Kong, China Taiwan, and Japan during that opening stage that linked China production resources into the international trading system, especially in textile and other labor-intensive industries. As China production base gradually became more expensive with an improved labor force, foreign investments also started to adapt in terms of technological sophistication to tap into the wealthier domestic consumer market and better-educated labor force. Among industries bought up by the more recent investments, the most prominent ones included auto-manufacturing ecosystems and computer, mobile phone and related electronics supply chain ecosystems. Lately the combined inward investments, which were recorded by IMF as assets investment positions, plateaued and even showed a slight decrease, reflecting slower domestic economic growth and international trade growth, rising domestic production cost, and certain competitiveness loss of foreign investment.

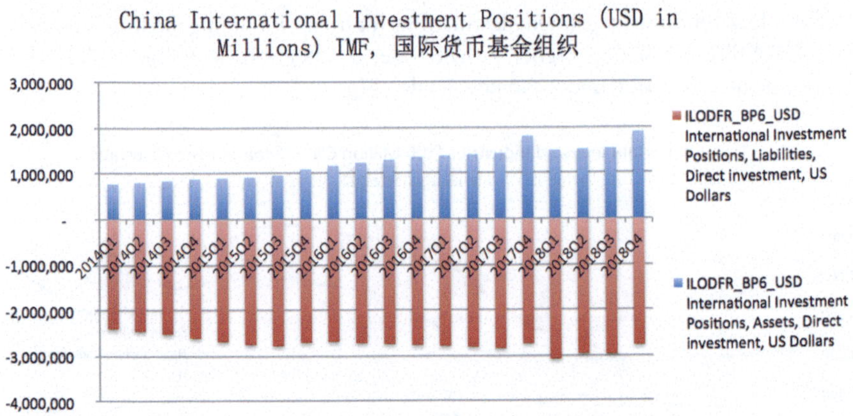

When analyzing foreign investment data, it is important to keep in mind that some of the foreign investments are actually recycled domestic capital flows looking for favorable treatment and protection given to foreign investments. Substantial portion of foreign investment from China Hong Kong, Virgin Islands and Cayman Islands could fit into that blurry category.

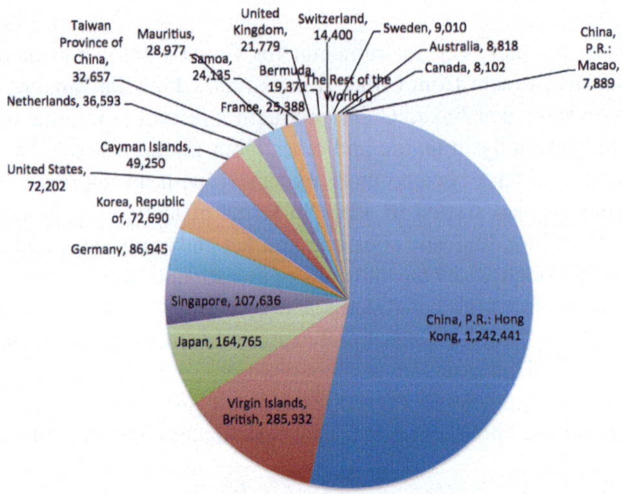

2017 China Inward Direct Investment Positions by Origin (USD, Millions) IMF 国际货币基金组织

Though less in quantity in comparison to those inflows originated from China Hong Kong and Virgin Islands but packed with more technological content, are those investment flows coming from industrialized economies, such as Japan, German, South Korea, Singapore and US. Capital flows into China from these industrialized origins contribute to a quite large portion of China's GDP. International auto companies and their joint ventures are responsible for the vast majority of domestically manufactured passenger cars, contributing to large amount of auto-related GDP. International tech companies also delivered large export volumes in PC, mobile phones and related electronics categories, contributing to export trade-related GDP. Therefore foreign investment flows' directional or amount change can have significant short-term economic consequences and long-term social consequences.

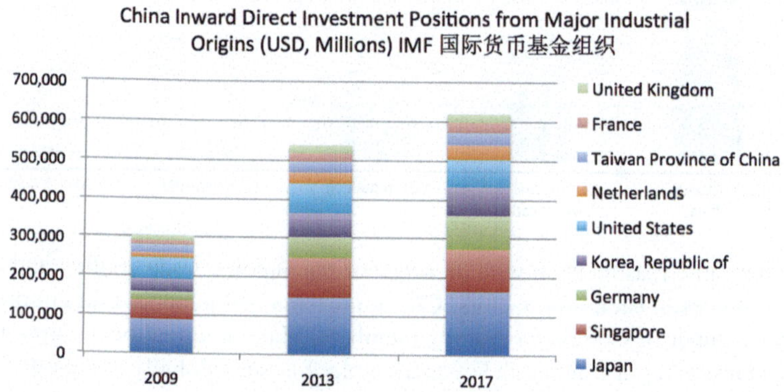

FDI usage per origin country/region data is available from NBSC. Since FDI usages from different origins specialize in different industries and congregate in different regional ecosystem, their year over year change offers useful insight into regional and industrial growth analysis.

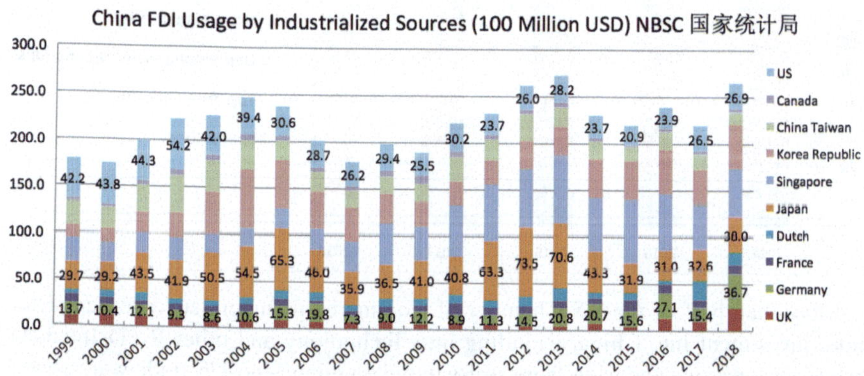

The largest investment source from Europe is Germany, whose auto and related investments flows can alter recipient countries economic fortune. Based upon 2013 German Chamber of Commerce survey, the main reason for foreign-owned enterprises engagement in China, was the presence of key customers, which included domestic market and global supply chain. Both German and Japanese brands had close to 5 million vehicle sales in China for year 2018. Volkswagen almost single-handedly created the modern auto supply chain in China and has maintained the market leader position in this largest auto market.

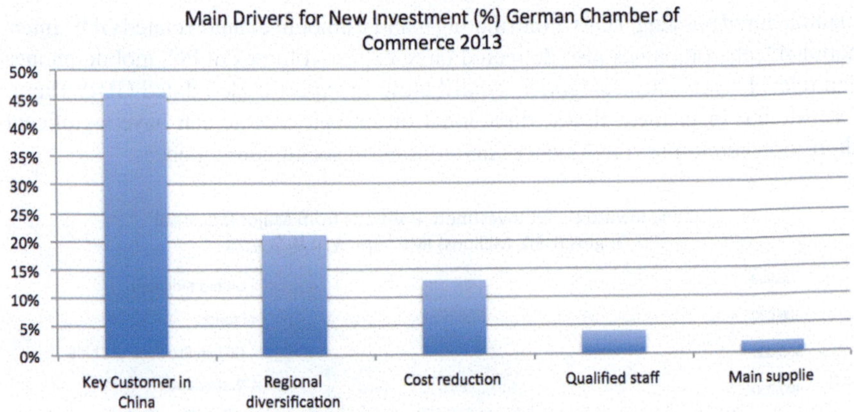

For the same reason, even with presence of the ongoing trade conflict and other negative domestic economic factors, China has remained a top investment priority for US Chamber of Commerce Survey members. Many multinational corporations will keep investing in China as a key market place to stay globally competitive.

More than half of the US Chamber of Commerce members surveyed expected more investment into China, including into Technology and other R&D Intensive Industries, one area enduring large stress in the ongoing Sino-US trade war.

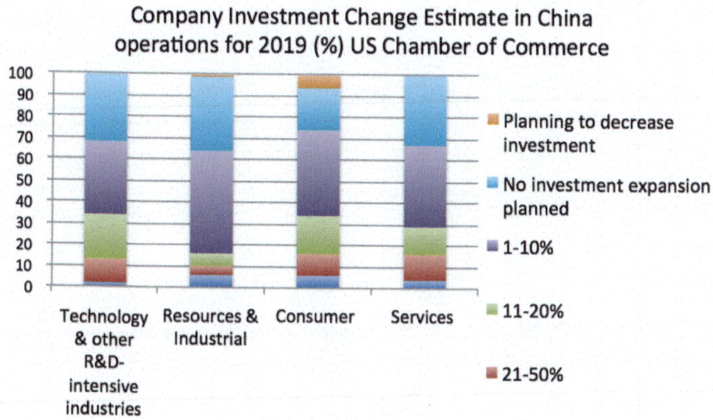

Continuous investment translates into continuous FDI inflows and regional plus industrial growth. The largest FDI destination is manufacturing segment, followed by real estate, a lot of which maybe Chinese capital recycled back though China Hong Kong. After coming down in 2016 and 2017, FDI into manufacturing recovered in 2018, a good sign for macro health.

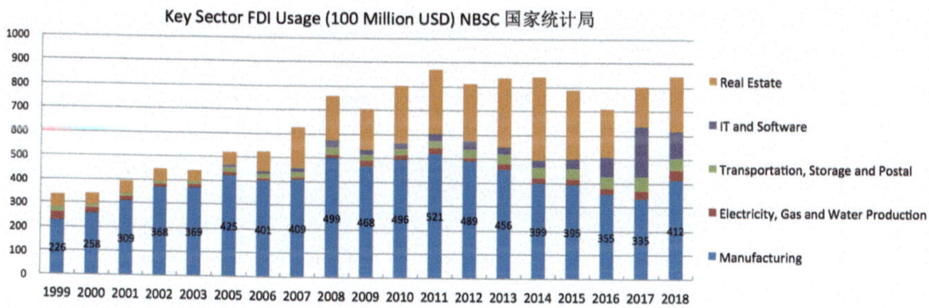

Company investment change estimate in China operations for 2020 (%) US Chamber of Commerce

Chapter 6
Investment Flows Dynamics by Demand Segments

The economy of China grew large and complex over the last 30–40 years, forming a structure quite unique in its own way. Within that economic structure, investments in terms of economic and financial resources are allocated in different quantities by diverse entity types based upon end demand originated from various sources. By measurement of GDP contribution, the most important investment event flows were real estate event flow, which had its demand generated by the domestic populace; fiscal event flow, which had its demand generated by governmental expenditure; and export revenue event flow, which had its demand generated by international consumers. Investment event flows allocated for more specific demand segments followed the lead of those three main event flow types. Smaller in comparison to the three main investment flows, some investment flows allocated for more specific segment demands are nevertheless also important for macro and industrial analysis and are detailed out in the following sections, which include high-speed trains, new energy vehicle, clean energy, aviation and shipbuilding, telecommunication and 5G, medical and educational Investment.

Using National Bureau of Statistics China data, by first calculating annual sales of commercial properties versus the annual total value of goods and services sold ratio, and the annual real estate fixed investment versus the annual total fixed investment ratio; and then apply those two ratios to goods and services share of GDP contribution, and investment share of GDP contribution, respectively, we can derive the share of direct real estate industry contribution to China's GDP. Before 2008, direct real estate share of GDP contribution was never above 16%, and since 2008 financial crisis, the number had increased substantially and was close to 25% in very recent years. Real estate sector acting as a stabilizing device to compensate the large economic down force was evident, as was the case in 2009, right after the financial crisis, and in 2016 and 2017, when the rising US dollar and pegged CNY exchange rate started to take large toll on manufacturing sector. By comparison, numbers from the US Bureau of Economic Analysis indicated the US total residential fixed investment, plus housing services, was in the range of 17.5–19% before the 2008 Great Recession.

X. Zhang, *Mechanical Analysis of China's Macro Economic Structure*,
https://doi.org/10.1007/978-981-15-3840-7_6

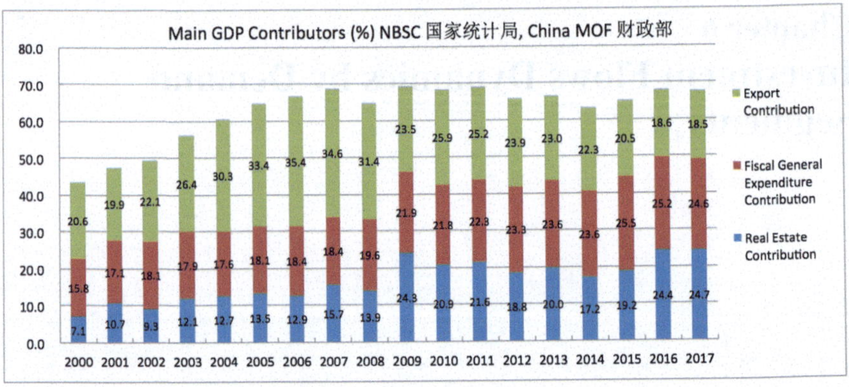

The effect of real estate industry on GDP contribution was even larger, close to 30% in 2017, if we include the fiscal local fund expenditure into the calculation, which was approximately 80% funded by real estate. Those funds were vital for local infrastructure drive. If we take simplification to the extreme, it was export revenue to real estate consumption to infrastructure expenditure that formed China's main economic event flow at the early stage of economic reform, hence export-related industrial index could be used to gauge macro growth condition. In more recent years, real estate activities became decoupled from export activities and its investment and consumption alone could be used to gauge a significant piece of macro economic condition.

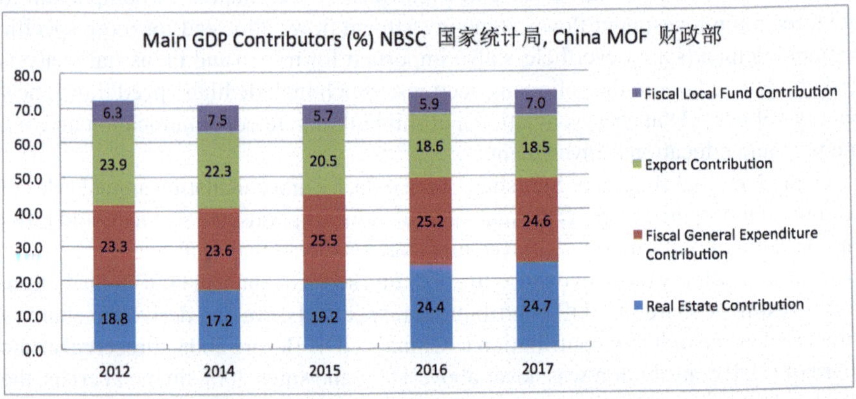

The other main important economic event flow types include fiscal and trade types that were discussed separately in earlier parts of this book. The majority of fiscal event flows went into local level expenditure. Large counter-cyclical fiscal spending stabilizes economy during down period. Specifically the revenue from the land usage right transfer not only powered local infrastructure, it was also derived from real estate activities hence good for predicting the investment flow within other demand segments. International Trade as a percentage of GDP has declined, and the net effect of trade (export minus import) is even much smaller than that.

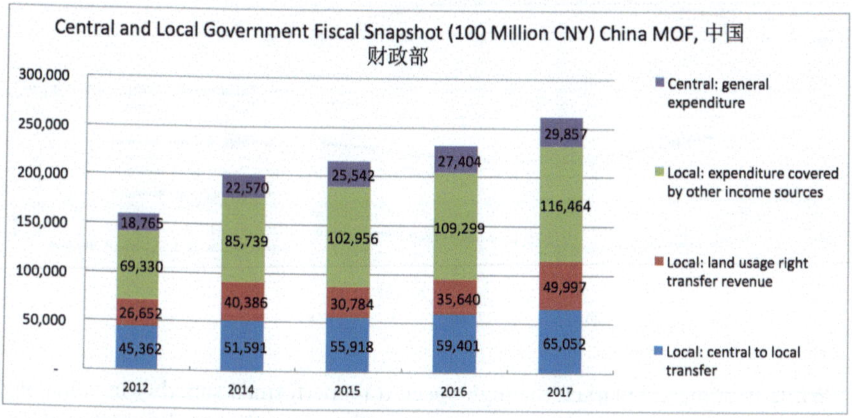

6.1 High-Speed Trains

Outside the main economic event flow types including fiscal, real estate, and export, within the more specific investment flow segments, high-speed train facilitates labor and population movement and is a game changer for a densely populated country with uneven geographical economic development level. In 2013 governmental reform to separate the ministry function from enterprise function per railway services, the Ministry of Railways was split into two, with the governmental function transferred to Ministry of Transport, and the railroad operations and development functions given to a newly created entity, China Railway. China Railway contracts out construction projects to China Railway Group Limited (CRECG) and China Railway Construction Corporation Limited (CRCC), and procures rail equipment from China Railway Rolling Stock Corporation (CRRC). CRECG, CRCC and CRRC are all listed commercial entities supervised by central SASAC. CRECG and CRCC are comparable in terms of engineering expertise coverage and business activities capacities, and they do more than just building railroads. On the other hand, CRRC is more focused on rail line, and its railway equipment revenue is correlated to China Railway's construction expenditure, implied from China Railway freight construction cost.

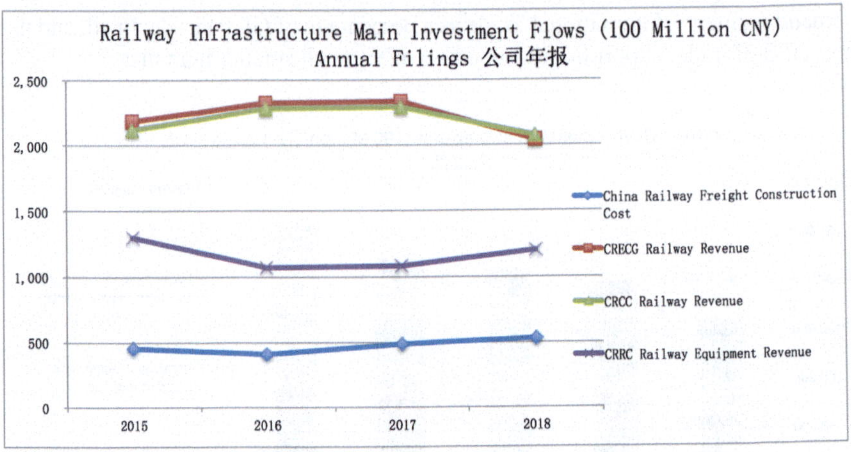

While in domestic market, the high-speed train performed superbly in balancing regional economic growth by shortening traveling time among different regions, with affordability overriding profitability concern, its export was hindered by high procurement cost for land in more economically vibrant countries and for equipment in less economically vibrant countries. Costly and financed by long-term debt, its continuous expansion and speed upgrades in domestic market, if can be sustained, will nevertheless be important for lowering both broad industrial cost and balancing regional economic growth, hence strengthening national economic competitiveness and supporting social stability.

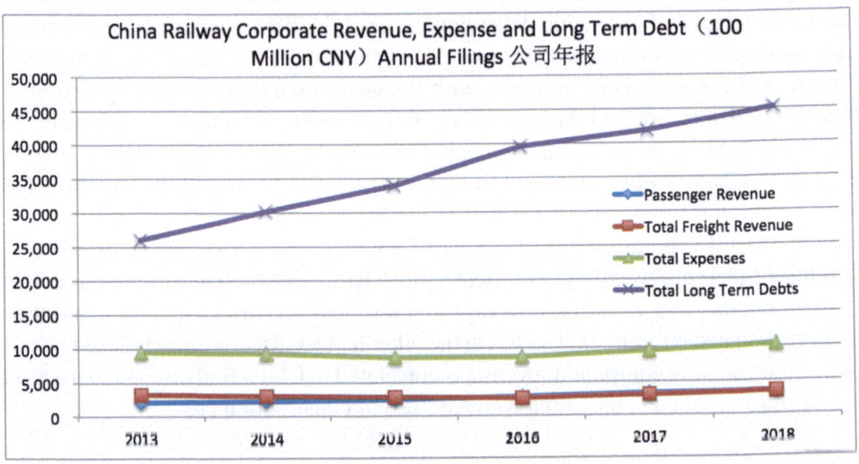

The train industry's capacity and competitiveness, which are important for its long-term success, can be assessed by CRRC's manufacturing statistics. CRRC had a severe over-capacity problem that was caused by fierce branch competition before its merger into current single entity form. Highest revenue was from EMU. With high-speed rail network gradually coming into completion, municipal demand for rapid transit will become more important revenue source. Engineering improvement in that segment will be interesting to watch possibly with global ramification.

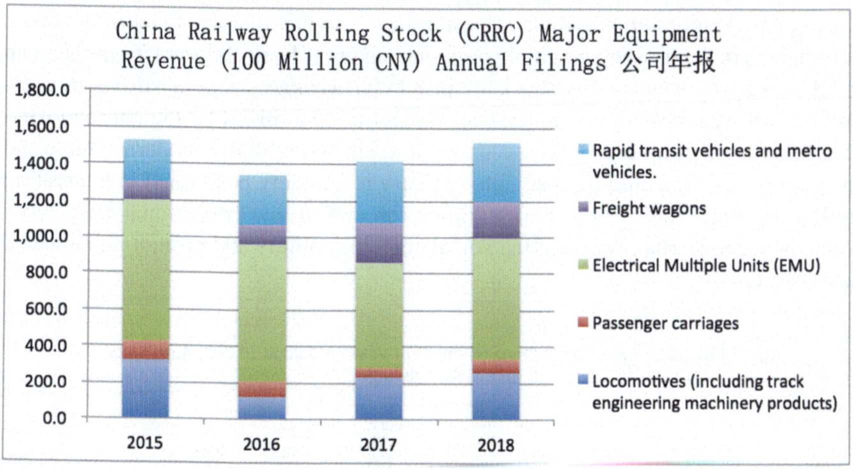

The shift from high-speed rail development towards municipal rapid transit development is even more evident when we look at the unit production numbers of different vehicle types by CRRC. The falling production level of the high-speed EMU units and rising production level of rapid transit vehicles started in 2016. Their in sync implementation and future improvement will be crucial for the continuous bringing down industrial cost and social cost, hence important for assessing China's national and regional developmental progress on both economic and social front.

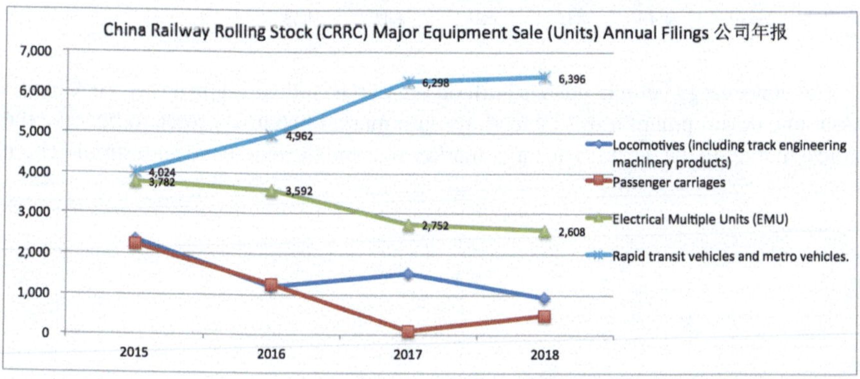

6.2 New Energy Vehicle Market

Another important growth area within the transportation industry is the new energy vehicle market. The push to develop and grow the new energy vehicle in China is driven by environmental concern for achieving tangible CO_2 emission reduction, energy security concern for reducing crude oil dependency, as well as industrial and employment concerns so domestic automakers might finally become somewhat more competitive at least in home market among global auto manufacturers and hence provide more employment opportunities. The fact that the share of domestic automakers in the passenger vehicle segment had never been above 44% with data up to 2018, was a constant reality check for the relative weakness of domestic automakers and overall weakness in manufacturing capability epitomized by the auto industry. Due to the large number of components required in assembling a modern vehicle and the large size of the auto market, auto industry is uniquely positioned in generating middle income employment opportunities for mid-to-low educational level labor force, hence important for breaking social class immobility and promoting balanced development.

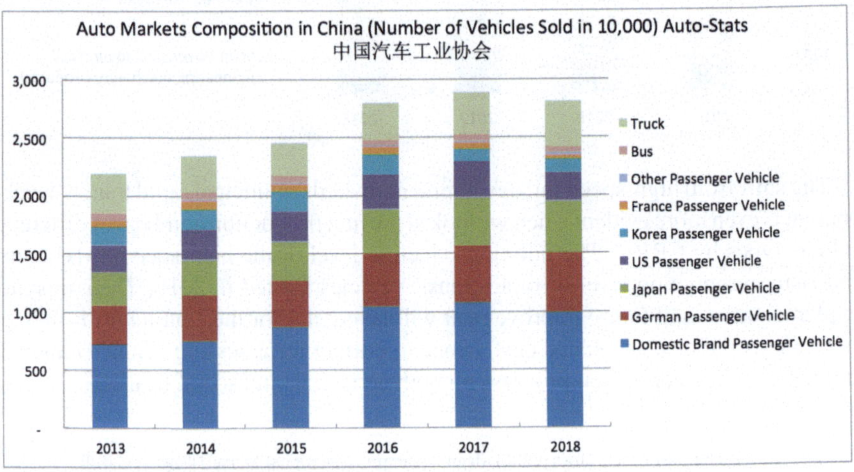

The new energy vehicle push is built on top of past industrial progress. As China's economic development moved ahead, its auto market had also grown to become the largest market in the world. The large market size and the extensive auto supply chain to support it provided foundations for the current new energy vehicle push. NDRC and MOF together with other agencies had designed and published policy initiatives with monetary incentives to encourage new energy vehicle introduction. Different levels of annual introduction incentive targets were set based upon 3 levels of local pollution level designation. The higher the local pollution level, the higher annual incentive targets set for new energy vehicle introduction for each specific region.

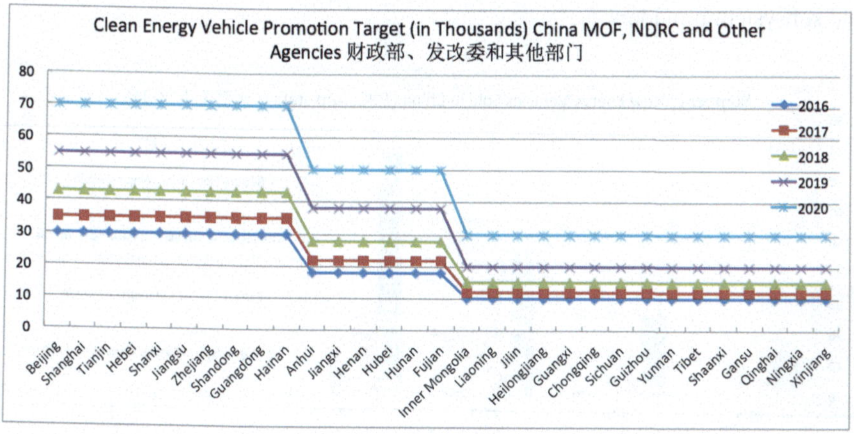

Unlike high-speed train system, the eventual scale of new energy vehicle application could be so enormous it has to be commercially viable for the long run to be a realistic transportation solution, and the main players in this new energy vehicle industry are expected to be private enterprises though policy incentives should be available for initial support. The push for new energy vehicle is fraught with technological and policy risk. For both passenger vehicle that includes car, MPV, SUV and crossover, and commercial vehicle that includes bus and truck, a battery electric vehicle has less mechanical complexity versus traditional vehicle, hence lower technological entry battier for domestic automakers and the preferred solution for new energy vehicle implementation. But battery technology may take on divergent paths and also be challenged by other technological possibilities. Two major battery providers in domestic market, Contemporary Amperex Technology Limited (CATL), which champions ternary lithium ion battery, versus BYD, which champions lithium ion phosphate battery, are both challenged by the possible adoption of hydrogen fuel cell that was championed by Toyota. Different battery technologies are compared on fire risk, material cost, low temperature usability, energy density, recharging speed and other factors. One hydrogen fuel cell disadvantage lies in its huge infrastructure cost requirement that could be a total waste if that technology is discarded later on. While German, Japanese and other global automakers excel in many technological subfields, the winner-takes-all risk forces battery/fuel cell solution providers, automakers and markets to work together for risk mitigation, and this reduces existing global player's monopolistic technical advantage. Even with uncertain market and technology risk, coordinated policy push, large market size supported by auto manufacturing ecosystem and strong battery solution providers, suggest promising development future in China for domestic new energy vehicle market, vehicle makers and subsystem providers.

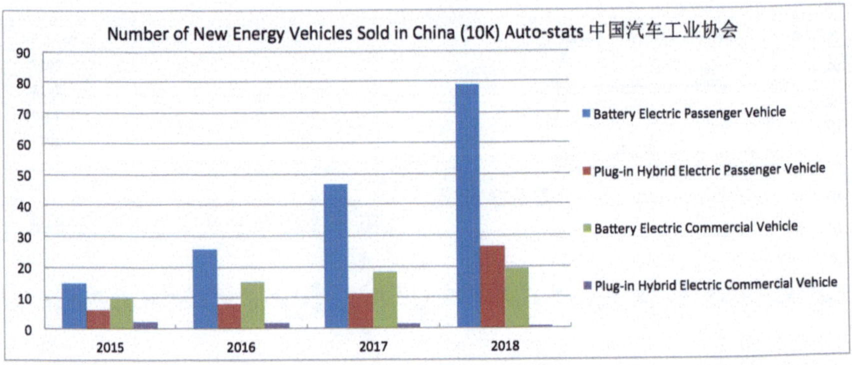

6.3 Clean Energy

Clean energy is another important area for making economic progress and generating potential employment growth. The increasing energy demand, on top of continuously improved living standard, coupled with pollution control concern, requires a cleaner set of energy supply solutions. The share of non-coal electricity supply increased from less than 20% in 2008 to close to 30% in 2018, a real achievement given the large size of the expanding domestic electricity market. The highest absolute amount increase for non-coal electricity supply came from hydro source, which has long-term application advantage but its full utilization is limited by uneven water resource distribution among different geographies and between different seasons in China. The other problem for dam projects is the increasingly high cost for resettling the affected population. The largest percentage increase came from wind and solar power, with their combined contribution took less than 10% in 2018.

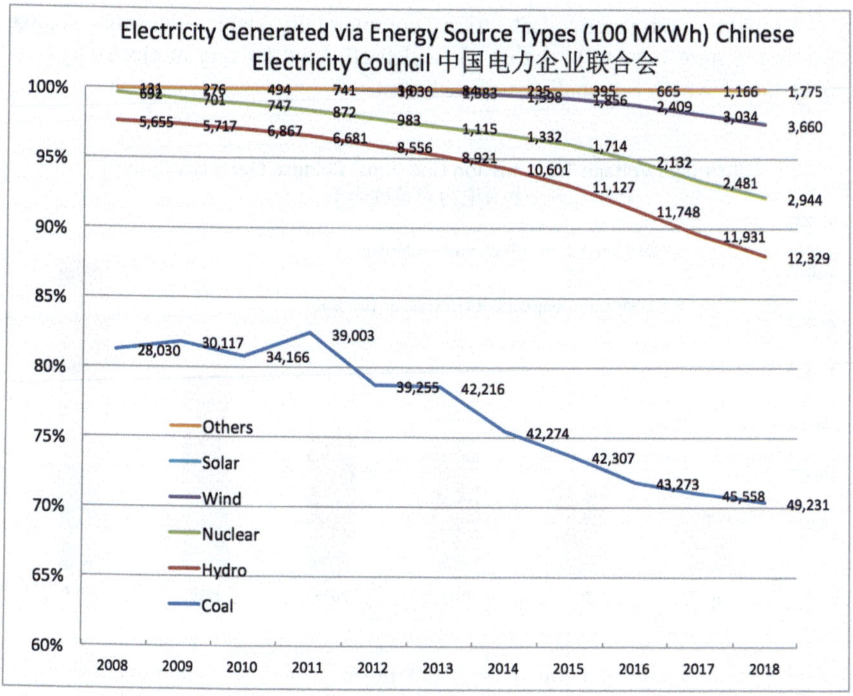

Underpinning the large electricity generation increase was the continued energy infrastructure investment. Investment figures showed that between 2012 and 2013 energy development priorities were reset, and more preference was given to wind and solar electricity sector. Investment is an important leading indicator for electricity generation capacity change.

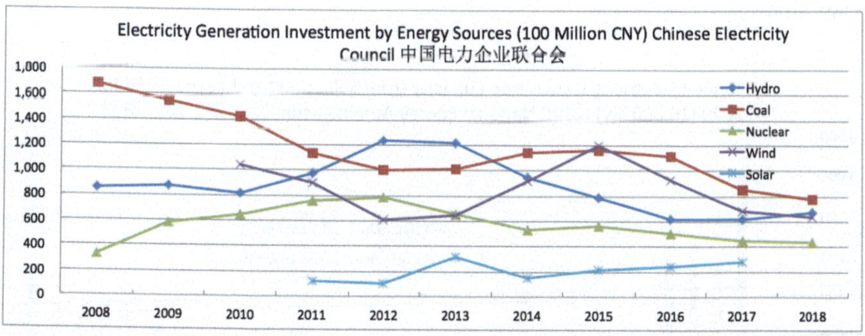

Effective electricity-related investment not only has to be quantitative with scale but also qualitative with technological improvement. For example, in the case of wind electricity, much of the wind energy resource is located in northwest part of China, while electricity end usage is heavily concentrated in the southeast coastal area. To make wind-generated electricity commercially viable, ultra-high voltage transmission lines have to be set up for scaled efficient delivery of electricity over long distance, which is a qualitative investment.

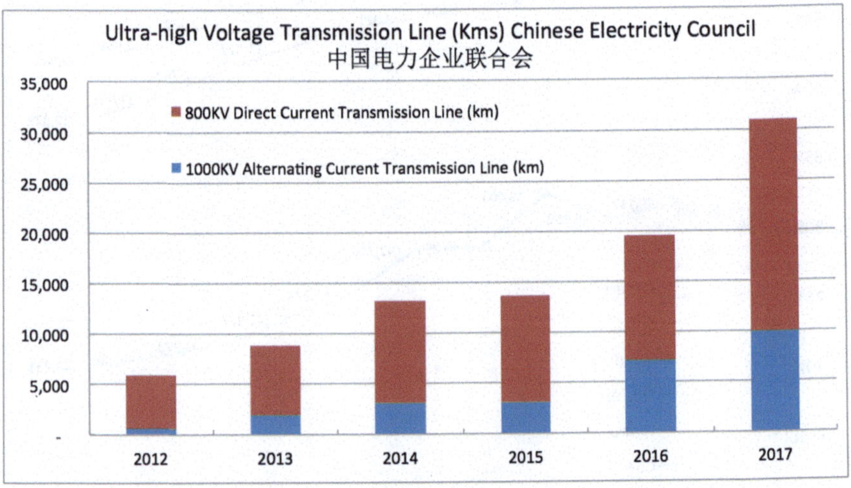

Both solar and wind-generated electricity power investment planning and implementation are geographical in nature. Open space in northern China, the so-called Three Northern Region (San Bei), includes Xinjiang, Inner Mongolia and Hebei, offers large quantities of wind and solar energy reserves that can be harvested at relative low cost due to open landscape and low population density, once efficient transmission delivery over the long distance is made available. These regions receive largest planned capacity. Coastal province Jiangsu has extensive mud flat area created by Yangtze River deposit, area that can be utilized for sea-based wind power generation.

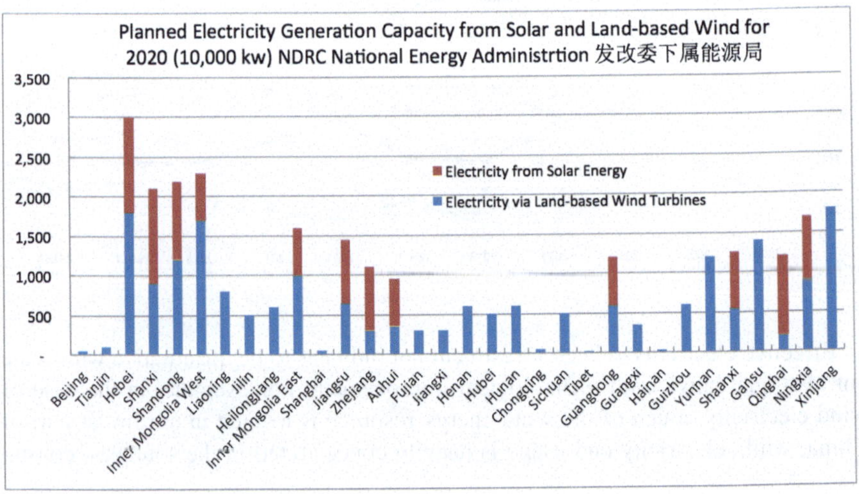

With basic transmission and other infrastructure put into place, with corresponding regional electricity generation targets planned out, electricity power operators roll out their production upgrades while equipment manufacturers provide some of the key underlying technologies. The dominant wind turbine technology provider in China is Goldwind, a private owned company that specializes in PMDD wind turbine technology. Overtime, its product category progressed from small turbines to larger turbines, illustrated by their reported number of turbines sold in different size categories.

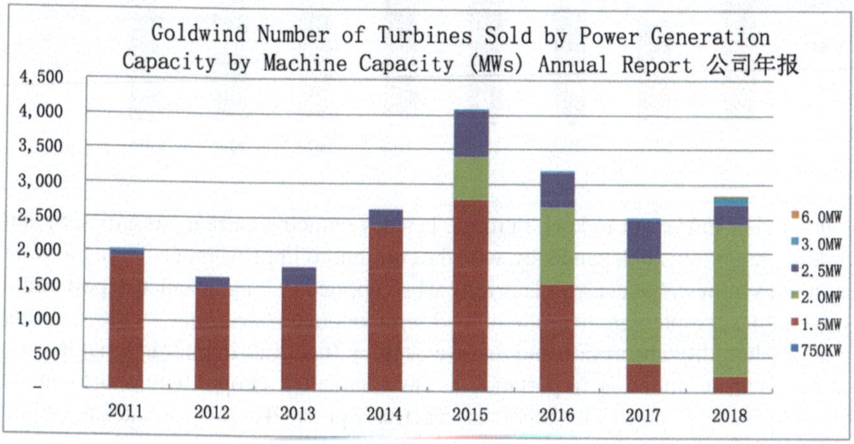

Goldwind's technological progress is even more evident when we look at the capacity installed data from its annual reports. The 750 KW machines and 1.5 MW machines had mostly disappeared. With 2.0 and 2.5 MW machines taking the largest share, and 3.0 and 6.0 MW gradually entered play. It technological growth is a result of international cooperation, with Vensys, a research institute purchased from Germany provides PMDD pioneering technology, Goldwind provides manufacturing capacity, and China provides the wind electricity market and infrastructure fund. Lacking any of the above components would not have created affordable wind turbine installation and Goldwind success story. With this development framework in place, the expansion of wind-generated electricity usage will likely continue, so will equipment providers' commercial success and related investment opportunities.

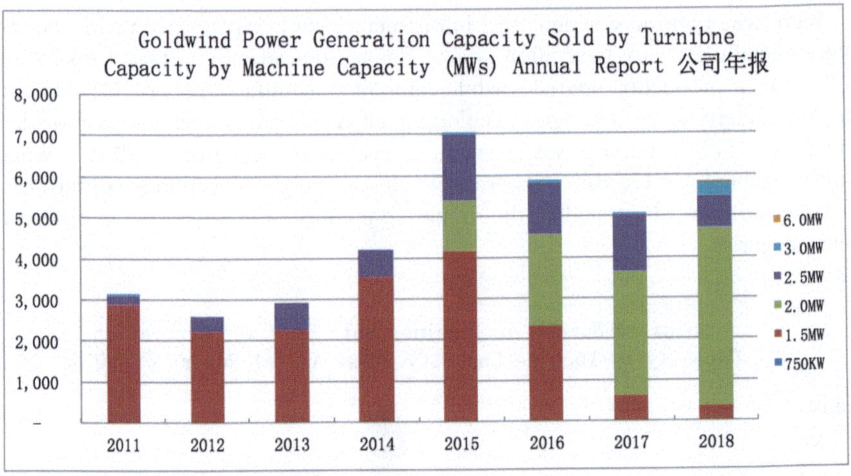

It is rather important to keep in mind, besides reducing carbon gas emission and crude oil geographical dependency, with the continuous improvement of transmission technology, renewable energy electricity when applied in long distance export could evolve into a complement to crude oil and semiconductor/electronics trade, offering monetary liquidity absorption and reserve pegging functions in international trading system. With its looming importance in environmental, geopolitical and financial areas, clean energy electricity becomes an actively pursued area by private and public institutions from all major nation states.

6.4 Aviation and Shipbuilding Ambitions

Besides the high-speed train system and new energy vehicles, the other transportation equipment areas that are making materialistic advancements include the commercial aircraft industry and shipbuilding industry. Different from high-speed train industry, which sets its ultimate goal for providing must-have affordable long distance transportation solution for the mass population thus requiring monopolistic scale and efficiency to optimize land appropriation process and minimize revenue shortfall, commercial aircraft and shipbuilding industries are not considered social goods to the same extent of essentiality, so they do not enjoy the same level of central planning support or resource backing, therefore have to be commercially competitive mostly by themselves.

The materialization of a competitive and modern domestic aircraft industry is more difficult than originally envisioned. The global aviation market was long dominated by two global players with technological know-how accumulation dating back to

WWII era. Even though China already possesses a sizable military aviation industry capable of manufacturing large transports and a large civilian aviation market, they do not easily translate into a functioning commercial aircraft industry. The crux of the issue is the creation of an extensive ecosystem that can deliver numerous parts and subsections of a large modern civilian airplane with quality. Sitting at the top of that ecosystem, a final system integrator will then manage those suppliers for delivering quality parts with precisely given specification for each production cycle in a timely fashion with an acceptable level of cost overrun. Commercial Aircraft Corporation of China Ltd (COMAC) located in Shanghai is striving to be such a system integrator, with its products including 70–90 seat ARJ21 into business and 169-seat C919 in flight trial. Tantalized by the possibility of at least having some domestic alternatives regarding mid-to-large civilian transports, for industry profitability, employment growth and security reasons, while it will be years before those domestic airplanes becoming competitive on global stage, China's commercial aircraft industry's advancement is materialistic and progressing.

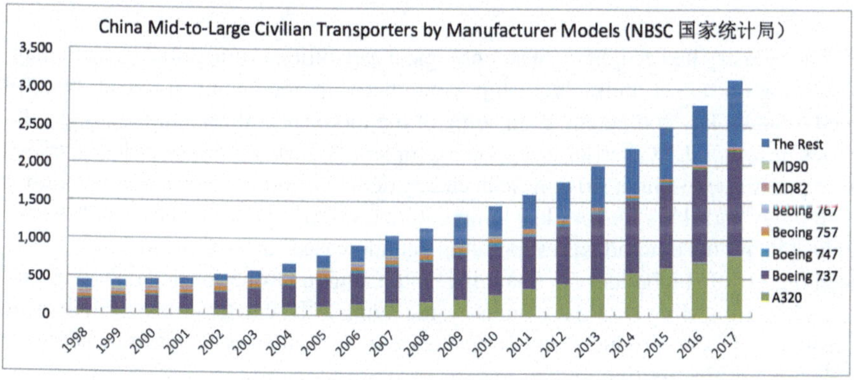

Comparatively, shipbuilding industry has less technological complexity but higher engineering and manufacturing labor intensity and China's developmental progress in this segment was faster and more pronounced. Some of the largest shipbuilders have emerged including China Shipbuilding Industry Company Limited (CSICL), China State Shipbuilding Corporation Limited (CSSC), CSSC Offshore & Marine Engineering Company Limited (COMEC), and Yangzijiang Shipbuilding Ltd. The industry, regardless at domestic or global level, was seriously weakened by the 2008 credit crisis that resulted the depletion of ship orders for international commerce due to lackluster international trade growth.

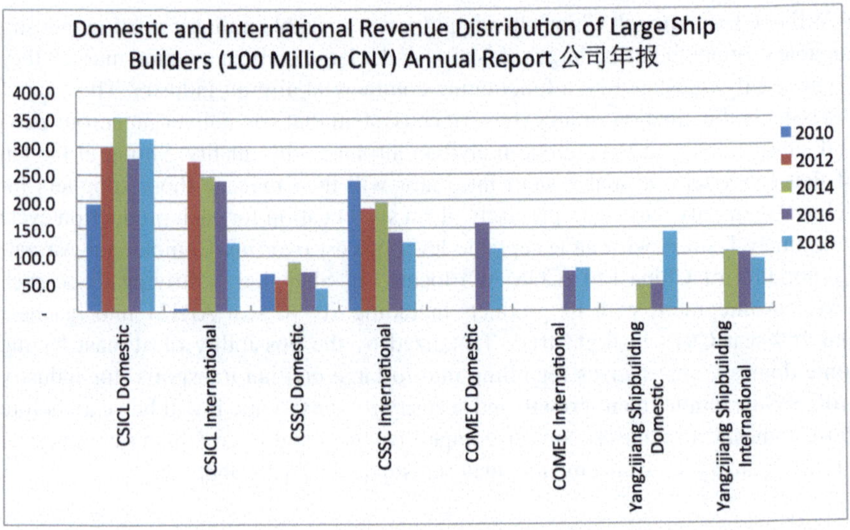

The industry had caught up in technological capabilities with global peers in manufacturing oil tanker, bulk-cargo ship, container ship and chemical tanker, but still need to attain key competencies in some of the more specialized shipbuilding categories, in which LNG carrier is a good example. LNG carrier recent order increases were partly due to China's rising clean energy demand, and LNG production requires technology and skills for very low temperature transfer pipelines, valves and storage tanks with reduced liquid gas evaporation and increased safety assurance. There had been reports of shipbuilders in Shanghai, and Xiangyu Group formed on top of previous bankrupt Ming De Heavy Industry, receiving LNG carrier orders or delivering finished LNG ship products, full competency in this category is yet to be achieved at the time of this writing.

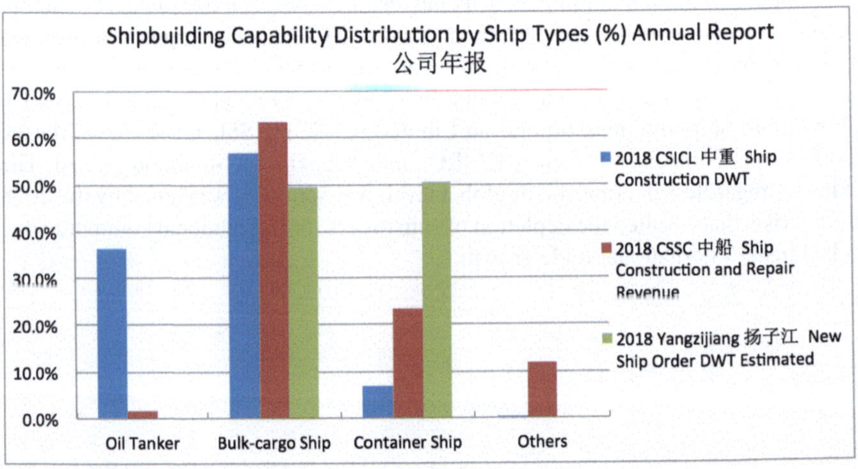

Looking forward, the steady progress of China's shipping industry is to be expected, so is the market entry of China's commercial aircraft industry, though probably at a slower pace. Industrial ecosystem investment opportunities, may either be for enterprises abroad working with domestic partners, or when in domestic territory, will probably be localized in Shanghai, Jiangsu and Dalian, for shipbuilding industry, and in Shanghai and Chengdu, for commercial aircraft industry.

6.5 Telecommunication and 5G

Just as large electricity market is the foundation to support domestic risky wind and solar energy development, and air travel market is the foundation for civilian aircraft industry development, large mobile phone and broadband end user markets are the foundations for China 5G and other advanced telecommunication technologies development. With the mobile end user number exceeding one billion, and broadband user number exceeding 250 million, the domestic telecommunication market is large enough for standalone technology and standard development with trial and error before international market deployment.

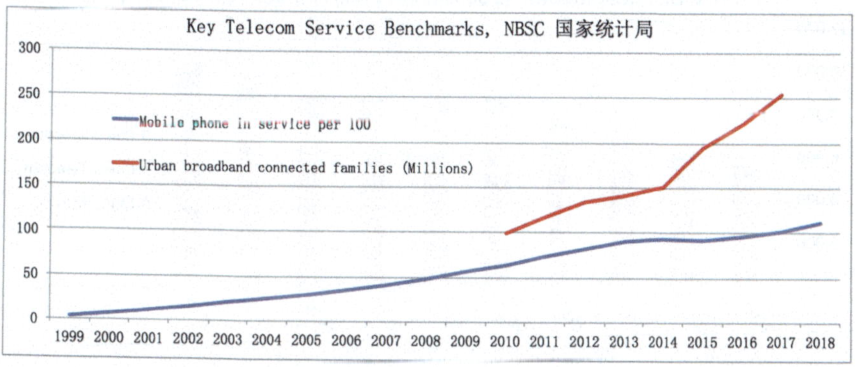

Three large operators dominate the domestic mobile telecom market, China Mobile, China Unicom and China Telecom. Besides China Mobile being much larger in the mobile market, three operators offer relatively similar products and engage in fierce price and offering competition.

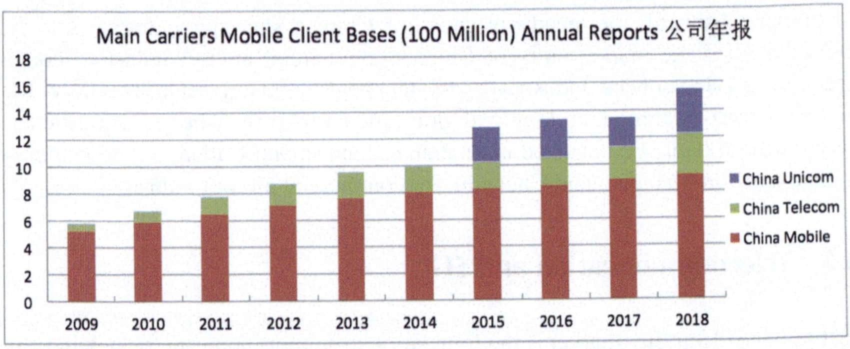

With the gradual saturation of domestic mobile market, the large operators' mobile business income plateaued, leaving them with strong incentives to identify new market points for differentiation. The situation is made more urgent when policy initiatives were put in place to drive down telecommunication cost for end users to reduce the cost burden during current economic growth moderation.

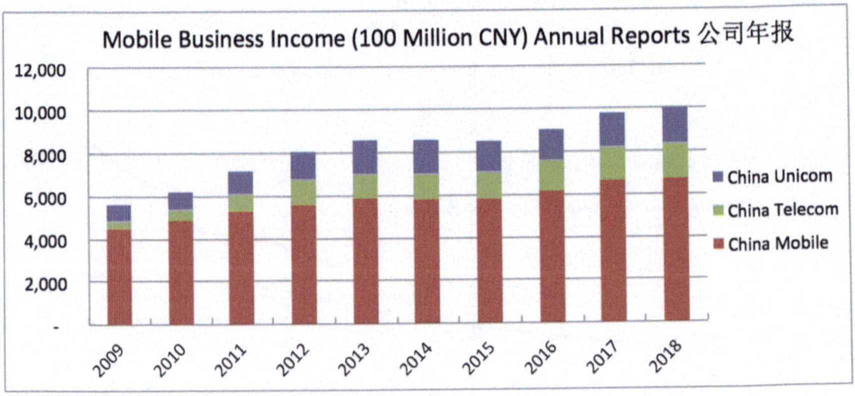

One possibility to position a mobile service company for acquiring relative competitive edge is by providing speedier data transmission over wider service areas. Prior the 5G rollout, total number of 4G base stations deployed had increased from less than 1 million in 2014 to close to 5 million in 2018. 5G base station deployment is expected to gather pace with related capital expenditure.

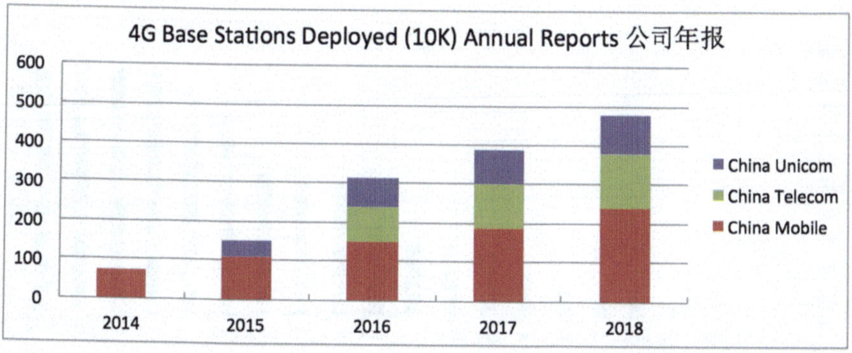

Internet of Things (IoT) is another area for telecom service providers trying to position their competitive differentiation. In an era where AI and big data service not only bring income growth potential, but also change the entire telecom industry landscape, capital expenditure and resulted deployment of smart connection had increased substantially.

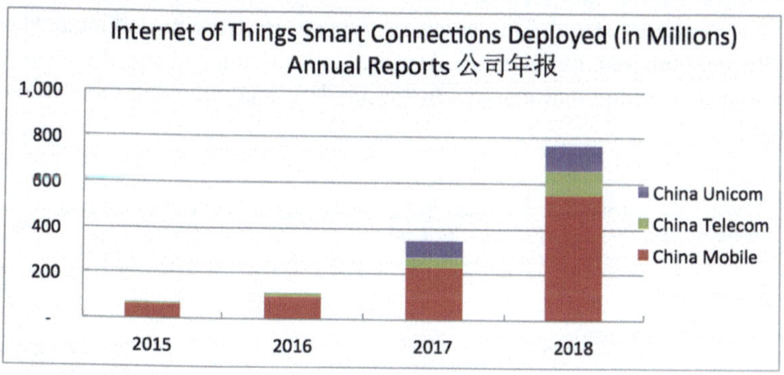

In a nutshell, large end user market and fierce competitive pressure led to three major operators continuously make large capital expenditure in mobile services and IoT domain. The resulted most up-to-date technology environment becomes a fertile ground for scaled end user equipment innovation and production including smart phones and network equipment. Looking forward, this large and competitive market will support and ensure China's smart phone industry and telecommunication equipment industry to perform strongly, bringing pressure to various global competitors, and produce regional and ecosystem investment opportunities to domestic and international investors alike.

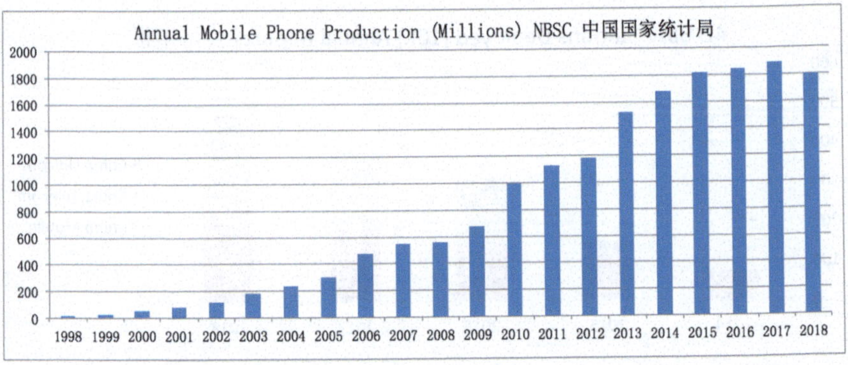

6.6 Medical Investment Prospect

As domestic economic and social development progressed, higher standard in medical services is also expected. The increased imports of medicine and medical equipment reflected both that higher medical service expectation and also domestic weakness in both developing and manufacturing modern medicine and modern medical equipment.

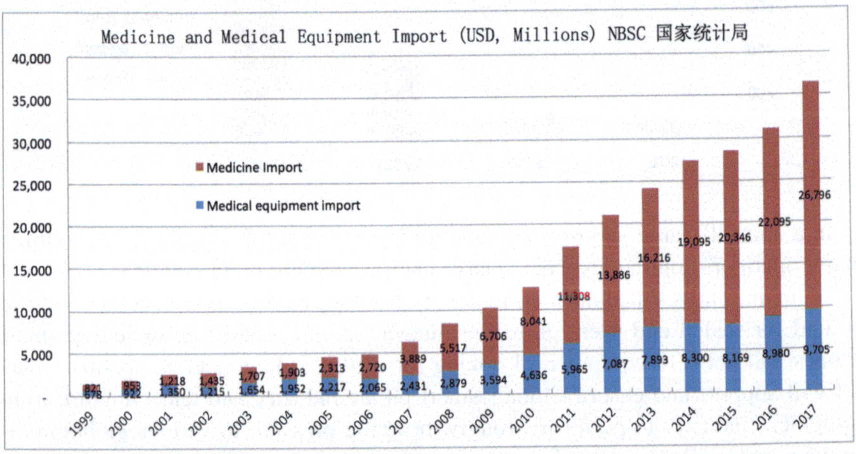

The imported medical supplies in 2017 approximated 245 billion CNY with much higher profit margin versus domestically produced medical supplies. During that year, the large and medium-sized domestic medical enterprises total profit was about 250 billion CNY. With the coexistence of the lacking quality domestic-originated medical supplies, high price and quality of overseas medical supplies, and large population need for affordable quality medical care, the social and commercial needs to create a capable medical industry for quality medicine and medical equipment are real and pressing.

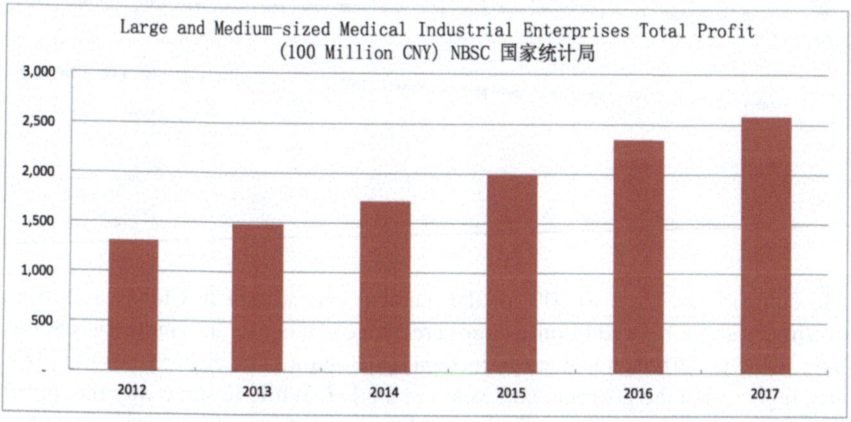

Citizen causes of death distribution can be used to identify where quality and quantity medical supply development are the most needed. The largest causes of death were cancer, cardiovascular system, cerebrovascular disease and respiratory failure. Some of these causes, such as cardiovascular disease, were closely related to aging. As a rapidly aging society, the domestic demand for medical supplies for aging-related treatment will grow substantially over the next several decades, creating prospects for investment activities.

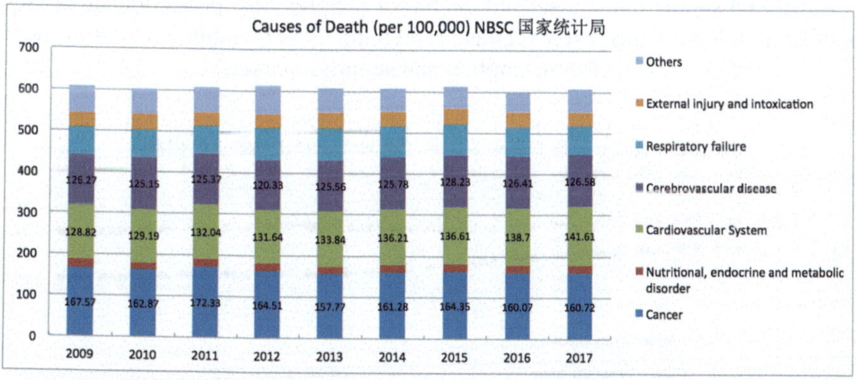

What caused the difficulty for domestic medical industry advancement is subject to debate. Besides weak IP protection, past lax regulatory oversight, many also thought that certain level of margin has to be maintained to induce technological research and development by the industry. Margin comes from the downstream medical service expenditure. In US, the medical expenditure from the government is less than half.

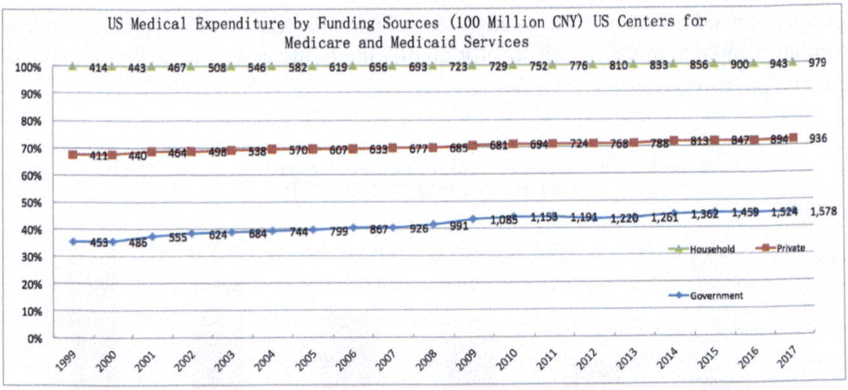

In comparison, close to 60% of the medical expenditure in China came from government support. In addition, a large percentage of the insurance industry is SOEs. These made governmental share in medical expenditure somewhere close to 70%, much higher than the governmental share in the US. While in some way the higher weight of public influence in medical expenditure made the medical service providers very efficient in promoting healthcare services throughout the vast expanse of country over a huge population, some of them very impoverished commoners in remote locales, the price control is extensive hence the main margin incentive for research development has to come from the scale factor. The realization of scale potential in medical supplies was hindered on two fronts: first, China is still a developing country by average income and living standard, hence most of the affordable medical supplies have to be generic, but the lacking of consistency test on generic medical supplies makes direct comparison of products from different suppliers difficult and that leads to a fractured supply market; second, on top of that, regional protectionism causes modification of basic med list at regional level related to expenditure reimbursement furthers segregates medical consumption and supplies market.

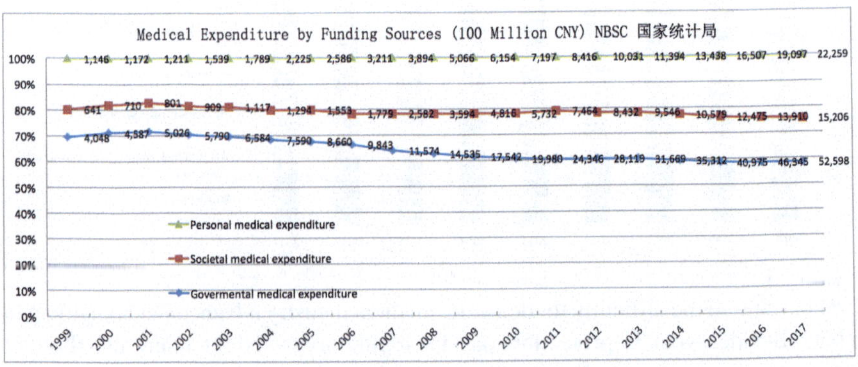

The governmental reform in the last couple of years has been trying to address those two issues. Consistency test is encouraged to promote best generic drug, and basic med list is compiled with the consistency result part of the consideration, and with minimum regional modification allowed. The potential benefit of the scale factor will therefore be gradually realized, encouraging research and investment in the medical supply industry. The combination of the need for medical service advancements, the condition created for inducing those advancements, and the technology difficulty in making those advancements, generates opportunities for pharmaceutical and medical technology providers and industry investors.

6.7 Educational Investment Prospect

A large and well-educated workforce is a prerequisite for a nation's industrialization. It took China more than a half century after the Opium War to end the Imperial Exam system focusing on history literature materials, and a nationwide migration to a modern educational system, with large portions of content dedicated to engineering, science, English, and other contemporary subjects, was only accomplished after the CCP took over, so as to give domestic workforce the necessary education required for comprehensive modernization. Building up and maintaining quality education system require sustained resource allocation in quantity, and that allocation has kept pace with China economic progress in the last several decades, a large portion of which came from fiscal sources.

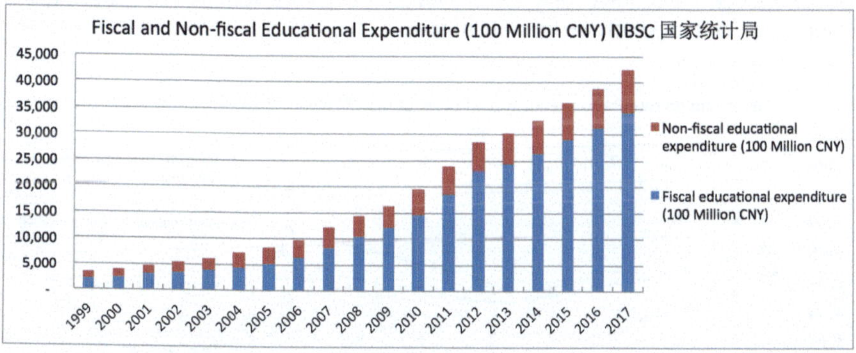

Percentage-wise, the largest portions of educational expenditure went to higher education, followed by middle and high school, and elementary school, reflecting cost requirement, perceived relative importance and subsequent allocation priorities. Any allocation mixture change within such a large system would be slow and arduous and requires a lot of planning ahead of time.

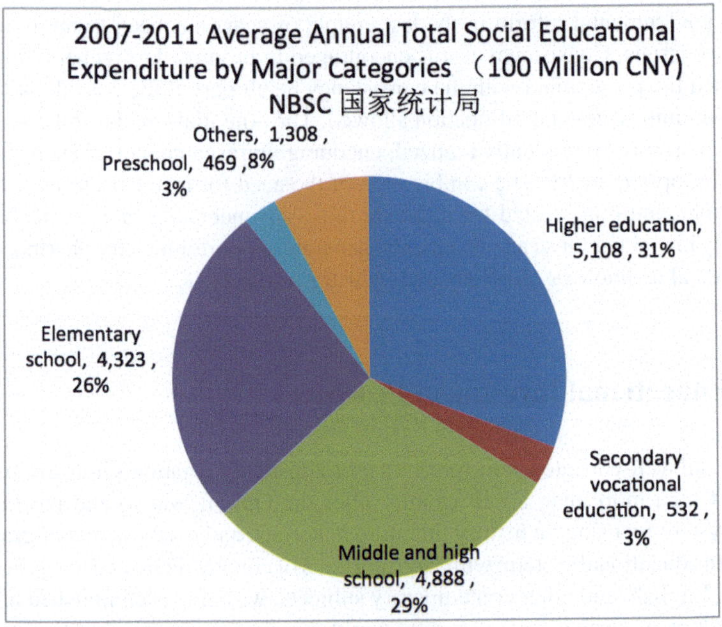

During the earlier phase of China's reform process, education was treated as another market industry and the proportion of fiscal support in educational expenditure was lessened. The consequence was higher student cost burden and less enrollment representation from rural and other lower income families. To address this social imbalance and other issues, fiscal support was increased and its weight in the total educational expenditure became higher.

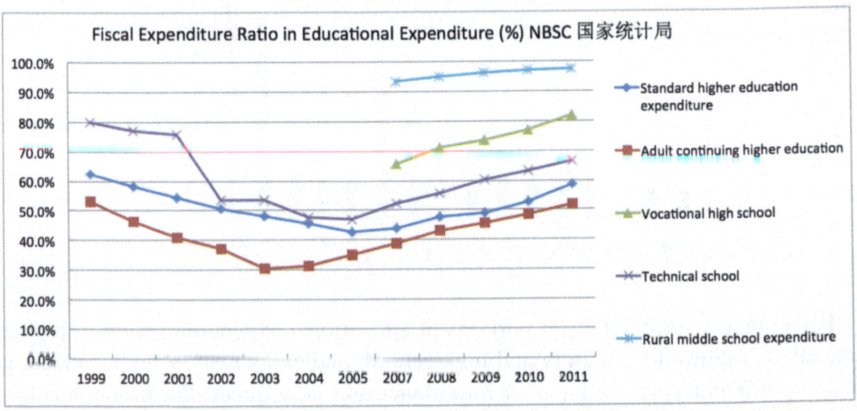

Besides broadening education's social outreach, public expenditure can also be utilized for furthering knowledge exploration in depth. If we use the number of Ph.D. candidates as an indicator for measuring the scale of advanced education and research, in the segment of engineering, science and medicine, the numbers had all doubled from 2004 to 2015, illustrating the increased support and demand for advanced studies in those important categories. But that increase is relative. Based upon US National Science Board study, the number of Ph.D. awarded in science and engineering in US was about 40,000 versus China close to 60,000 for 2014. Taking into account US capability in attracting world talent and solid research environment, the quantitative edge in China is not enough to change the existing US advanced research dominance at global level. Hence the domestic investment into advanced research and education still has a long way to go.

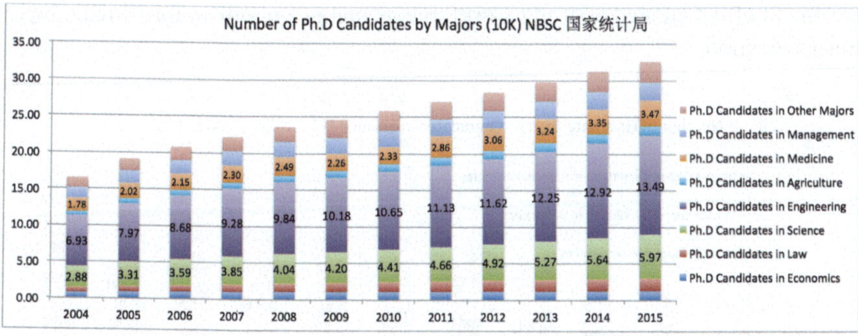

Compared with Ph.D. level engineering studies that can be advanced and theoretical, master degree level engineering studies are more directed towards application. The increase of master degree education in engineering from 2004 to 2015, showed there was a fundamental engineering skill market demand at work, besides the high-end research that could be more influenced by fiscal policy initiatives.

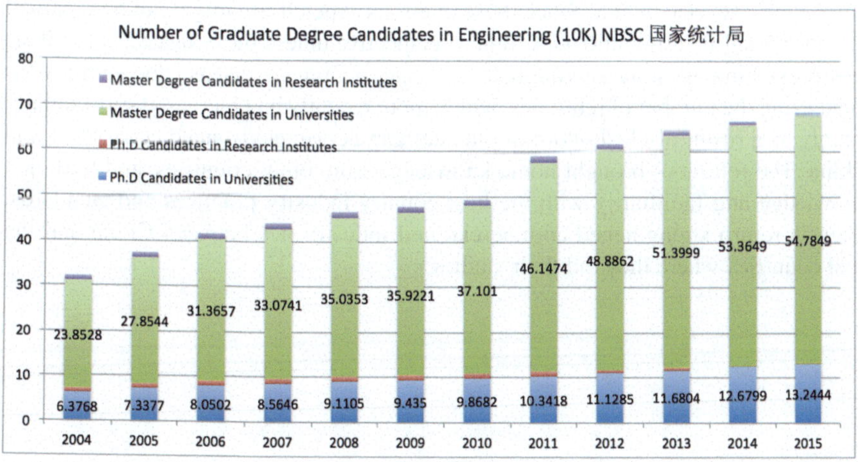

The progress of graduate level education was also evident in the area of science, when measured by the number of Ph.D. and master degree candidates. Advanced educations in both engineering and science are expensive, requiring large sums of investments from public, educational institutions and individuals. Here the traditional Chinese value on education played an important role. Fiscal and institutional educational investments increased the level of education of workforce and that benefited industrial growth, families and individuals holding traditional Chinese belief in education responded to the increased growth demand by furthering individual education level, hence creating a virtuous cycle. This combined social educational investment effort created a strong workforce as one of the pillars for China's rapid industrialization.

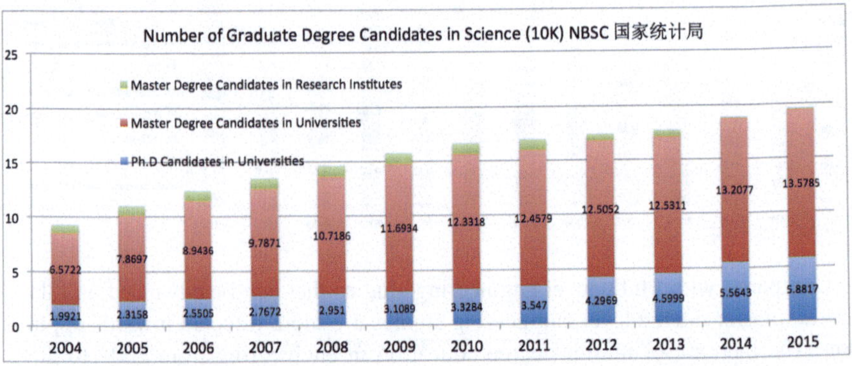

In addition to the domestic educational expenditure with its statistics collected by NBSC, there is also large overseas educational expenditure, which would be mixed into China's service deficit. Since those overseas expenditure might not be regarded as educational investment from China's perspective unless the educated individuals return to China, we may approximate the scale of China overseas education investment using the number of returnees, which more recently had increased substantially mainly as a result of closing developmental gap between advanced economies and China. The returnees brought home knowledge from other countries, and with that knowledge and familiarity with the host country industry practices and standards, often in return strengthened commercial and industry ties between China and the host countries where they did their studies.

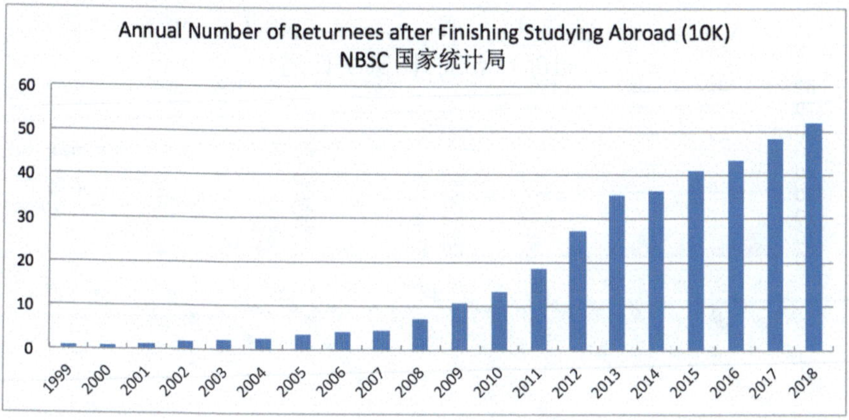

The very large sum of educational investment is spent unevenly within China, due to higher population density in coastal provinces, higher industry demand in well-developed regions and other reasons. To invest in educational industries in China, investors or education service providers need to first map where their targeted end clients are, either by the level of income, e.g., as an international school group looking for high income family student, or by the client industry concentration, e.g., as an investor funding a mechanic trade education shop, or by population congregation, e.g., as a test prep service group with a keen sense on high school graduate population density.

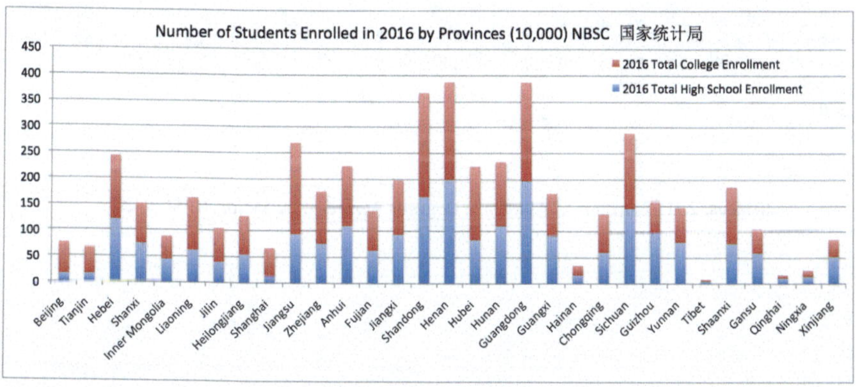

Lower than college on the educational ladder, the associate level education is nevertheless just as important for creating a skilled manufacturing labor force. Large numbers of associated degrees are awarded each year in different categories, including finance, medical, education, manufacturing and civil construction.

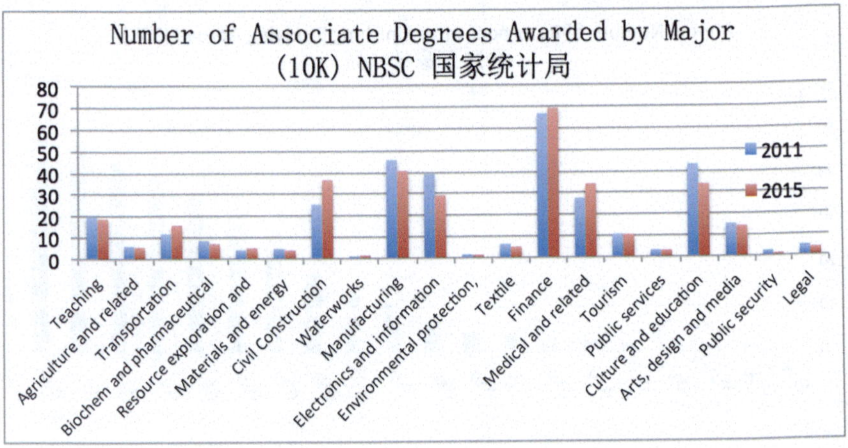

The ups and downs of number of associate degree awarded in different industries, which were sensitive to segment demand change, from 2011 to 2015, showed the difficulties in manufacturing, and increasing role of public spending, in transportation, civil construction and waterworks. These signals are important for analyzing industry trends and possible education investment opportunities.

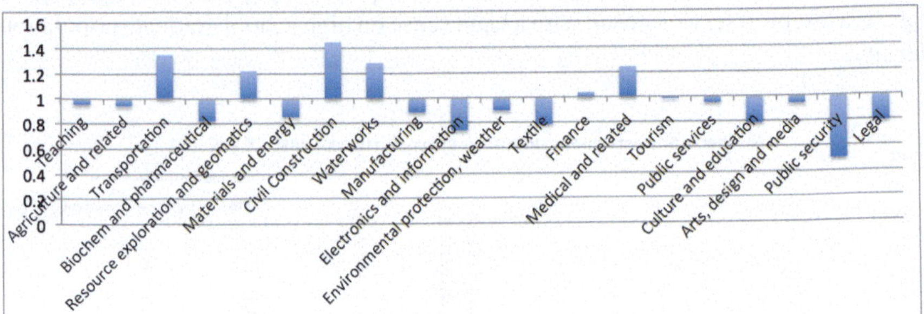

2015 vs. 2011 Number of Associate Degrees Awarded by Major, NBSC 国家统计局

Chapter 7
Balanced Investment Flow Dynamics on Artificial Intelligence

The global competition engaged in by major industrial powers in the filed of artificial intelligence is so fierce and the impact of AI technological revolution on social and economic development so profound, the discussion of the investment into artificial intelligence segment is worth its own chapter.

7.1 The Global AI Industrial Revolution

7.1.1 The Age of Big Data, Machine Learning and Robotics

The purpose of large datasets had moved beyond simple application in corporate efficiency improvement. Since the defeat of Lee Sedol by AlphaGo shook the world in 2016, the general society had ruminated over the possibility that the power of machine learning used in model regression tests, with large dataset collection made possible by internet and mobile devices, could enable artificial intelligence to challenge humans in performing various complex tasks, such as object recognition for self-driving vehicles. Realizing the profound ramification brought by this technological breakthrough, major industrial powers took actions and the battle for technological supremacy became so heated it could be regarded as one of the if not the main contributing factor to the raging global trade war and possible decoupling of electronic supply chain that was the hallmark business model after the World War II.

7.1.2 US Drive on Technological Supremacy

The US has been the pace setter in AI technological development, backed up by the size and vibrancy of its technological research. In 2016, US Executive Office of the President and National Science and Technology Council (NSTC) jointly published

X. Zhang, *Mechanical Analysis of China's Macro Economic Structure*,
https://doi.org/10.1007/978-981-15-3840-7_7

"Preparing for the Future of Artificial Intelligence" document. In that document, it stated that "it is very unlikely that machines will exhibit broadly-applicable intelligence comparable to or exceeding that of humans in the next 20 years, it is to be expected that machines will reach and exceed human performance on more and more tasks". To better prepare the US for the future, the document was drafted "to foster inter-agency coordination, to provide technical and policy advice on topics related to AI, and to monitor the development of AI technologies across industry, the research community, and the Federal Government". Around the same time, NSTC also published "The National Artificial Intelligence Research and Development Strategic Plan" document, defining "a high-level framework that can be used to identify scientific and technological needs in AI, and to track to progress and maximize the impact of R&D in AI, looking beyond near-term AI capabilities toward long-term transformational impacts of AI on society and the world". The US AI development approach is centered on providing a robust legal framework, setting up public database, providing AI training and testing resources, ensuring safety and security and committing long-term research investment. On top of that development infrastructure, the market itself would then decide what products to develop and which future developmental directions to take. Some areas of particular interests included autonomous vehicles and aircrafts, cybersecurity, AI weapons and human-AI collaboration.

7.1.3 German and High-End Closed-Loop Manufacturing Supply Chain

A leading industrial nation with extensive international trade exposure, Germany faces competitive pressure from both incumbent industrial powers such as US, Japan and newly industrialized powers such as China and South Korea. To maintain German and broader European industrial resilience in an uncertain international environment, the country continuously innovates to keep its lead in both quality improvement and cost reduction, and uses strengthened core technological edge, industry standards and other moats to protect key segments, especially the auto industry, which faces intense international trade pressure. In a document "Final Report Summary—RACE2050 (Responsible innovation Agenda for Competitive European transport industries up to 2050)", funded by European Commission FB7-Transport program, specifically mentioned was "EU eastward enlargement in 2004, the efforts to create the European Single Sky, the Commission's high ecological vehicle and product standards or the on-going harmonization of the rail market can be assumed correlating strongly with the rise of China's competitiveness". Especially under the current condition, the large trade surplus exposure of German auto industry to the US market, including those generated via factories in Mexico, is a huge motivator for German manufacturers to make their products globally more competitive hence possibly less reliant upon a single market.

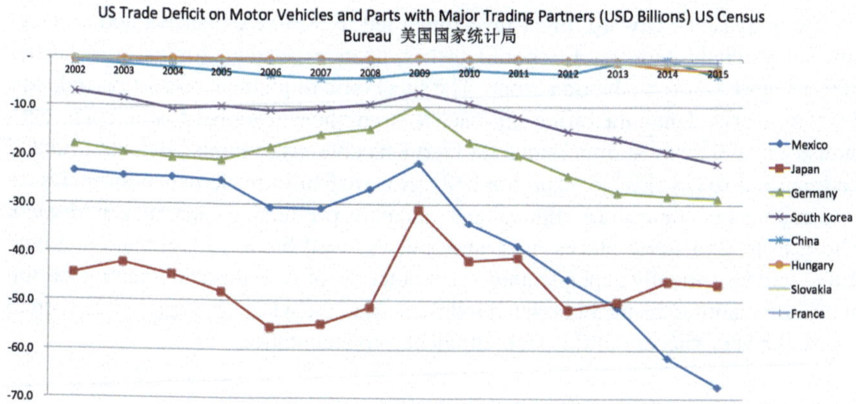

The German answer to the global industrial competitive pressure is Industry 4.0. It is a comprehensive innovative effort to further harmonize production chain, reduce cost and strengthen technological moat. In essence an AI technology revolution with a manufacturing industry focus, the Industry 4.0 concept was first put forward by German government in 2011, and was advocated as an integrated interconnection of processes in production, logistics and services spanning across different large manufacturing industries and countries in Europe. Based upon public discussion, the implementation would probably first start in auto, auto supply industry and logistics, then in medical, medical technology, electrical engineering, mechanical and plant engineering, energy systems, and later in the chemical and aerospace industries. Industry 4.0 was built on top of successful German manufacturers' eastward investment expansion since EMU into Mid-Europe where educated labor cost was lower and room for GDP growth was higher.

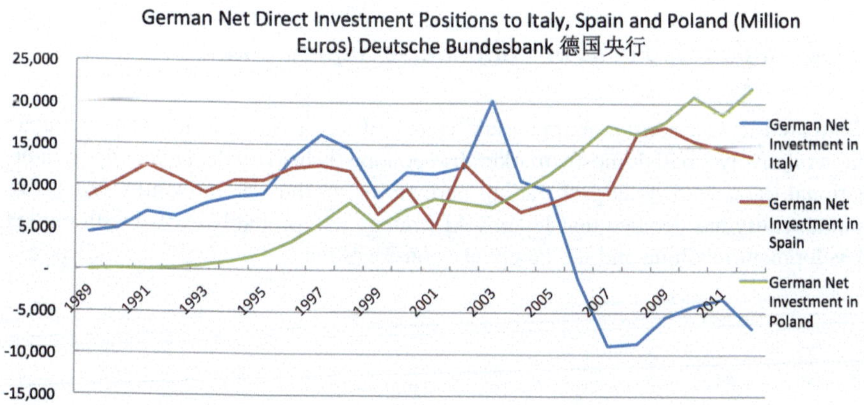

The increased eastward direct investment led to a more expansive and efficient auto supply chain. Industry 4.0 should further enhance the technological entry barrier of German-led auto production group. The successful implementation of AI/Industry 4.0 computerized manufacturing approach to strengthen the global position of its auto industry is of uttermost importance for German economy, with its 2015 auto-related trade surplus to US close to 30 billion USD, close to 5 million German brand vehicles sold in 2018 in China, and additional auto and parts production capacities in Mexico, Mid-Europe and other places. In a nutshell, the well-being of German economic future will be critically dependent upon the outcome of AI industrial implementation in its auto manufacturing and related industries and the whole government is keen to secure the very success of this technological implementation.

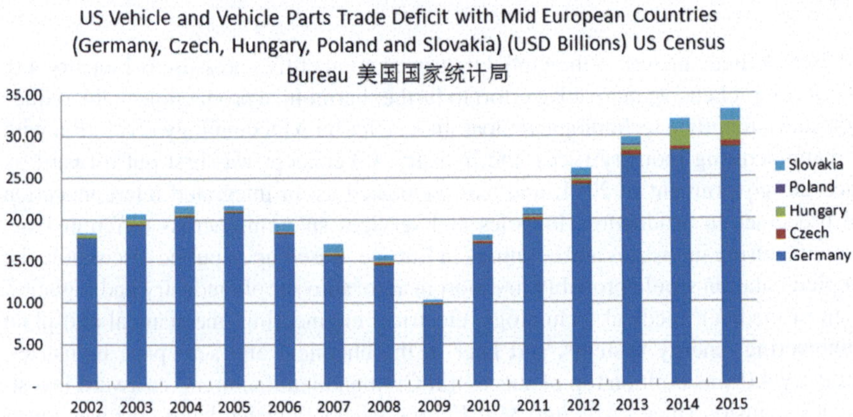

7.1.4 *Japanese Focus on Automotive Supply Chain*

Compared to Germany manufacturers having EU as its large home market, Japan has a relatively small domestic market. Its economy is heavily dependent upon international trade with its largest trading partners being the US and China. This economic reality has decided that Japan's AI strategy will probably evolve with market development in China and US taken into consideration.

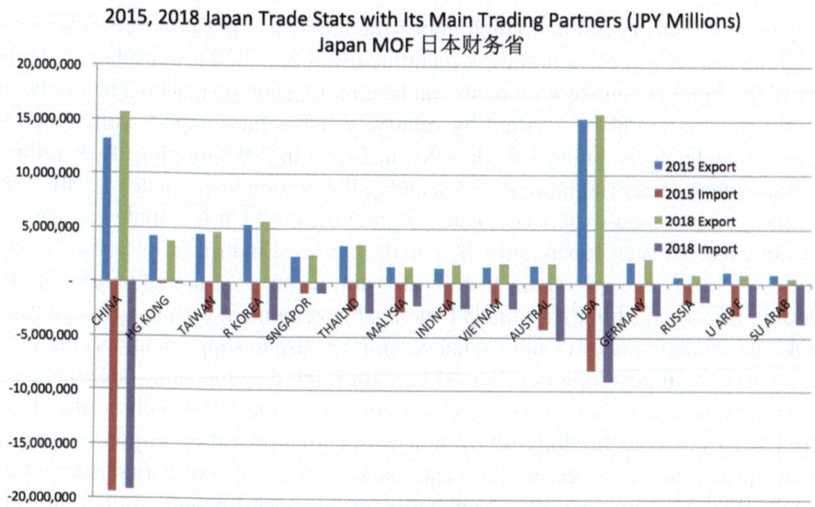

As illustrated by its trade data, the Japanese export-driven economy takes in raw materials and minerals as input and produces manufactured goods as output, the largest category of which is transport equipment, i.e., automobiles and related products. Unless this paradigm is significantly shifted by some technological force, e.g., clean energy, military robotics, the single most important deliverable of Japan AI strategy might be to steer its automobile manufacturing segment for the future with particular attention given to China and US markets development.

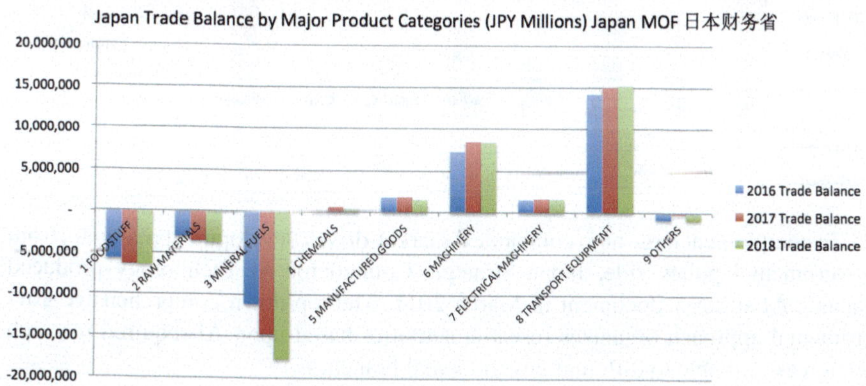

Japan auto industry differs in their deployment postures in China versus US market. China has an extensive domestic manufacturing base and lower labor cost, and more of the Japanese auto components can be directly sourced in China before being assembled. This could be verified by relatively lower auto export from Japan to China, while Japanese brand vehicle sales in China in 2018 hit close to 5 million. The Sino-Japan industrial labor division and collaboration also run deep, with large machinery import and export between two countries, which is a trade pattern that does not exist between Japan and US. The deeper level industrial interconnectivity signifies a possible supply chain forming for auto-centric AI manufacturing sector including Japan and China, a mutually beneficial development with Japan's aging and shrinking population needs China's manufacturing base to supplement its core competency industrial development. For AI breakthrough development, large Japanese auto companies try to source new technologies from the US. Catching the future using US-based AI technology innovation with China providing important supplementary production engineering base and market base, and continuously deploying AI technology to strengthen its auto manufacturing capability and product offering, could be the preferred solution for Japanese auto makers in the current technological competition.

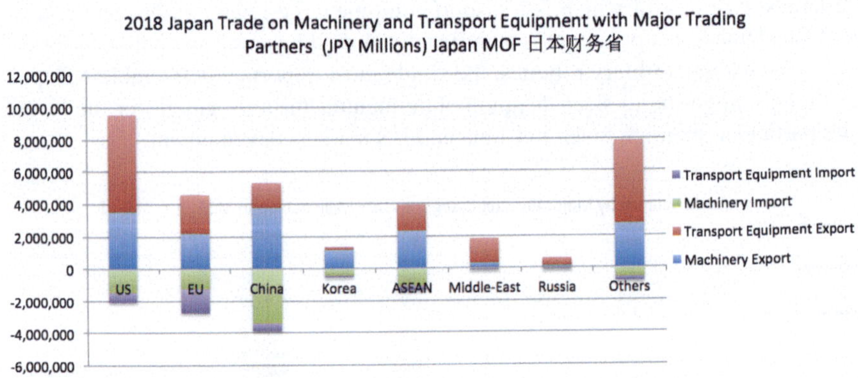

To complement large auto companies' market-driven development roadmap, from governmental policy side, Japan Strategic Council for AI Technology produced Japan's AI strategy document in March 2017. The top-down comprehensive governmental approach organizes research activities based upon AI-required research resources available to different governmental branches.

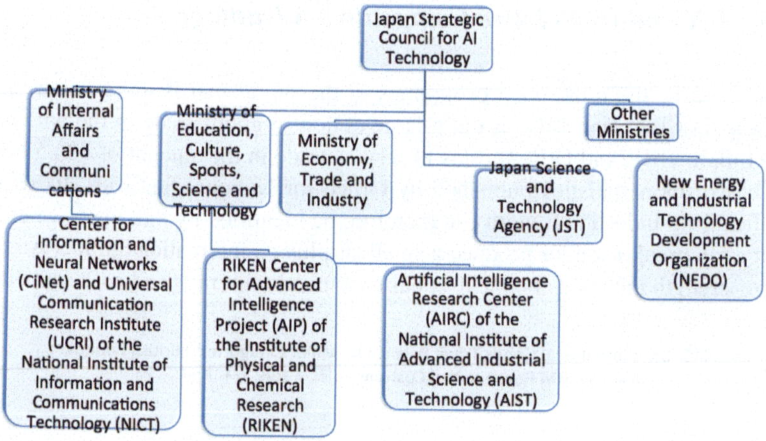

The focuses of the governmental AI strategy included big data infrastructure, robotics, manufacturing improvement, energy efficiency, household usage and Internet of Things. The implementation objective for phase 1 was AI product development. The objectives for phase 2 and 3 were product rollout, and creation of AI value creation ecosystem, respectively.

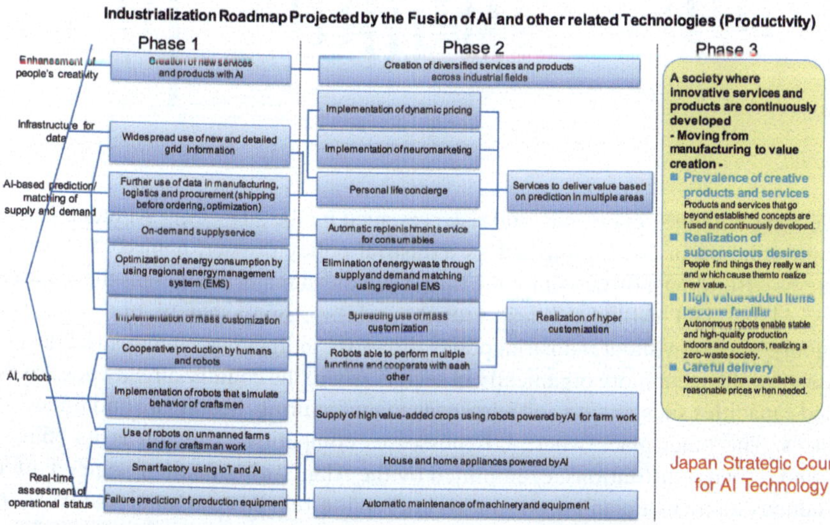

At global level some of the key Japanese AI players might be worth tracking for include Softbank, a technology portfolio investor, Toyota, a leading auto manufacturer, FANUC and Yaskawa, two leading robotics manufacturers. Sourcing innovative technology development from North America would be critical for Japanese AI technology development, which has a domestic environment facing dwindling and aging population and relatively weak software development ecosystem.

7.1.5 UK and Its Relative Competitive Advantage

UK has one of the most open economies in the world that is quite unique in its own way. For the year 2018, it ran a large deficit in goods trade in the amount of 138.8 billion GBP, and large surplus in service trade in the amount of 106.5 billion BPs, based upon statistics published by Office for National Statistics. Its relative manufacturing industry strength can therefore be identified by looking at where the country can break-even, or produce a small surplus on international trade. Areas of relative strength included chemicals, pharmaceuticals, aircrafts and parts and others.

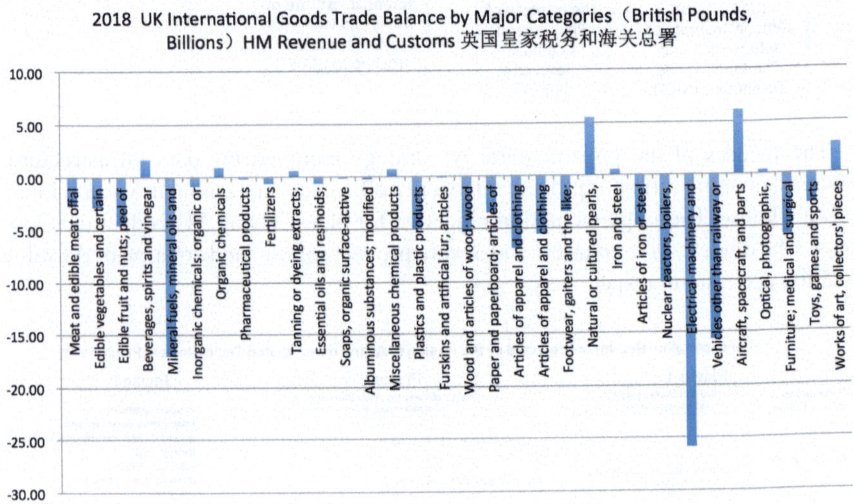

Sensing both the opportunity and risk presented by the advancing AI technology, UK government in 2017 published its industrial policy dossier, named "Industrial Strategy—Building a Britain fit for the future", listing 4 major challenges the country faces: AI and data revolution; clean growth; mobility; aging society. In this market economy, with or without industrial policy directive, indigenous AI industrial development would occur more organically in sectors where the country already possesses scaled capacities such as auto and aerospace manufacturing, healthcare and financial services. The other place where UK possesses competitive strength is its education and research institutions, exemplified by the Alan Turing institute, named after the famous mathematician known for his encryption-related computational work in WWII era. UK has a relatively small domestic economy and industrial sectors versus other large manufacturing countries, hence its objective would be to participate in the technology innovation with cutting-edge programs that can attract large capital and talent infusion to move development into commercialization or production stage without jeopardizing domestic technology employment.

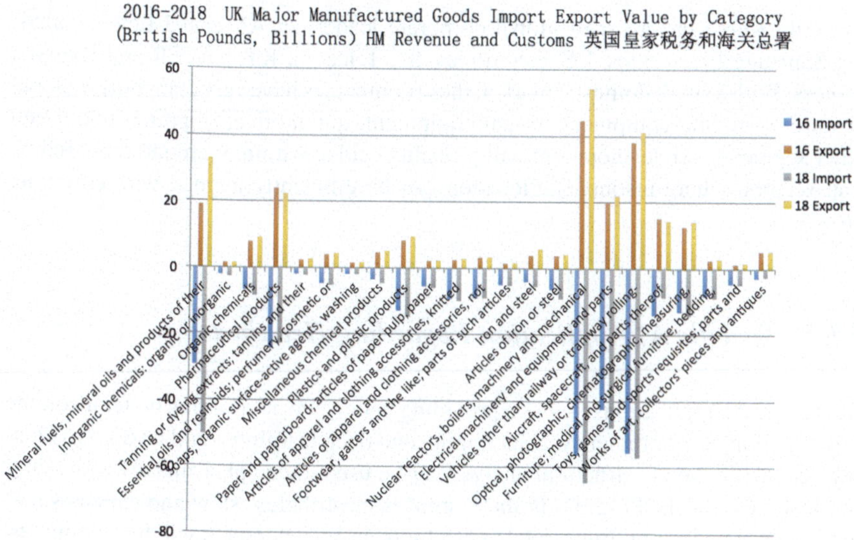

7.1.6 *France, Canada, South Korea and Other AI Competitors*

These countries are grouped together without separate listing not for their lack of future potency in the raging global AI competition, but are here because of the difficulties in getting published analytical industrial data.

Among them, France has a good mathematical education base and an extensive manufacturing base covering aerospace, transportation and military industries, but it does not yet possess a Google equivalent for big data or Apple/Huawei equivalent for mobility supplies, both of which are important areas related to AI development. Its AI enterprises will probably congregate in its largest cities such as Paris with harmonizing data structure being taken as the first industry step, hence the sectors making fast development progress might be healthcare, where sovereign regulation is a must-have, or aerospace, transportation and military segments where EU might want to have more indigenous and unified development within its boundary.

As early as April 2015, Canada Information and Communications Technology Council (ICTC), published its white paper on AI, titled "Artificial Intelligence in Canada—Where do we stand". Canada has relatively small domestic economy but also houses some of the very competitive research universities and institutions. Farming, fishing and mining are among its most important industries. It is likely within Canada AI will find its application in natural resource exploration, mining robotics, agricultural and marine resource management, while potential brain drain to the south has to be managed vigilantly to retain its AI talent pool.

South Korea has a list of global corporate leaders in AI-related fields, including Samsung Electronics, LG Electronics, SK Telecom, KT, NAVER and Hyundai Motors. With a small domestic market, these companies have very competitive global posture in mobile equipment, visual equipment, automotive, shipping, portal and other segments. AI development will probably evolve within or around these industrial sectors, where resources allocation can be efficiently aligned with corporate growth.

7.1.7 *Specific AI Application Regarding Healthcare*

Healthcare AI applications focus on providing better care, identifying better medicine and improving care efficiency. Data mining and deep learning could be used to identify new medicine via structural analysis, or be used to decipher images with better and faster diagnosis. Progress in these areas is nevertheless slow and expensive, as IBM Watson had learnt. But capital expenditure and development will be continuous, especially in aging industrialized economies, including China, where the need for better and more efficient care is urgent.

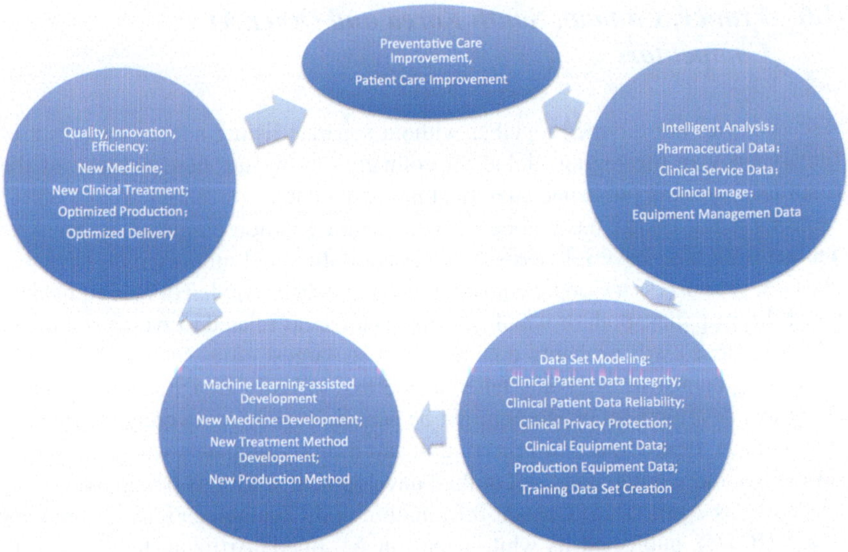

7.1.8 *Specific AI Application Regarding Agriculture*

Another specific area that AI application has great potential is agriculture-related AI development, with the application chain starting from data analytics, field management, planting harvesting automation to supply chain management. Geographically this development may start in countries where industrialization has already reached certain stages hence AI field support can be readily available and the efficiency offered by AI makes a difference. An application example is ground humidity survey combined with individual plant irrigation control can bring agricultural practice to unprecedented level of sophistication. Agricultural segment AI development is unique in its scale requirement since generally low cost in this business poses as a barrier to commercial application of AI technology.

7.1.9 *Military Lessons from Empire's Past Hubris*

The most worrisome development within the AI technology revolution, besides privacy loss, is its military application. Drone swarming has already spread to conflict arenas. While it does present a current technological advantage to advanced industrialized nations, the more rudimentary form had also fallen into the hands of the ragtag. AI military implementation may overwhelm the nuclear-strutted MAD in a couple of decades. Past empires in history often resorted to technological superiority in search for security and dominance, and failed when overstretched and resistance equipped with potent countermeasures stiffened. The discussion regarding different industries' participative responses to this wave of military technology advancement is worth a separate book.

7.2 Current International Successful Models

Leading countries have based upon their distinctive legal, business, research and education, and other characteristics created quite unique technology development models best suited to each country's development need.

7.2.1 Flourishing US Academic Innovation and NBRE

The core strengths of US innovation are the openness and the quality of its education and research institutions and IP protection-driven capability in efficient risky capital allocation to successfully commercialize those innovations. Top engineering schools, including Stanford, MIT, CMU, Cal Tech etc., produce top-notch research. To translate research innovations into products, a place such as The National Robotics Engineering Center (NREC) plays a vital role. NREC is an operating unit within Carnegie Mellon University's Robotics Institute and "works closely with government and industry clients to develop and mature robotic technologies from concept to commercialization. A typical NREC project includes a rapid proof-of-concept demonstration followed by an in-depth development and testing phase that produces a robust prototype with intellectual property for licensing and commercialization". This is a very efficient process built on top of strong legal protection on IP quite unique to US, which cannot be easily emulated by other countries.

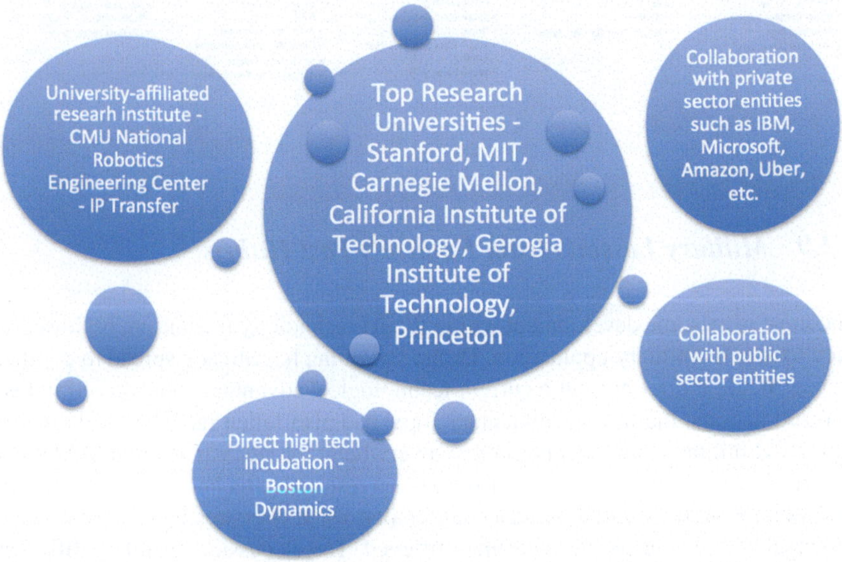

7.2.2 AFWERX

AFWERX is another US mechanism to bring innovation directly to client requirement. It is a US Air Force platform to bring innovator, funding, military clients and project management and logistics (legal, etc.) to the same place. Proposals can be submitted during a virtual meeting where the problem is introduced. Open, efficient and effective, this model was emulated by many around the world.

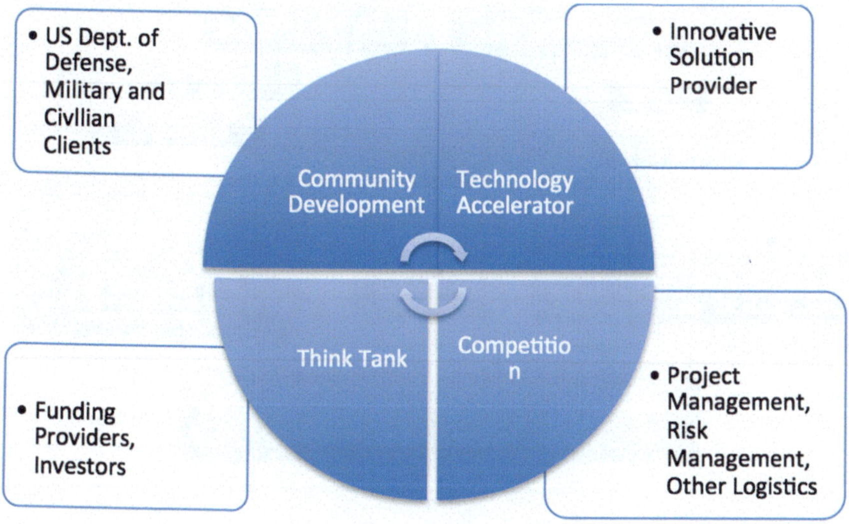

7.2.3 DFKI

German Research Center for Artificial Intelligence (DFKI) is a non-profit public–private partnership playing a critical role in German AI technology drive. Its website describes itself as "Based on application-oriented basic research, DFKI develops product functions, prototypes and patentable solutions in the field of information and communication technology", which makes it analogous to NREC in US. But DFKI is also very different from NREC since it is not managed under a university. Being a public–private partnership it has more direct governmental and industrial oversight and involvement. It receives funding from government agencies including the European Union, the Federal Ministry of Education and Research (BMBF), the Federal Ministry for Economic Affairs and Energy (BMWI), the German Federal States and the German Research Foundation (DFG), and receives cooperation from industrial partners as well. Twice a year, a committee of internationally renowned experts (Scientific Advisory Board) audits the progress and results of state-funded projects. DFKI is critically involved in both domestic Industry 4.0 and AI solution development, and international research projects that advance German industrial competency. For example, working with Japan on German "Industry 4.0" and Japanese "Society 5.0" including cognitive robotics could advance German understanding of Japanese mastery of robotics hardware, and working with Lenovo on LENOBOT ("Helpdesk of the Future") would enhance German industry position in speech recognition development in Chinese-speaking arena, an essential and competitive market for German auto industry.

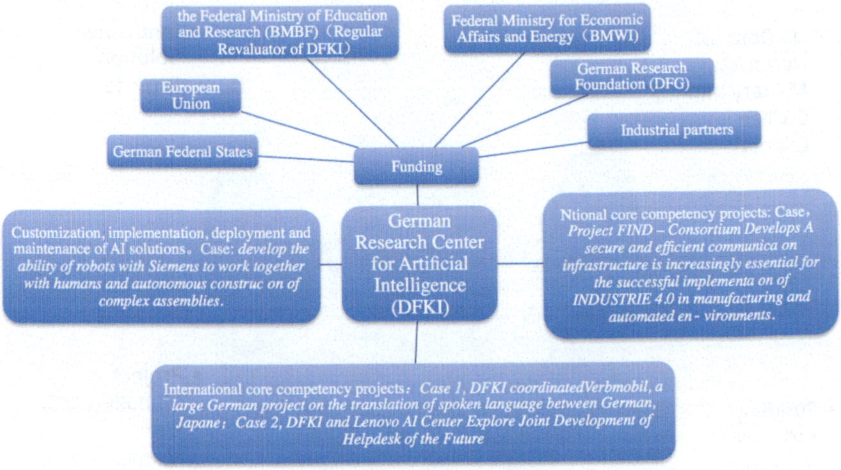

7.2.4 Alan Turing Institute

As stated on its website, this British Institute is an independent charity, established as a joint venture between the universities of Cambridge, Edinburgh, Oxford, University College London, Warwick and the UK Engineering and Physical Sciences Research Council. The Institute aims to become a major force in the development of the dynamic new discipline of data science, in terms of advanced research, leadership training and public conversation influencing.

It might be possible to decipher the future directions of UK AI development by looking at what are considered as core competencies of this institute: system architecture, security and robustness, core statistics, complex structure in data, machine learning and artificial intelligence, mathematical modeling of complex systems, understanding human behavior and ethics of data science and artificial intelligence. It might also be relevant to decipher where these listed development might be commercialized by listing the challenges the institute is striving to take: revolutionize healthcare; deliver safer, smarter engineering; manage security in an insecure world; shine a light on economy; make algorithmic systems fair, transparent, and ethical; design computers for the next generation of algorithms; supercharge research in science and humanities and foster government innovation.

This is quite different from NREC or DFKI model. With broader coverage on interdisciplinary data science research and training, using training and its associated revenue to create a talent pool and ideal pool, thus attracting top talent and capital, the institute tries to channel UK core competencies into industries where commercialization mostly possibly might make an impact.

7.2.5 The Current AI Ecosystem

A brief introduction on AI industry is probably useful before its industrial investment flow can be discussed regarding such a heavily technical field. AI industry might be considered a 3-stage ecosystem, which includes infrastructure layer, data model layer and application layer. Each layer is extensive and technically complicated with its own sub-ecosystems. The infrastructure layer includes chips, network and cloud computing. Among different types of chips, CPU technology, represented by Intel and AMD, is relatively mature and powerful, but is better suited for commands storage and execution, and less suited for data storage and analysis. GPU technology, represented by Nvidia and AMD, was originally designed for graphics processing, thus a good fit for AI task. FPGA technology, represented by Xilinx and Altera, is a programmable design, a compromise between efficiency and flexibility and often used for cloud computing and security. ASIC technology, represented by Google TPU, Intel VPU and Cambricon NPU, is specifically designed for AI, but burdened with long developmental cycle and low level programming inflexibility. Also included in the physical layer, are various types of sensors to gather different kinds of signals, signals that can be used to measure changing humidity, temperature, light and magnetic, or used to detect force, gas, liquid and location. Known industry leaders include BOSCH, Honeywell and others. Sensory that converts external environmental readings into useful data at simplest level needs to make a choice on whether using analog output, which is continuous but noisy, versus digital output which is discrete and often appears less natural but also is less noisy when transmitted across distance. Different industry leaders could specialize in either analog or digital devices. Cloud computing and different generations of network can also be considered as part of infrastructure layer.

Above the infrastructure layer is the data model layer that converts complicated signals into useable datasets. This is where visual and audio processing, deep learning, machine learning and natural language processing (NPL) reside.

Application layer on top of data model layer is very extensive, which at least includes robotics, self-driving, intelligent living, intelligent financing, intelligent medical services, security services and others. Robotics includes industrial robots, service robots and specialty robots. Self-driving application includes air, land and marine machinery.

7.2.6 General AI Investment Risk and Return

Infrastructure layer technology, such as chip technology and network technology, has become a heated area of industrial competition and trade conflict. Success in this layer requires scale of production to spread the cost originated from heavy research, building up vertical supply chain and extending horizontal ecosystem, hence the investment success rate is low and the odds strongly favor the incumbent with market dominance. High risk and high return, scale requirement and long investment time horizon are common characteristics for investment into infrastructure layer.

Data model layer is more talent-intensive therefore applications within this layer are often developed among a congregation of mathematical talents from elite universities and research institutes that often reside in large metropolis. Investments prefer to go into segments where potential future application of the chosen projects can be broad. For example, visual recognition projects are popular among investment community since the output can be used for financing transaction facial recognition, security clearance and public security management with profound impact.

Application layer investment decision is often made based upon whether the investment recipient is an incumbent in an existing industry revolutionized by AI or a new entrant into completely new fields enabled by new technologies. Robotics, self-driving automobiles all have strong incumbent bias due to their technological difficulty required in the product manufacturing process. New entrants can quickly build up their advantages in fields that are relatively new without incumbent competitors. For example, flying drones and intelligent livings have become hot areas where Internet giants have entered these new fields and made their presence felt.

7.3 Popular AI-Related Investment Areas in China

AI investment flows in China can also be analyzed using the 3-stage ecosystem investment framework. If we use widely published research paper citation as a benchmark for comparison, China still lags behind US on basic AI research. But powered by big data, expansive manufacturing capacity, well-educated workforce, giant Internet enterprises and their ample funding capability, the country has made strides in many application layer fields and gradually extended into model layer and infrastructure layer. Even with the ongoing trade conflict, development in voice AI, visual recognition, smart living, self-driving vehicles, AI drones, and robotics, would likely continue due to the strong pushing technology forces and pulling market demand. Since independently verifying industry data is very difficult for these areas, much of the discussion here will be based upon public information available on web and less quantitative versus other chapters within this book.

Funding can come from large Internet companies, private equities supported by domestic and international Internet companies, funds supported by SASAC capital and banks. Different funding sources have their own preferences, with large Internet companies being the most aggressive, standard PEs always looking for the exit, SASAC capital looking for long term investment, and banks being the most conservative.

7.3.1 Voice, Visual and Big Data

AI investments into these areas are very popular in China. Some of the leading companies specializing in voice and visual AI segments include Beijing SenseTime, Beijing Megvil, Shanghai Yitu and Hefei IFLYTEK. Important domain expertise could be either facial recognition or AI-supported voice translation. Industry applications range from banking clients or online payments ID authentication, public security, smart phone ID authentication, smart living and some other areas. The expansions in voice and visual areas are likely to intensify in the coming years and drastically change how we live our daily life.

7.3.2 Voice and Sensory Electronics

Within this area, being inexpensive and well designed with newly available technologies, smart speaker has quickly become the center of smart home device battlefield and linchpin of the evolving home appliance ecosystem. Burning investment in scale, Baidu's Xiaodu, Alibaba's TMall Genie and Xiaomi's Xiaoai compete fiercely in this space. They can offer voice-initiated search on music, weather and other contents, connect to home devices and make online payments.

7.3.3 Self-Driving Vehicles

Both traditional auto manufacturers and Internet companies are pursuing the development of self-driving vehicles. Many of the self-driving passenger vehicle prototypes have kept their components for human intervention, which make these vehicles costly and therefore give advantages to traditional automakers that possess mature driving technology manufacturing knowhow. One solution for cost management is shared driving since it can lower ownership cost by increased passenger carry. Cargo delivering self-driving vehicle does not have to worry about passenger safety and can be deployed with less technical difficulties in industrial park. For both self-driving cargo vehicle and passenger vehicle are viable only if there is a system to support them and it is possible they gain their acceptance in China via policy and extensive manufacturing help. Capital investments into those vehicles, vehicle components and system components will keep up their pace.

7.3.4 AI-Enhanced Airborne Vehicles

This is a competitive segment for both economic and security reasons. At international level, large industrial economies including China, Europe and US all possess core technologies required for making airborne drones, but at the low and medium range of the technological spectrum, China DJI is a clear leader for civilian application. As with all innovations, this space is fraught with risk, and new competitors with better battery or visual technology could quickly emerge and change market dynamics quickly. With DJI being well capitalized and holding market dominance, new investment into airborne drone segment probably would come either in the form of niche specialization or being complementary to DJI at system level to avoid a risky investment bet.

7.3.5 Industrial Robotics

Though larger quantities of robots are being manufactured each year in China, domestic manufacturers often act as system integrators with relatively less technology input and thus receive thin profit margin. There have been complaints about 2-tiered pricing scheme from domestic robotics manufacturer with perception for being charged a higher price by global technology suppliers. The core competencies required in robotics include motor, controller and gearbox, all prerequisites for precision movement control with the right combination of torque, speed, position and mechanical durability. 4 global robotics leaders excelling in these areas, including Swedish ABB, German KUKA, Japanese FANUC and Japanese YASKAWA, dominate the Chinese robotics market. One interesting exception is the strain wave gearing, also known as harmonic gearing. At the relatively low to mid level technology spectrum, this component is nevertheless widely used in robotics. LeaderDriver, a domestic manufacturer in this area managed to achieve technological success and helped to lower the total cost of robotics manufacturing in China.

With a large manufacturing base and an aging workforce, investment into China industrial robotics, especially regarding the three core technology areas, is expected to rise continuously, befitting the overall trend towards higher level of domestic industrialization. Traditionally automobiles manufacturing segment is a preferred place to put robotics into scaled industrial application. Since foreign automakers dominate Chinese auto market, their quality preference and path dependency make the threshold for domestic component adoption into industrial robotics much higher, therefore even with policy support, successful robotics technological and capital investments in China need careful calibration.

7.3.6 *Service Robots*

Successful service robots that possess deep market penetration are those with strong domain differentiation, in contrast to some beliefs that this segment might present low entry barrier for new entrants. Large sub-segments include medical, client service and educational service robots. Being that the medical robots are expensive while cost structure of China healthcare industry is still overwhelmingly fiscal supported and therefore very cost-conscious, the entry barrier for medical robots investment is substantial.

Educational service robots investment might enjoy more success. Entrants include robotics start-ups testing water in the educational area, industrial robots manufacturers extending professional education into more generic educational area, toy makers providing robotics education service and other entities venturing into robotics education. Foremost it remains difficult to decide what constitutes a good robotics education use case; secondly, there is the issue regarding how to bridge the gap between high robotics expenses versus relatively low educational budget available from broad income spectrum; complicating the situation even further, is a general lack of technological capabilities by many existing robotics manufacturers. Hence an investment decision into educational service robotics will be challenging.

7.3.7 *Investment Methodology and Risk Return Profile in Summary*

Investment flow into AI areas needs end customer demand to become successful. Domestic infrastructure level investment was drastically stimulated by the fear caused by the ongoing trade conflict, as many companies are made aware of the risk of losing access to key components, which can include operating systems, chips, essential chemical ingredients and others. Data model level investment into voice recognition and visual recognition areas linked to various application layer products is supported by both commercial and government demand. Based upon China economic scale and capital availability these areas will possibly see the greatest success. Other application level investment into AI drone supported by global demand, industrial robotics supported by manufacturing ecosystem demand, and service robotics supported by individual consumer demand will also likely grow in the foreseeable future.

Therefore investment return assessment should be based upon the final customer demand forecast, with some of the key elements being governmental procurement, which may be derived from various 5-year plans, manufacturing requirement, which can be assessed by industrial and corporate analysis, and consumer demand based upon population purchasing studies. One key risk factor is the availability of investment capital, which can come from Internet giants, governmental fund, global and domestic private equity funds, each with their own investment risk preferences and investment time horizon. Other risk factors include policy change, cultural preference, both of which impact final customer demand, and ramification from a protracted trade conflict.

Chapter 8
The Eternal Journey Towards Sustainable Economic Structure

At the time of this writing, the global economy has entered the state of greater uncertainty with prolonged monetary easing, financial leverage, trade conflict, technology rivalry, and contest for industrial supremacy. Among the change agents leading to these uncertainties, technology is one of the most prominent. It is advancing at such a quickening speed that gaining control of its core components may possibly translate into advantageous positions in industrial supply chain and global capital allocation process, thus provide tempting sense of security for industrial powers looking into the future world of unknown. Facing the changing world, with different history background, China would pursue its social and economic developmental path with its own distinct set of priorities.

8.1 History as the Guiding Management Rationale

China has had a long tumultuous history. Learning from the past to prevent decision makers from repeating previous mistakes had always played an important part in policy deliberation process during the imperial era. And that learning from the past part remains just as important today. Some key developmental considerations based upon history lessons include emphasis on national unity, centralized fiscal control, hierarchical administrative structure, SOEs, class mobility, technology independence, key resources independence, real estate restraint, and environmental sustainability.

National unity preempts regional identity. National unity is considered not only critical for the survival of the nation state, it is also perceived as an economic necessity. Infrastructure works along the Yellow River and other major rivers had been carried out throughout the Chinese history to prevent flood disaster and to manage irrigation due to uneven water resources distribution between seasons and among different regions. The Grand Canal was constructed and maintained as the old super highway linking together the most fertile land on China east coast. Without national unity, these large infrastructure projects on major rivers, the Grand Canal, and the modern

X. Zhang, *Mechanical Analysis of China's Macro Economic Structure*,
https://doi.org/10.1007/978-981-15-3840-7_8

era high-speed train project, could not be accomplished. Maintaining national unity was and is considered critical for national economic survival.

Central fiscal control is essential for maintaining national unity. Though the form and degree of the central fiscal control could change from time to time to calibrate the subtle balance between central control versus local initiatives. Through history, whenever national fiscal control over regions was lessened to reduce central budgetary pressure, many times the country would fall into internal conflict and civil war would breakout. The transfer payments from central government and large policy bank projects can all be considered different forms of central fiscal control over regional government.

To effectively implement central control, the current form of top-down bureaucracy structure will likely remain. It had produced astounding efficiency in country's industrialization process in the past. Though inherent problems such as corruption control and bureaucratic inertia have led to pressure for loosening up, significant change on anything that worked well before will likely be slow and careful.

State-owned enterprises would persist, though the whereabouts, forms and extent of their industrial presence may change from time to time. State-owned enterprises had often been part of fiscal mechanism to collect revenues in industries being monopolistic in nature, e.g., salt and iron industries during Han dynasty. The large sum tax revenue collected might be used as transfer payments for funding various government initiatives. SOEs often do not excel in materialistic innovation, and are better suited at being a well-funded platform where private enterprises can operate on. Hence corruption control is critical to maintain the fairness and openness nature of these platforms.

Promoting social class mobility is forever critical. Education is an important method to produce class mobility. In the education system, the Imperial Exam of the past was being perfected for hundreds of years to inject class mobility into the otherwise strictly hierarchical high society, and current National Entrance Exam is close but not as effective. To maintain progress on class mobility, other methods have been pursued. Top among them, urbanization is not only considered an important industrialization initiative, it is also viewed critical to alleviate social divide stress between urban dwellers and rural population.

Technology independence is considered important for both industrial capabilities and sovereign defense. Without technology independence, cost to build comprehensive industrial ecosystem will often be too large and the quantity of Chinese demand alone can push the price to such an extent that it can distort the market to the point of being dysfunctional.

Key resources independence has to be maintained. These include agricultural products, commodities, and other materials. Simply because China has such a large population and ensuring demand, without reasonable level of resource independence, if supply is ever disrupted for any plausible reason, domestic social and economic impact could be severe.

Real estate industry dependency has to be controlled. While important for local economic development and employment growth, real estate industry had become disproportionally large within the domestic economy and consumed that much resources, it reduced the economic dynamics within other segments of the economy.

Environmental concern has become a top priority. The cumulative environmental damage of the past economic growth was so large, that hundreds of years of past deforestation and more current air, water pollution are being addressed at an impressive speed.

8.2 International Lessons for Industrial Structural Imbalance

Useful lessons can be drawn from both domestic and international experience. The top international lessons relevant for this changing time may include imperial expansion per wealth gap, market return expectation per industrial imbalance, and efficiency versus perceived fairness concern.

Imperial expansion may enlarge wealth gap. When a country takes on global responsibilities for a variety of reasons, the return management for diverse external adventures quickly becomes complicated. Various interest groups grow more powerful and their arguments more difficult to follow. The domestic interest becomes only part of total concern for the country, and the general public can be sidelined in policy discussion that may affect them. Hence the return from external entanglements for an empire will often benefit the elite more due to their more active participation in policy formulation process.

Market return expectation may lead to industrial imbalance. To assess industrial policies more consistently hence make policy stipulation process more manageable across the board, global powers, especially those in the more recent times, often moved towards market liberalization with financialization, not only because of their global reach enabling them to leverage on vast incoming resources, but also it then becomes easier to manage different interest groups using financial benchmarks and market forces that can be more quantifiable and open hence less controversial. The monetary market return method will then reduce capital available to those more mature but less profitable industries, making domestic economy less balanced. A good example would be Boeing, even being a large duopoly with ample revenue and a strong technology moat, it can be peer pressured by domestic tech giants to generate higher capital return, leading to extensive outsourcing practices, demonstrating the difficult side of a pure market economy.

Efficiency may destroy perceived social fairness. The very efficient global supply chain, which brings US innovative population and technology capital, Japan, Korean and Singapore equipment builders, and China's manufacturing engineering capacity and labor together to generate the unprecedented global industrial growth around PC and telecommunication equipment, has also left other social groups of global population less content. The affected mid-to-low tier manufacturing labor in US became the major political supporters for the current trade conflict and the affected innovative group in China became the aspiring population emigrating from China to US and other industrialized countries.

8.3 Balancing Need for Long-Term Structural Stability

Learning from the past lessons led to the balanced social and economic development agenda being given a top priority and designed to address a plethora of difficult issues. On the government administrative side, balanced development objective calls for balance between centralized versus decentralized form of governance. Centralized control brings governance stability, which defined a large part of China's history, an example of which would be reining in local government leverage. But over emphasis on centralized control alone will reduce equality in internal dialogue flow thus may hinder dynamism of regional economies.

Balancing between top-down versus bottom up management styles requires much broader effort in its social context versus balancing between central and decentralized governance styles. Top-down style in governmental and corporate management brings efficiency, which was often cited as an important contributing factor to China's past economic progress. The trade-off is in the inherent difficulty in bringing up unforeseen but game-changing innovation event that tends to occur bottom up. The shift towards less top-down and more bottom-up management style will be gradual but is quintessential for an industrialized economy. There is a limit on how much an industry can develop by compensating for the lack of materialistic indigenous innovation capability with fast learning, streamlined execution and efficient industrial ecosystem.

Another balancing issue pertaining to technology is balancing the need between indigenous technology self-sufficiency versus system openness. Requiring full tech self-sufficiency or not, comes down to the question as whether it is realistic to build up an insulated parallel technology universe by Chinese talents while the talents from rest of the world might work collaboratively on many fronts, and to what extent technology should be developed domestically to insulate domestic industries from potentially disruptive international events.

The extensive introduction of technology application into industries and daily life has changed wealth distribution pattern among the population. To rebalance wealth distribution requires adjusting the relative development priorities between social fairness and efficiency. In that balancing process, China is gradually modifying its development agendas in more resemblance to those of German and Japanese models.

Another balancing issue regarding social progress is adjusting the relative development priorities between industrial growth and environmental sustainability. In that balancing process, many steel mills were closed and deforestation process was reversed. It is both domestic and global responsibility to save the environment for future generations. Some other important balancing items include weighing global interests versus international security initiatives cost, and real estate economic contribution versus segment dependency.

8.4 Possible Sketch of a Complex Investment Decision Tree

The balancing action items listed above are only a small portion of the current broad social and economical development agenda for a country as large and complex as China. Mechanically, to implement the whole list of development agenda including those balanced growth items, government plays the central role of organizing resources starting with sets of deliverable targets, which are defined and specified based upon central committee published statements, and many of the targets are made available to the general public in various 5-year plans from central government, regional government, ministries, and others. Being macro in nature, many of the specific regional and industrial objectives relevant for macro and industrial analysis are neither quantitative nor exact and should not be expected to be so. But since these objectives reflect the desired balanced approach listed earlier within a social and economic development framework for China, they still have quantitative expectations and boundaries for optimal level of achievement. The level and boundaries of the objectives form the basis for creating the large picture of China's changing macro and industrial economic structure.

The mechanical process of Chinese economy, summarized at the highest level, starts with the central committee's published statements, combined with years of extensive consultation (a) within different executive branches, (b) with academia, and (c) with the general public, being translated into NDRC and different levels of governmental 5-year plans. To fulfill those plans, Ministry of Finance would provide financial resources for the general budgetary expenditure and local government would provide additional resources for the local fund expenditure. PBOC monitors and injects monetary liquidity into banking industry to fund the more general economic activities. Policy banks finance those initiatives not commercially viable but critical for the long-term national development. SOEs operate on commercial terms, produce large tax revenue, but act more as platform upon which private industries would thrive. Private industries, some of them very competitive in the high tech industries, are market driven and provide the largest amount of employment critical for the growth and stability of this populous nation.

In each planning and implementation stage, central and regional government, NDRC, Ministry of Finance, PBOC, NBSC, other ministries, and agencies, would publish lists of documents and statistics that can be applied to understand and keep track of the progress of the development targets delivery. The health of macro condition and various Industries can be further assessed based upon banking data, industrial association data, both being supplemented by leading corporations' released reports. Data regarding more mature industries is more readily available versus more fast-moving technology industries.

Based upon mechanical analysis using data from different principal players at different progressive development stages, a more fundamental and dynamic macro and industrial picture can be drawn for insightful investment condition assessment in China. Would China be able to implement balanced social and economic agenda successfully, leading to improved quality of lives, promoting innovation, and controlling corruption? Would US be able to maintain its technology lead, reduce wealth inequality, and still keep its vibrant market capital-driven economy open to China? Would advancing AI technology produce a divided world, segregating countries, regions, and ethnicities based upon possession of technology and capital, or would it bridge the social and economic gap between the Haves and the Have-Nots? Given the complex and fluid nature of the current global economic order and the sizable influence of Chinese economy to the global economic growth and balance, the importance for that reaching clarity on China economic mechanics cannot be overstated.

Specific End Notes

All data used in charts within this book are from public sources. All charts are noted in chart titles for their data sources, side by side in both English and Chinese. Using the following chart as an example, which illustrates China annual mobile phone production volume. Data was sourced from NBSC, short for National Bureau of Statistic of China, 中国国家统计局 in Chinese. The purpose for doing so is to facilitate advanced readers to corroborate the content and further their own academic and empirical research when needed.

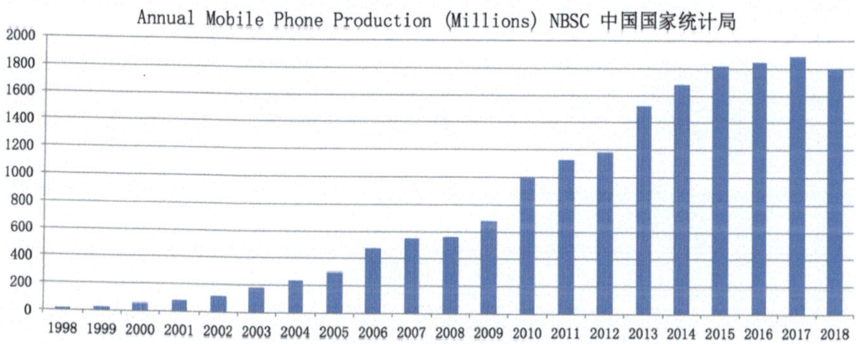

X. Zhang, *Mechanical Analysis of China's Macro Economic Structure*,
https://doi.org/10.1007/978-981-15-3840-7

The manufacturer's authorised representative in the EU is Springer Nature Customer Service Centre GmbH, Europaplatz 3, 69115 Heidelberg, Germany. If you have any concerns regarding our products, please contact ProductSafety@springernature.com

Printed and bound by CPI Group (UK) Ltd, Croydon, CR0 4YY
25/09/2026
02222901-0001